IMAGES
of America

NASHVILLE INTERIORS 1866 TO 1922

IMAGES
of America

NASHVILLE INTERIORS 1866 TO 1922

Amelia Whitsitt Edwards

ARCADIA
PUBLISHING

ISBN 978-0-7385-0220-5

Published by Arcadia Publishing
Charleston, South Carolina

Printed in the United States of America

Library of Congress Catalog Card Number applied for.

For all general information contact Arcadia Publishing at:
Telephone 843-853-2070
Fax 843-853-0044
E-mail sales@arcadiapublishing.com
For customer service and orders:
Toll-Free 1-888-313-2665

Visit us on the Internet at www.arcadiapublishing.com

Contents

Introduction

In 1981, the American Association of State and Local History published William Seale's landmark book, *The Tasteful Interlude: American Interiors through the Camera's Eye 1860–1917*. The importance of this book for all those with a penchant for the decorative arts is incalculable. House museum curators working in this time period were especially grateful for this work since it provided them with yet another tool for creating truthful interior settings. While the Seale book covered the entire country, this publication only covers the Nashville, Tennessee area. Both books cover the same time period.

Interior photographs were generally made by professional photographers until flash bulb cameras became widely available after World War II. Early amateur photographers were not equipped with the lighting necessary to make interior photographs. It is believed that all of the photographs in this volume were made by professional photographers, although some of their names are unknown.

The first daguerreotypes were made in Nashville in 1841 when an artist named Moore set up his camera at the Union Hall Hotel. None of the photographs shown here are believed to have been made until after the Civil War. The earliest interior photographs are those of Belmont Mansion between 1866 and 1877.

During the 50-year period covered by this book, affluent Nashvillians, who could afford the services of a professional photographer, decorated their houses in a great variety of styles. The Victorian and Edwardian periods are general terms used to describe this time period when the historic revival styles dominated the decorative arts market. Revival styles that are represented in these Nashville interiors are Gothic Revival, Renaissance Revival, Louis Fourteenth, Fifteenth, and Sixteenth Revival, Greek Revival (sometimes called American Empire), and the Colonial Revival. Mixed in with the revival styles are examples of the creative styles developed during the Arts and Crafts and Art Nouveau movements. Non-European influences to be seen in these photographs are Anglo-Japanese, Egyptian Revival, and various Turkish and Near Eastern designs.

Other published works containing collections of early Nashville interior photographs are *Art Work in Nashville*, *The Souvenir Album*, *Tennessee Centennial Exposition*, and *Some Representative Women of Tennessee* by Annie Somers Gilchrist.

ACKNOWLEDGMENTS

I have relied heavily upon previously published sources for information on the decorative arts, as well as for biographical material about the people who inhabited these interior spaces. Since this book has no footnotes, credit to the authors and their works has been given in the list of sources that follow the photographs and text.

Many others have been generous enough to lend me their treasured photographs and to share with me their knowledge. To the following list of people I express my sincere gratitude.

Robert L. Acklen
Mark Brown, Director, Belmont Mansion
Fletch Coke
John L. Connelly, Davidson County Historian
Debbie Cox, Metro Nashville Archives
Wilbur F. Creighton Jr.
Laura Benson Davis
Angie Cantrell Ezell
Mike Fleenor, Tennessee Historical Commission
Percy Warner Frazer
Elizabeth Z. Fryer
Susan Gordon, Tennessee State Library & Archives
Margaret Greenlee
Opie E. Handly
Janet Hasson, Curator, Belle Meade Plantation
Mary Glenn Hearn, Nashville Room
James Hoobler, Tennessee State Museum
John Mitterholzer IV, Director, Historic Nashville
Terri Johnson, Metro Nashville Hist. Commission
Bill Kelly, Metro Nashville Historical Commission
Marsha Mullin, Curator, The Hermitage
Polly Trammell Murphy
Richard C. Plater Jr.
Jean Farrell Prueher
Steve Rogers, Tennessee Historical Commission
Emma C. Rose
Fran Schell, Tennessee State Library and Archives
Mike Slate, *Nashville Historical Newsletter*
Thomas P. VanStraten, Nashville Area Chamber of Commerce
Margaret L. Warden
Ruth R. Warner
Larry West
Ridley Wills II

A special thanks to Mary Rimlinger, my typist, who by magic can turn horribly handwritten pages into an orderly, readable, correctly spelled manuscript.

One

Country House Interiors

1. Belmont Mansion
2. Belle Meade Plantation
3. The Hermitage
4. Clover Bottom Mansion
5. Burlington
6. Renraw
7. Royal Oaks
8. Overton Hall / Crieve Hall

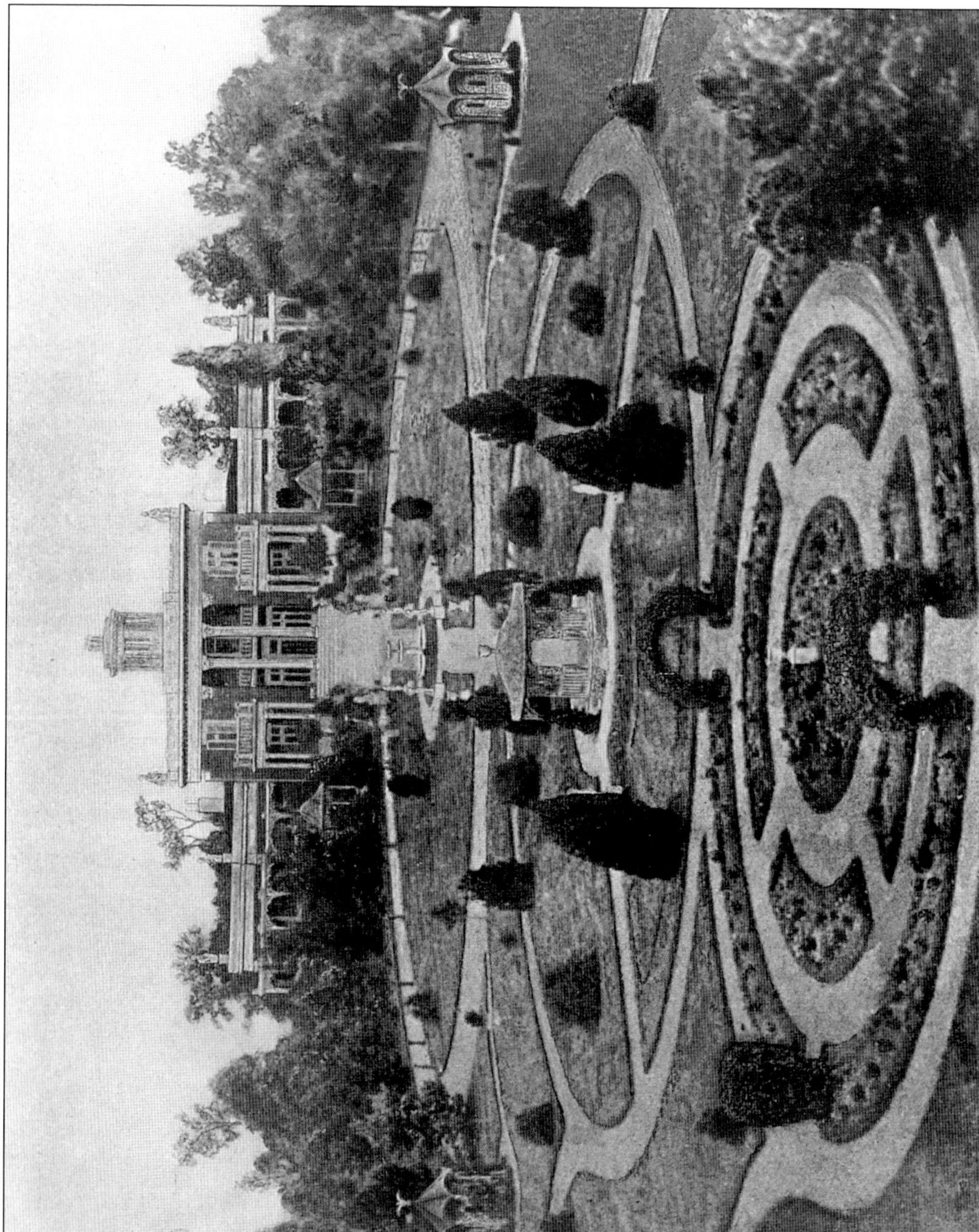

Belmont Mansion

The home of Adelicia and Joseph Acklen stands today on the campus of Belmont University surrounded by attached early-twentieth-century college buildings that were added by a previous school, Belmont College for Young Women.

In the late 1850s, the Acklens employed Nashville architect Adolphus Heiman to enlarge a small summer villa on this spot. Their grand Italianate mansion was the showplace of Nashville until 1887, when it was sold by Mrs. Acklen shortly before her death. Never serving as a farm or a plantation, the grounds were designed for amusement and pleasure. Other buildings gracing the gardens were a bowling alley and an art gallery, a greenhouse, a bear house, and an alligator pit.

The interior photographs of the Front Hall and the Grand Salon at Belmont Mansion were made by early Nashville photographer C.C. Giers. They are the earliest known interior photographic views in the Nashville area. Although the photographs are not dated, they fall between 1866 and 1877. The earlier date may be established by the date that the statuary arrived at Belmont and the later date by the year that the photographer, C.C. Giers, died.

The Belmont photographs are prime examples of the value of photography in the recreation of a historic house interior. While written documents indicated the existence of a fountain and eight paintings in the Grand Salon, their location in the room was unknown until these photographs were discovered.

An 1860 document written by Mother Frances Walsh of St. Cecilia Academy described the Grand Salon as a "spacious reception hall, the surroundings suggestive of Oriental luxury. The floor tessellated, a miniature fountain in the center sent up its misty spray." One photograph shows the fountain in the bay window and settled forever the question of its location.

Architect: Adolphus Heiman
Photographer: C.C. Giers,
Photographed: c. 1870
From the collection of the Belmont Mansion Association

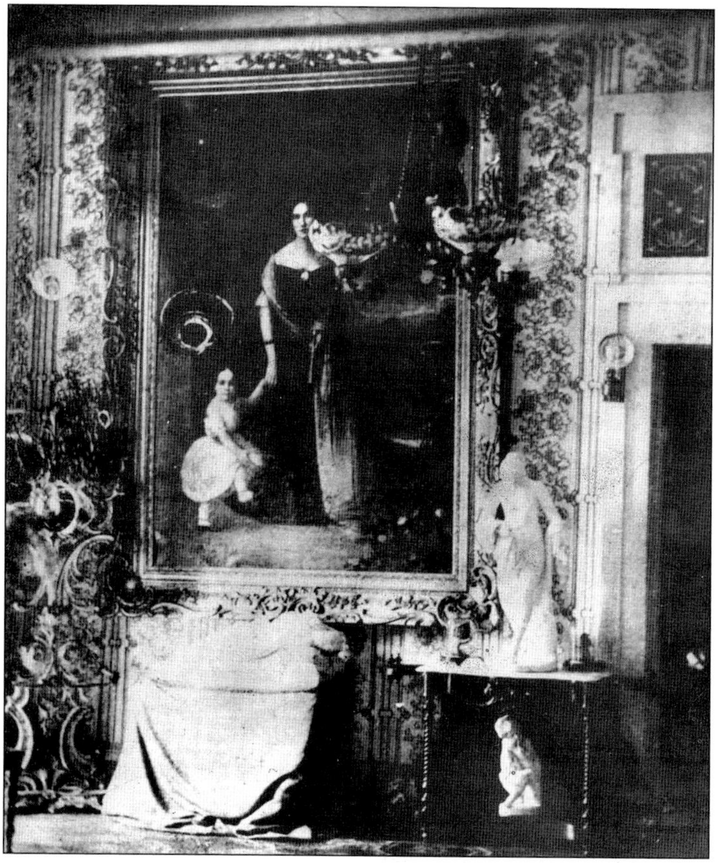

The location of the large oil painting of Adelicia Acklen and one of her children, painted by Bush of Kentucky, is unknown today. Under this painting is a marble sculpture by W.H. Rinehart called *The Sleeping Children*. It is probably the finest piece in Adelicia's collection in spite of its nineteenth-century sentimentalism. This piece occupies the same position in the house today as it did when this photograph was made. Seen beside *The Sleeping Children* is a copy of *Atlanta Adjusting Her Robes* by the artist Jean Jacques Pradier. Although this statue was sold to a Nashville family in the 1887 sale, it has not been located and returned to Belmont.

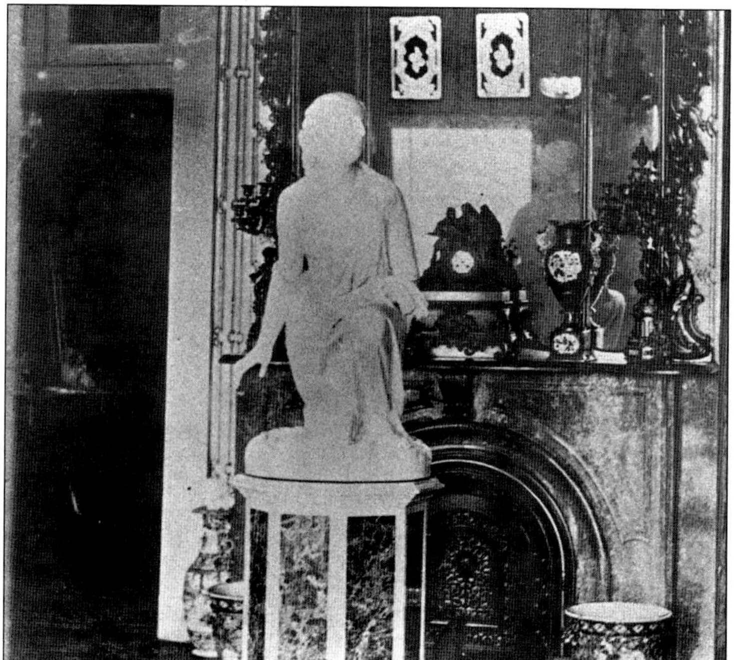

Visitors to Belmont Mansion are greeted at the front door by a life-size marble statue called *Ruth Gleaning Wheat* by the American sculptor Randolph Rogers. The Venetian glass in the doorway, as reflected in the mirror, has remained intact over the years. The original wallpaper has been reprinted and rehung; the mantel clock and candelabra have been returned by family members.

When this photograph was made of the Grand Salon, Mozier's statue *The Peri* dominated the room from its center position under the gasolier. Shortly after Mrs. Acklen's death in 1887, it was moved to the Acklen mausoleum in Mt. Olivet Cemetery. *The Peri*, a "fallen angel," is from the Irish poet Thomas Moore's poem "Paradise and the Peri," published in 1817. While most of the decorative art themes at Belmont were from the Bible or from Greek and Roman myths, a few, such as *The Peri*, come from contemporary literature.

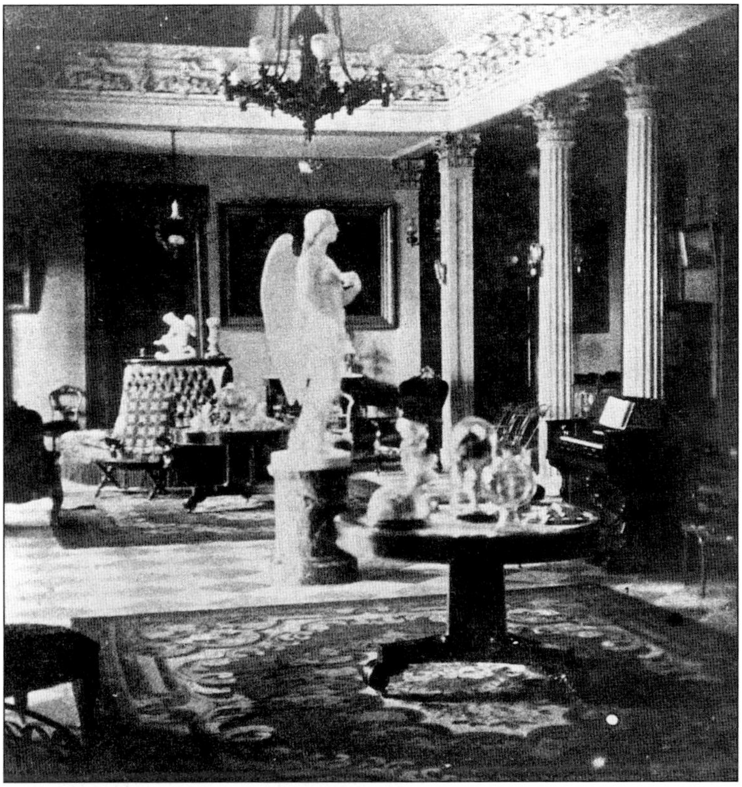

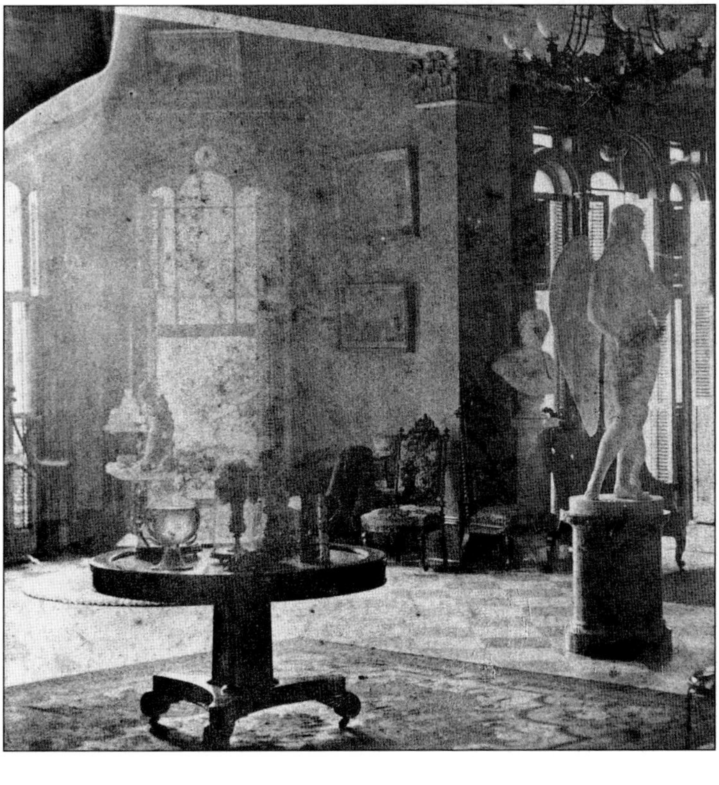

In 1881 a correspondent of the *Louisville Courier-Journal* listed six paintings together in the Grand Salon: five Venetian views by Canaletto plus *The Marriage of Jacob and Rachel.* These six paintings fit neatly into the bay window area; half of the arrangement is shown in this photograph. Three other paintings are listed separately: two are shown in the photograph above.

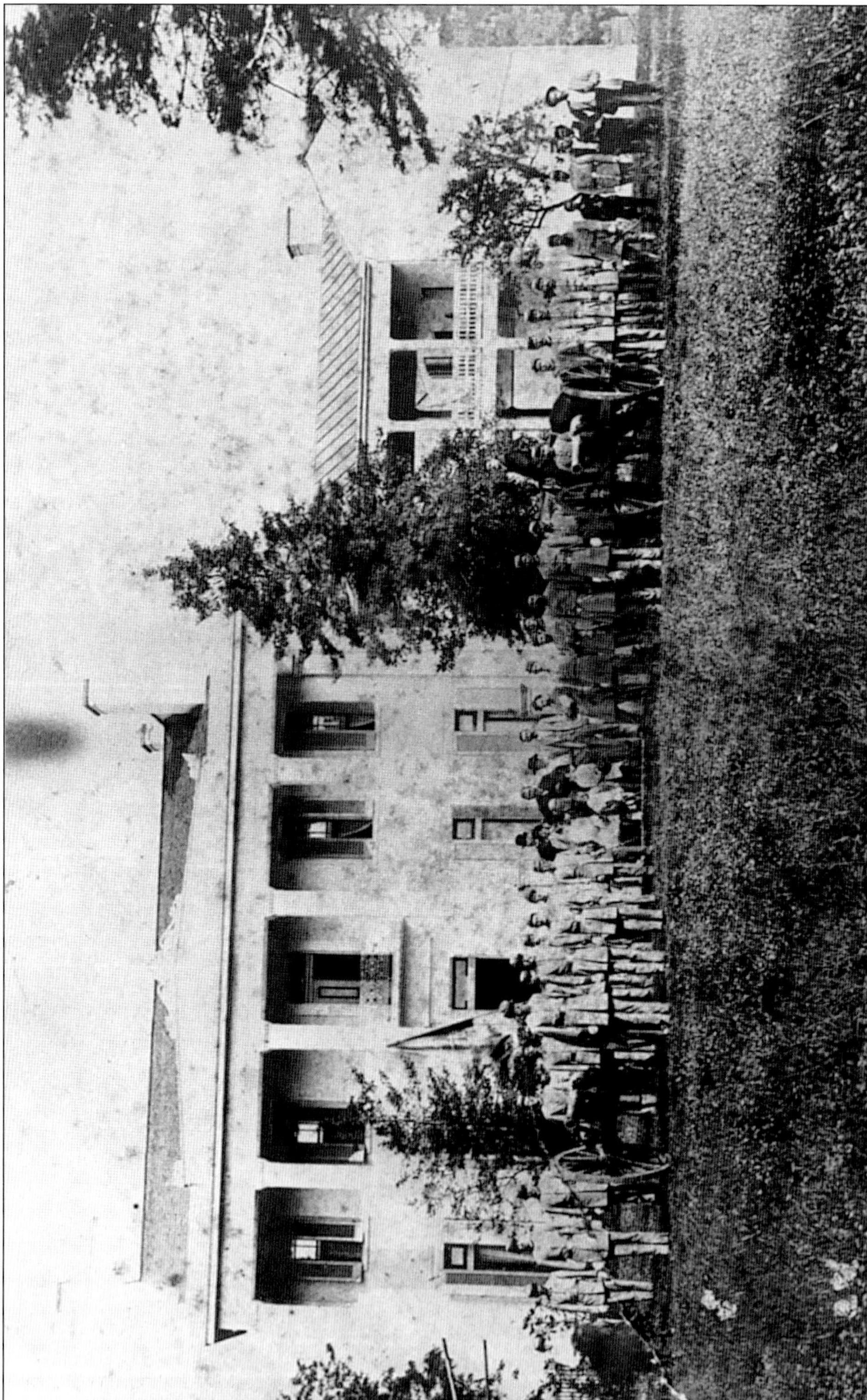

BELLE MEADE PLANTATION

The Hardings of Belle Meade Plantation came to the Nashville area in the 1790s. John Harding and his wife, Susannah Shute, lived in a double log cabin on Richland Creek, where his son, William Giles Harding, was born in 1808. John built a brick house near the log cabin in 1820. As he prospered, he continued to add to the acreage. Early on, Belle Meade became famous as a nursery for thoroughbred horses. By 1840, William Giles Harding was master of Belle Meade. After his first wife died, he and his sons moved back to his family home. William and his second wife, Elizabeth McGavock, had two daughters, Selene and Mary Elizabeth.

After the mansion was damaged by fired in 1852, it was rebuilt and enlarged on a grand scale. In the decade before the Civil War, Belle Meade was not only a premier stock farm but also a premier location for social events.

After the Civil War, Selene Harding married William Hicks Jackson, who assumed much of the responsibility in the management of the plantation. The fame and lavish lifestyle of Belle Meade continued until after the turn of the century. The interior photographs were made c. 1900. In 1903, the estate passed out of the Harding family hands. Over the next 50 years, several families occupied the mansion. In 1953, the Association for the Preservation of Tennessee Antiquities assumed responsibility for preserving the estate. Today it is open to the public as a museum house.

Photographed: exterior 1884, interiors c. 1900,
From the collection of A.P.T.A.—Belle Meade Plantation

Page 14: This photograph is of the reunion of the Harding Light Artillery at Bell Meade in 1884.

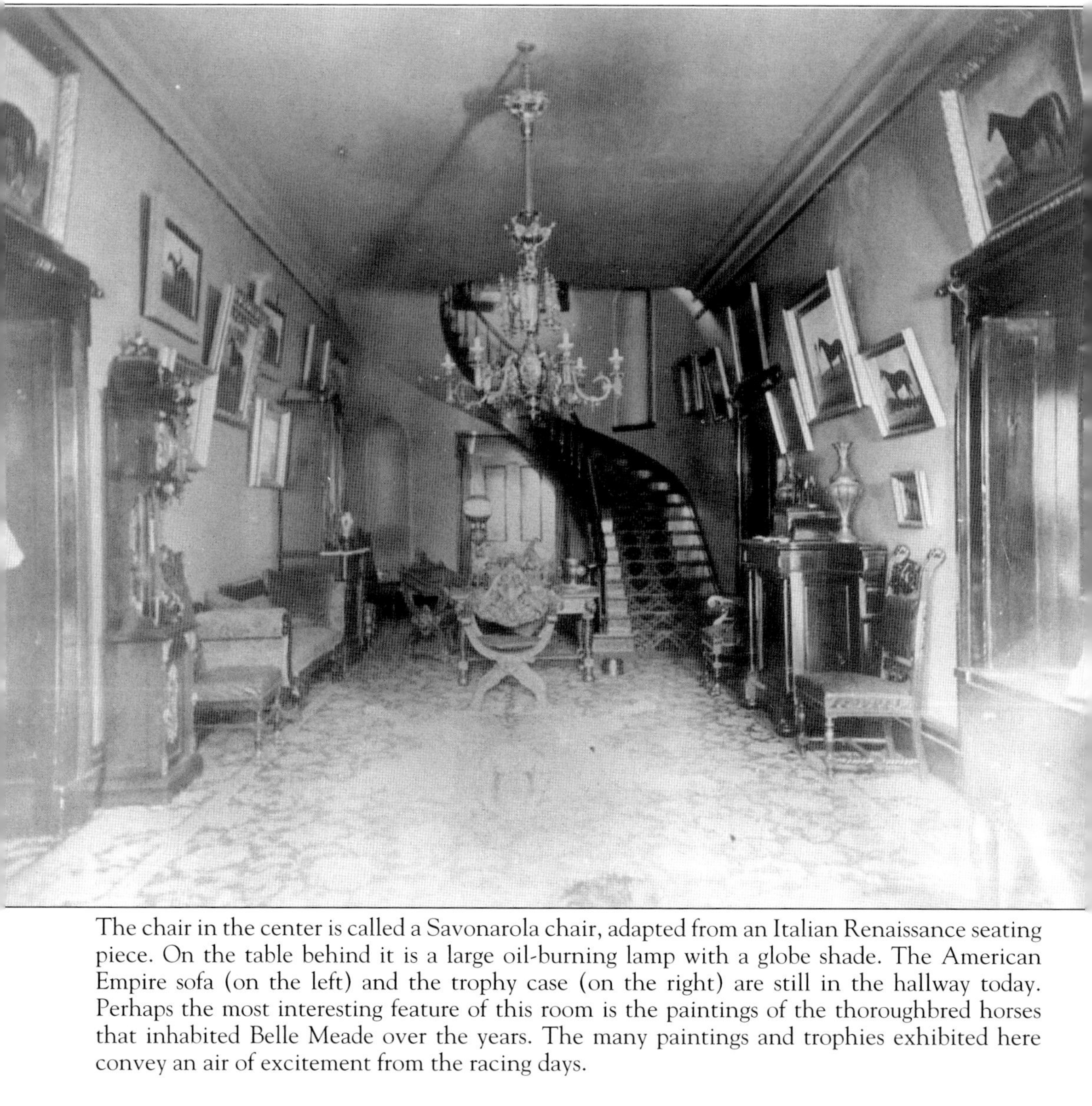

The chair in the center is called a Savonarola chair, adapted from an Italian Renaissance seating piece. On the table behind it is a large oil-burning lamp with a globe shade. The American Empire sofa (on the left) and the trophy case (on the right) are still in the hallway today. Perhaps the most interesting feature of this room is the paintings of the thoroughbred horses that inhabited Belle Meade over the years. The many paintings and trophies exhibited here convey an air of excitement from the racing days.

Page 17: An invitation to dine in this room was much sought after by Nashvillians during the nineteenth century. The dining room furniture is a Victorian Revival style adapted from English Renaissance furniture. The table and case piece mimic the Elizabethan furniture of the seventeenth century. The chairs are a combination of styles with cabriole legs and strap work carving. On the mantel is a portrait of Selene Harding Jackson. Over the sideboard hangs a portrait of William Hicks Jackson.

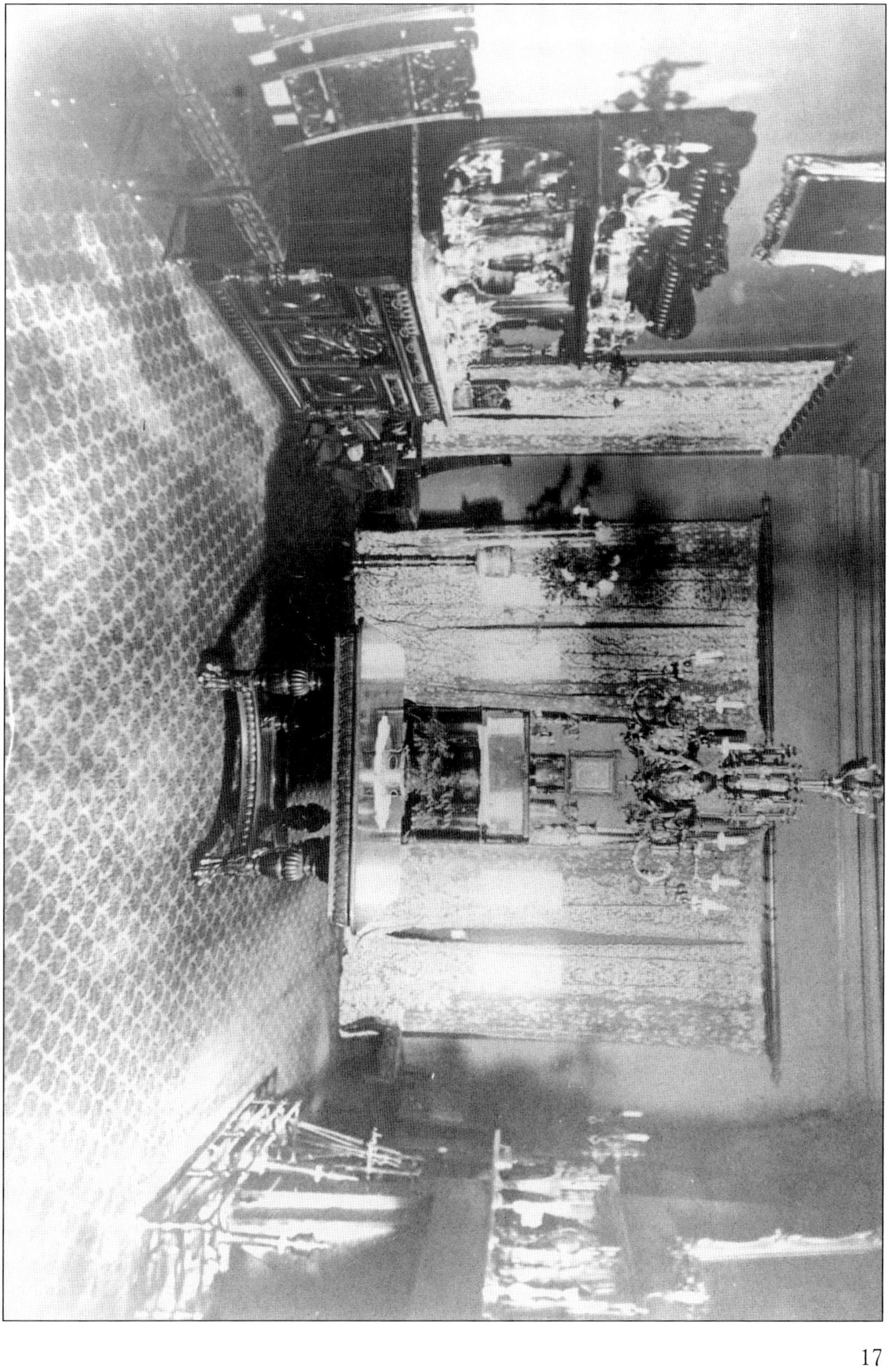

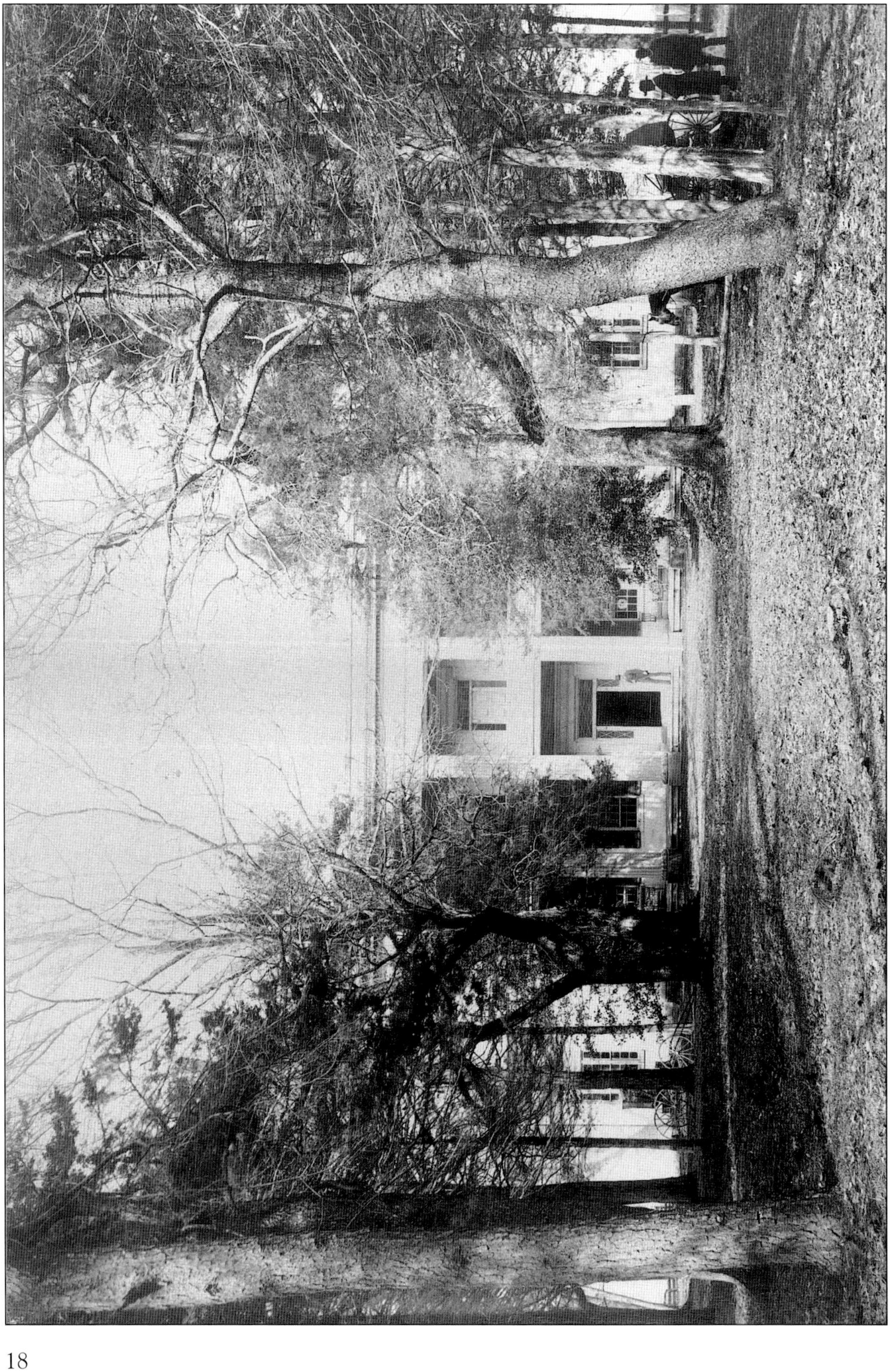

The Hermitage

Confederate Colonel Andrew Jackson III, grandson of President Andrew Jackson, employed Otto Giers to photograph the hallway, parlor bedroom, and dining room at the Hermitage in 1892. The next year, he moved with his family to Cincinnati, leaving the rooms shown here, as well as the entire house, completely empty.

After President Jackson died in 1845, his son, Andrew Jackson Jr., sold the property to the State of Tennessee with the understanding that he and his wife would live out their lives there. He died in 1865; his wife, Sara York Jackson, died in 1887. In 1889, the State Legislature passed an act giving the care and keeping of the Hermitage to the Ladies Hermitage Association (LHA). Colonel Jackson and his family continued to live there while the LHA tried to raise funds to purchase the furnishings. Since the organization was unsuccessful, he moved in 1893. By 1897, the LHA was able to start buying back President Jackson's furnishings. This house today is completely furnished as it was in President Andrew Jackson's lifetime.

By the time the rooms were photographed in 1892, President Jackson had been dead 47 years, the Civil War had taken its toll, and the property had been poorly maintained since. While the President's bedroom was still arranged the way it was when President Jackson died, it looked decidedly bare with no lighting or personal items evident. Even the colorful scenic wallpaper in the entry hall was in need of repair. Called Telemachus in the Island of Calypso, it tells the story of Telemachus as he searched for his father, Ulysses. This wallpaper was not only highly prized by President Jackson and his family, but is documented to have been in three other Nashville houses: the W.G.M. Campbell house on Lebanon Road; Rokeby, where the Upper Room now stands; and remnants still cling to the walls at Belmont Mansion.

Photographer: Otto Giers
Photographed: 1892
From the collection of the Ladies Hermitage Association

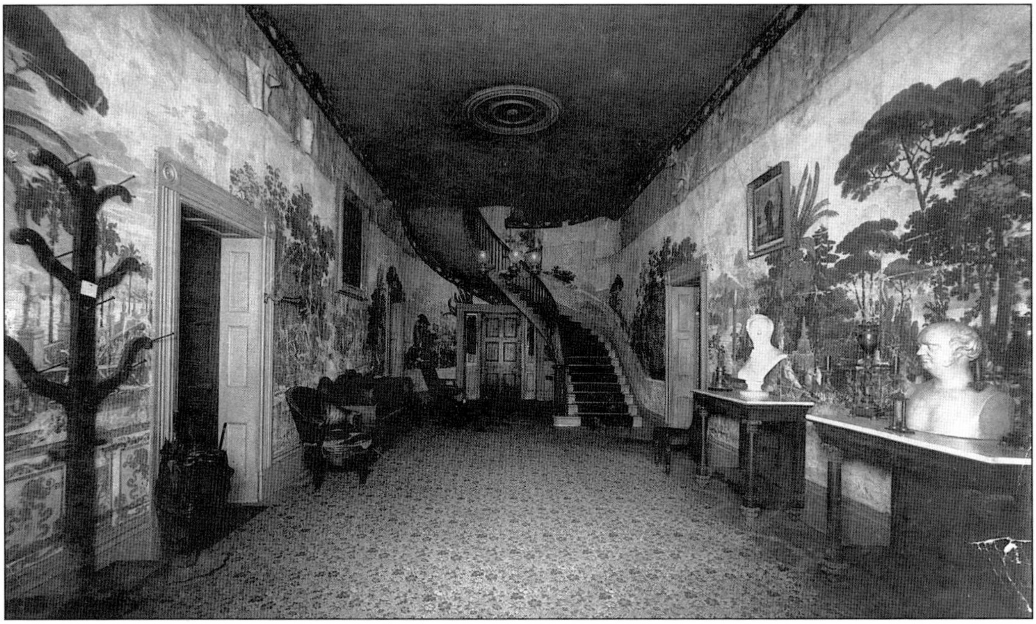

The front hall is dominated by the Telemachus wallpaper manufactured by duFour in France. The marble bust in the foreground is of Jackson's secretary of the navy, Levi Woodbury. The statue to the rear is of Lewis Cass, his secretary of war. The small barrel chair on the left was given to Andrew Jackson by President George Washington. President Jackson's family sold the chair to Mt. Vernon, where it may be seen today.

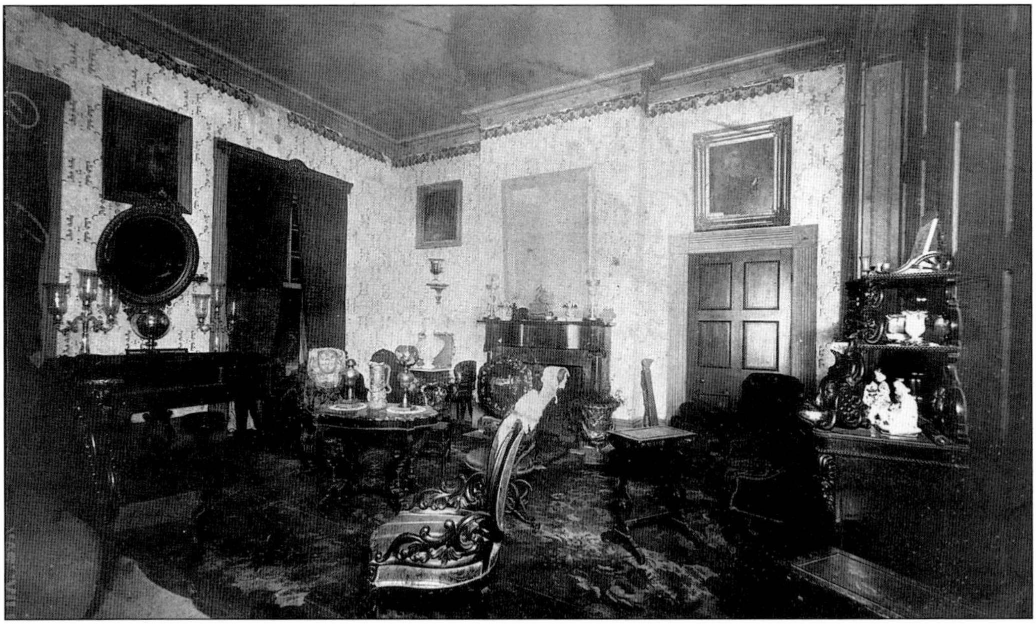

Hanging in the front parlor at the Hermitage in 1892 were three fine portraits by Ralph E.W. Earle. Two are bust portraits of Rachel Jackson and the President. The other is a portrait of Andrew Jackson on his horse, Sam Patch. A heavily carved Rococo Revival chair and étagère are in the foreground. On the étagère are two perfume bottles, in the shape of figurines, by French potter Jacob Petit.

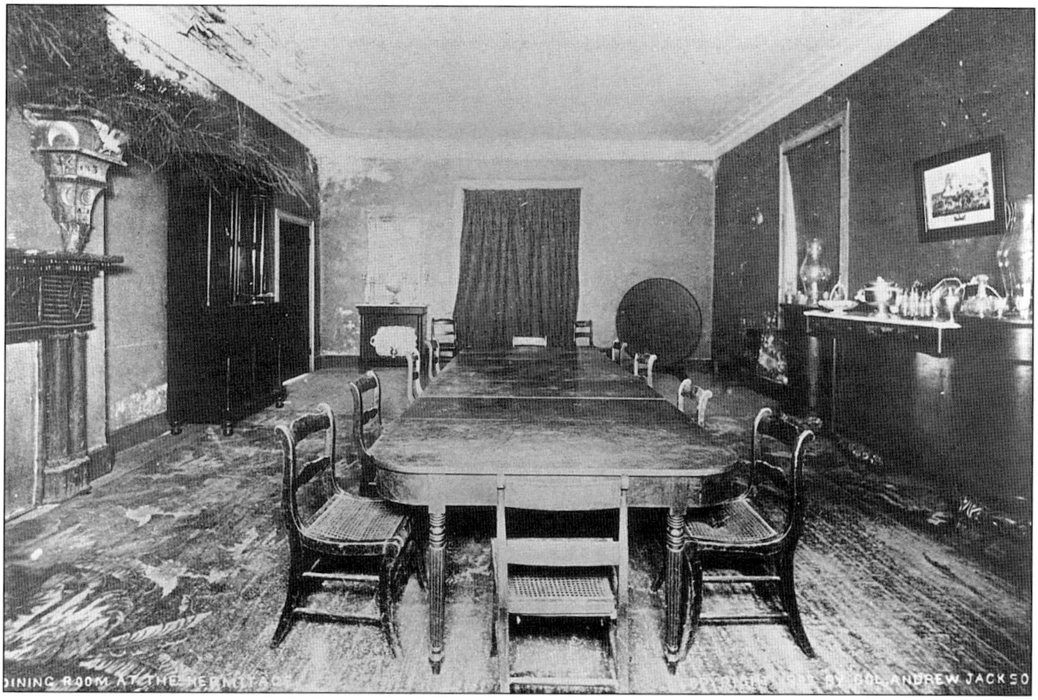

Cane bottom Klismos-style chairs surround the Sheraton banquet table shown here. Despite its dismal appearance, the silver and candles on the American Empire sideboard indicate the room was still in use. The wall urn over the mantel filled with dead foliage was actually an outside downspout converted to an interior vase.

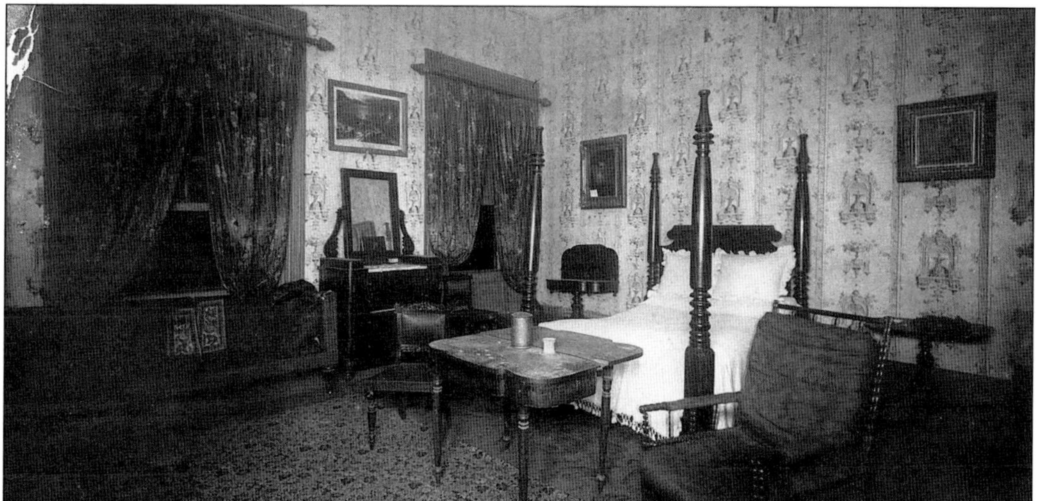

The wallpaper shown here is believed to have been hung in the 1850s over wallpaper that was hung in 1836, when the Hermitage was rebuilt after a fire. In a recent restoration, this wallpaper was removed and the 1836 wallpaper restored. The chintz window hangings seen here have been reproduced and rehung. The easy chair with spool turnings was covered in a damask fabric and the sofa and straight chair in horsehair. On either side of the four-poster bed are portraits of the President's granddaughter, Rachel, and his son, Andrew Jackson Jr.; both paintings are by Ralph E.W. Earle.

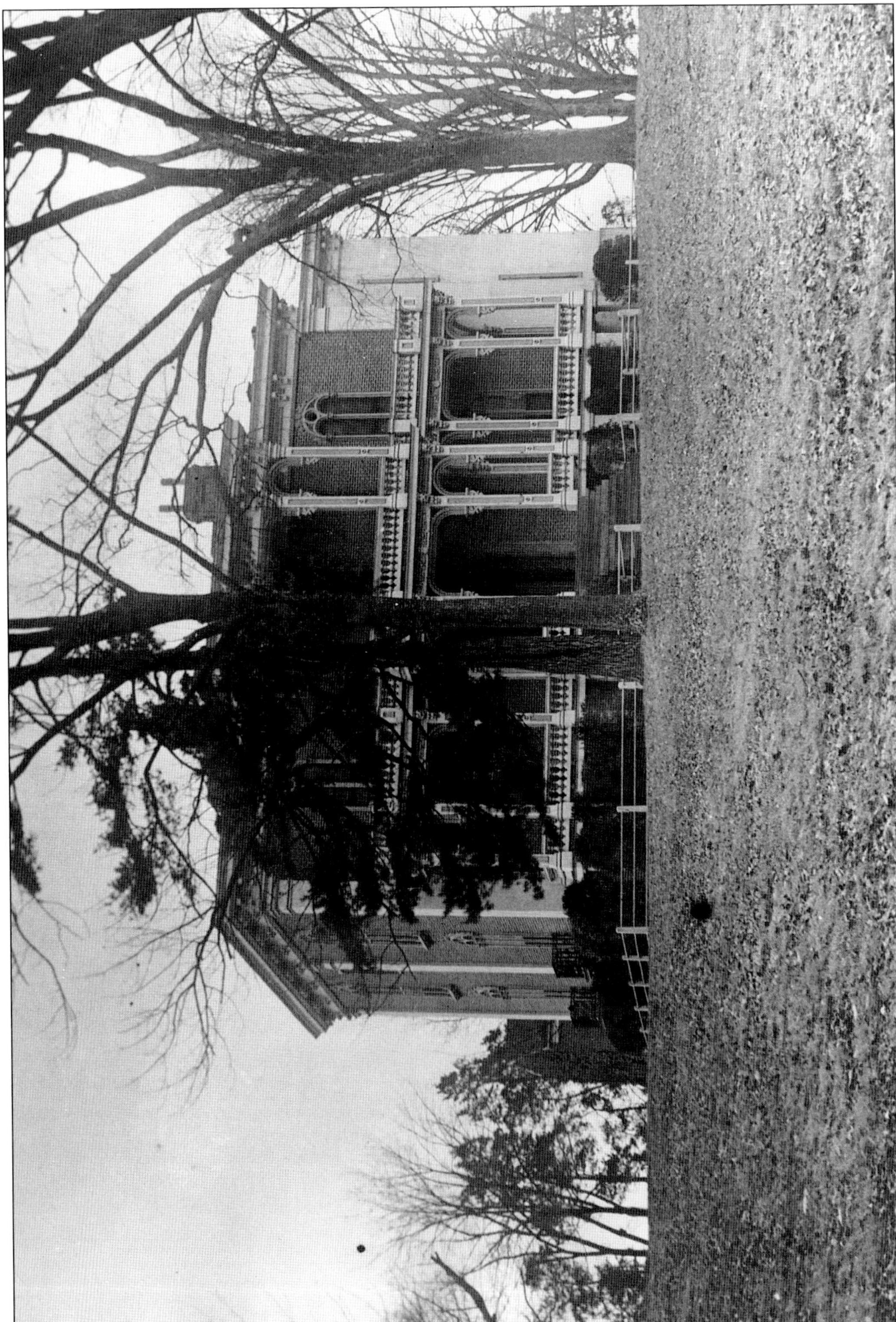

Clover Bottom Mansion

The house pictured here was built in 1858 to replace a former home on this site that had burned on February 7, 1859. Built by Dr. James Hoggett, it contained 23 rooms with 14-foot ceilings, sliding doors, and Italian marble mantels. In *Architecture in Middle Tennessee*, James Patrick calls the style of Clover Bottom "an Italianate development of the Federal plantation house." Long before this house was constructed, Clover Bottom Plantation had played a significant role in Nashville history.

John Donelson, one of the founders of Nashville, had claimed this land for his homesite shortly after his arrival here in 1780. After he abandoned the property because of an American Indian attack, it was claimed by another, and eventually was sold to the Hoggett family. Part of the tract near the Stones River became the Clover Bottom Jockey Club, with Andrew Jackson as its most famous member. Jackson also operated a tavern and a boatyard near the river in the early 1800s before his military and political careers thrust him onto the national scene.

Mr. Andrew Price, who bought the Clover Bottom property in 1882, was an outstanding breeder of trotting horses. He also owned sugar plantations in Louisiana. Clover Bottom was his summer home. The property was sold in 1918 to the A.F. and R.D. Stanford family. In 1949, it was acquired by the State of Tennessee. The house is now the office of the Tennessee Historical Commission.

Photographed: *c.* 1910
Exterior photograph: Tennessee State Library & Archives
Interior photograph *c.* 1910
From the collection of R.C. Plater

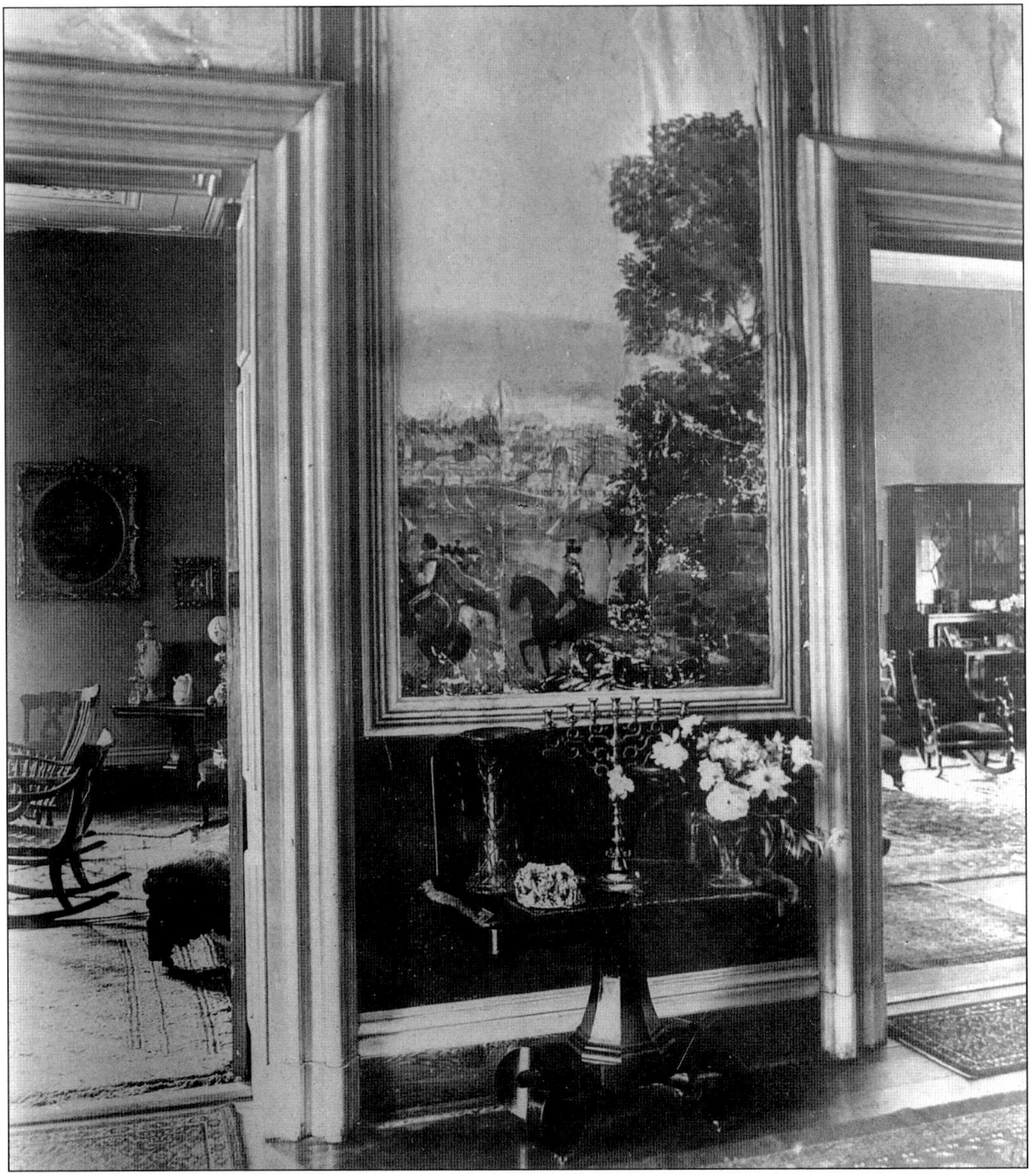

Two interior photographs were made during the residence of the Price family at Clover Bottom. The hallway walls were covered in a scenic wallpaper called *The War of Independence*, which was first manufactured by Zuber in France in 1838. From this hallway photograph we can glimpse both the front and back parlors connected by sliding doors.

Page 25: The two portraits seen here are of Edward J. Gay and his wife, Lavinia Hynes Gay, the parents of Mrs. Andrew Price, mistress of Clover Bottom at the time these interior photographs were made in the early 1900s. The portraits now hang at Arcadia Plantation in Thibodaux, Louisiana. The Oriental area rugs and rocking chairs seen here were typical of the decoration of similar rooms in this time period. The only lighting fixture is the double oil lamp in front of the window. *Aphrodite of Melos*, also known as *Venus di Milo*, adds a note of Old World elegance to this room.

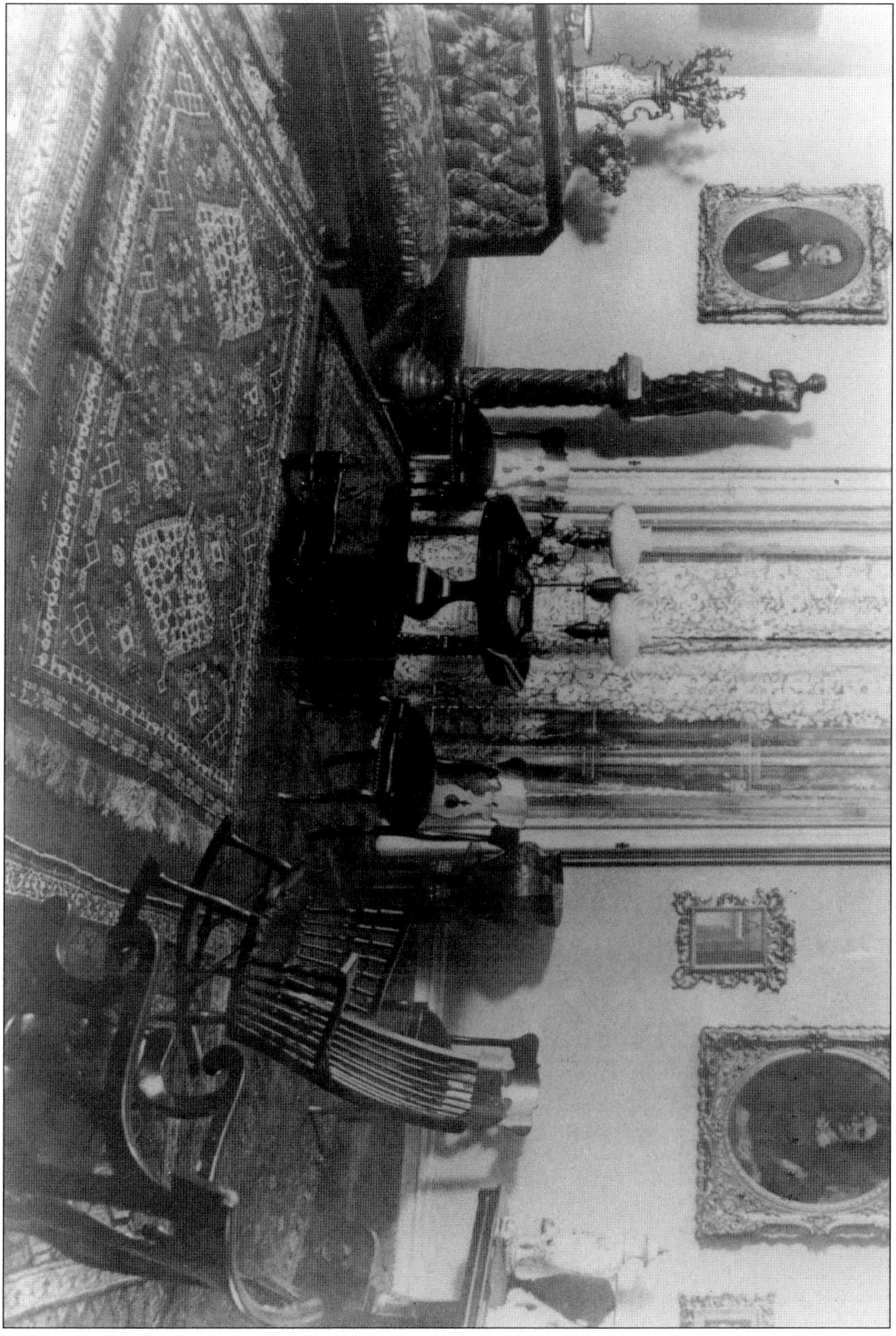

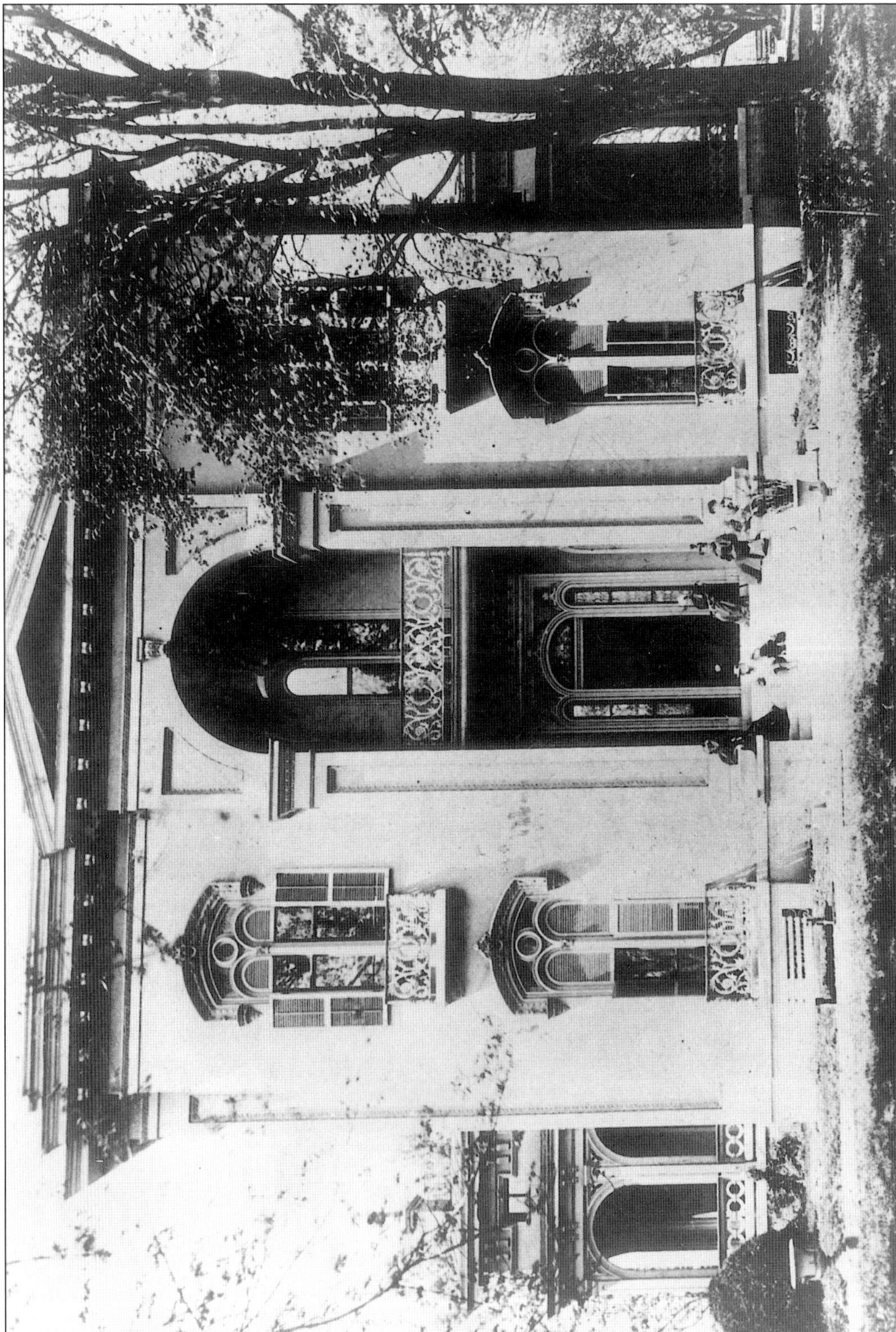

BURLINGTON

Burlington, the Elliston-Farrell house, was razed in 1932 to make way for the new Father Ryan High School on Elliston Place. Joseph, the first Elliston to occupy this property, was an early Nashville silversmith and mayor of Nashville. He was also a member of the committee that selected William Strickland as the architect for the Tennessee State Capitol Building. Family records describe the style of Burlington as Italian Renaissance and credit William Strickland as the architect.

The house pictured here was built in 1859 by Joseph Elliston's son, William R. Elliston, after the death of both Joseph Elliston and William Strickland. An earlier house that occupied this site was incorporated into the new house built of stucco on brick. The dominant feature of the facade was the great two-story arch of the entrance. This two-story arch entrance was a feature of other buildings in the area: the Giles County Court House in Pulaski (1850) and the Adelphi Theatre in Nashville, both designed by Adolphus Heiman. The influence of the Burlington facade was also seen on the facade at Kingsley on Murfreesboro Road, remodeled by the Weaver family in 1860.

The three interior photographs shown here appear to have been made when Elizabeth Boddie Elliston (1820–1904) was interviewed by a newspaper reporter in 1899. She was shown in one of the photographs sitting in a rocker by her fireplace. Over the mantel hung a portrait of her late husband, William Robert Elliston. Their descendants continued to live at Burlington until it was demolished in 1932.

Photographed: c. 1899,
From the collection of Jean Farrell Prueher, Tennessee State Library & Archives

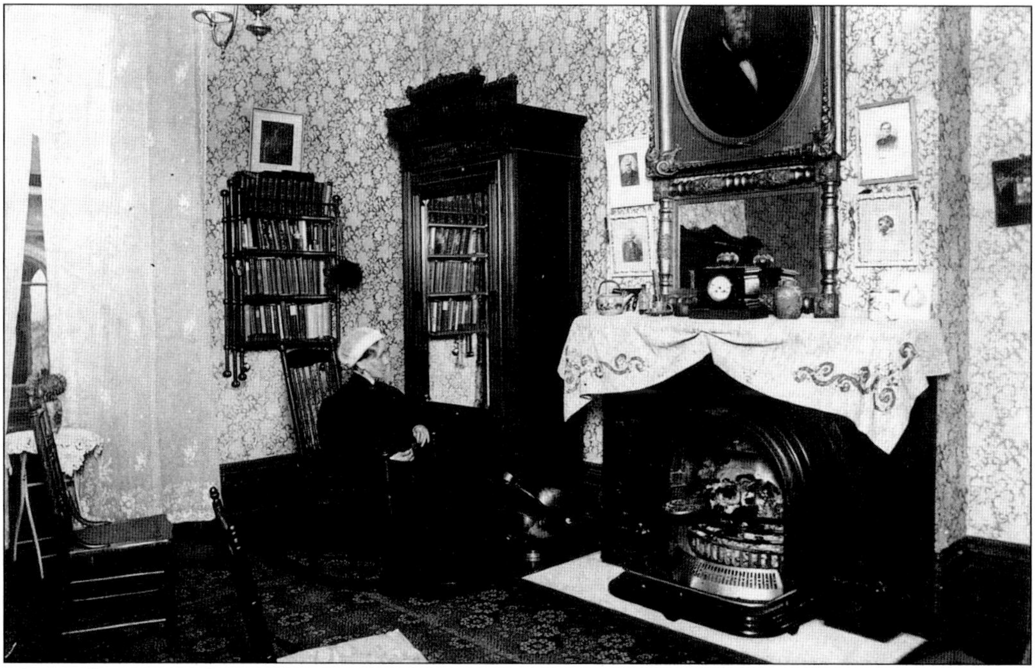

The wallpaper in this room is similar to an American pattern of the 1880s where the manner of William Morris and the Japanesque taste have been blended. Under the portrait is a mantel mirror flanked by framed family photographs. The mantel shelf is draped in a fancywork linen scarf and displays an Oriental ginger jar and tea pot. The large bookcase is one of a pair and is now in the collection at Belmont Mansion.

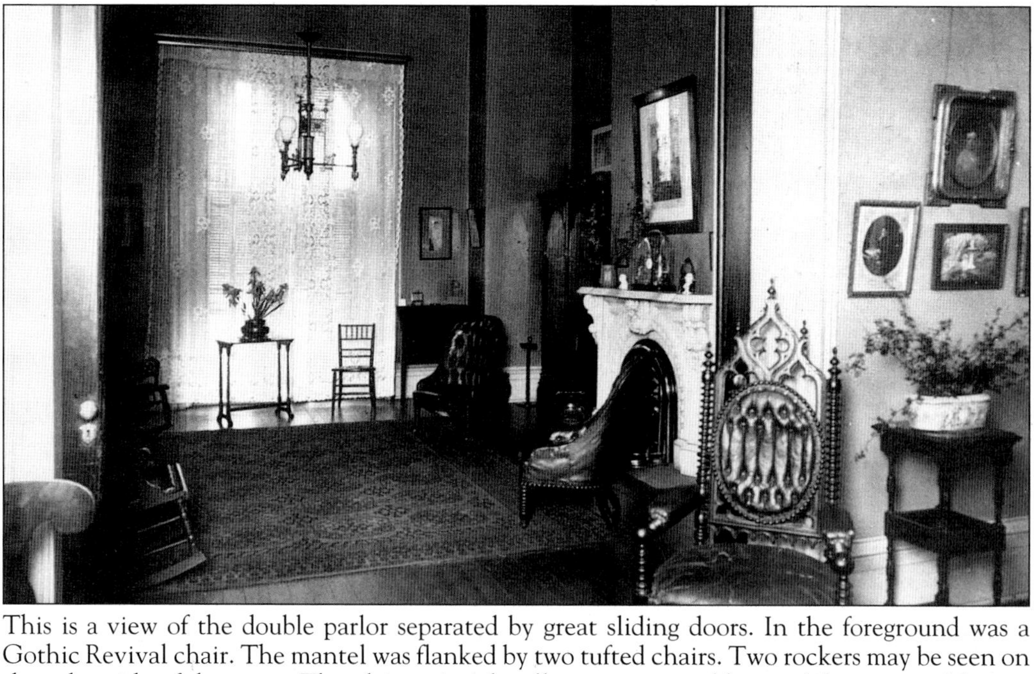

This is a view of the double parlor separated by great sliding doors. In the foreground was a Gothic Revival chair. The mantel was flanked by two tufted chairs. Two rockers may be seen on the other side of the room. The plain painted walls were crowned by an elaborate entablature. The Italian marble mantle had a clock under a glass dome.

The curved staircase at Burlington had a niche on the landing. In this photo, we can see the great arch leading to the staircase, as well as the elaborate cornice in the Gothic style. Reflected in the pier mirror is a scroll back sofa covered with black horsehair.

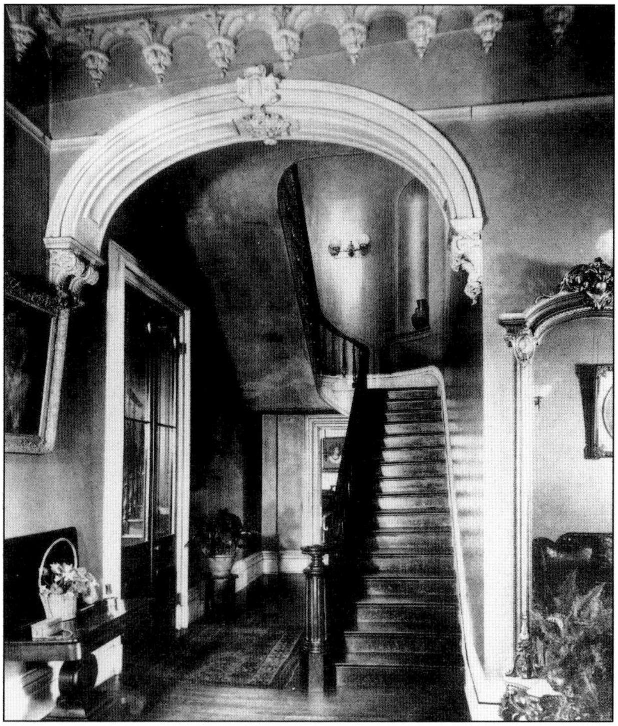

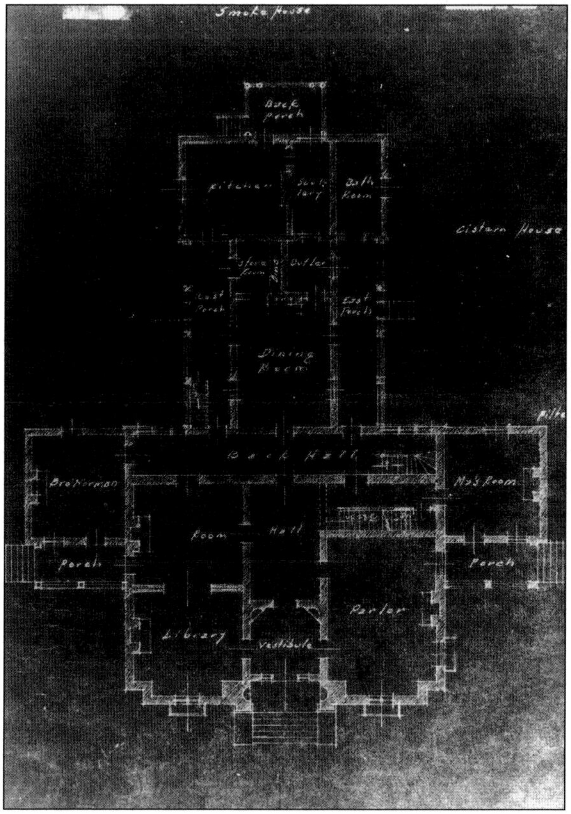

Nashville architect Donald Southgate, who married Lizinka Elliston Farrell, drew this floor plan of Burlington.

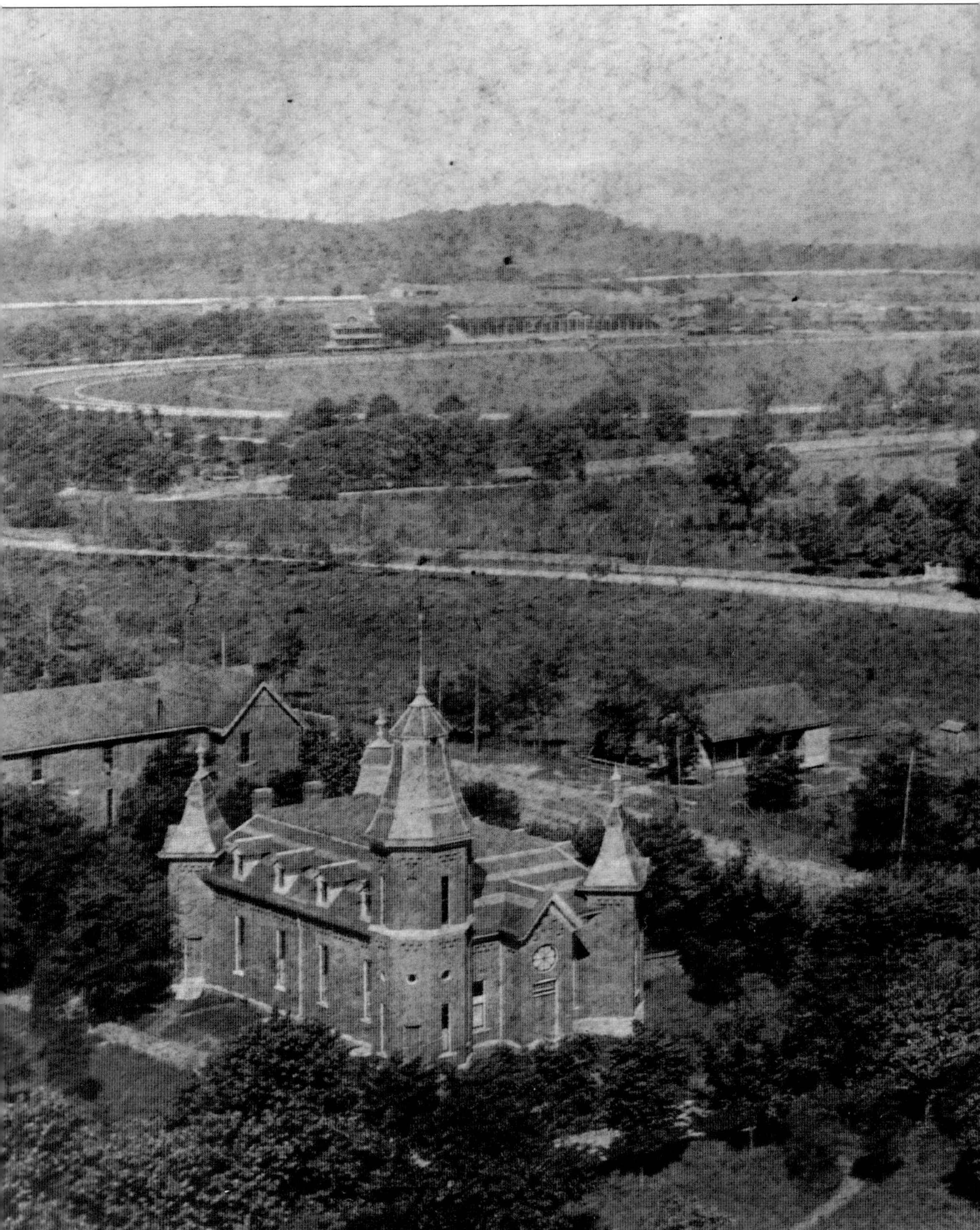

The gate and rooftop of Burlington may be seen in the center of this early photograph. The house on the right was the home of an Elliston daughter, Lysinka Buford, and her husband, Edward. It

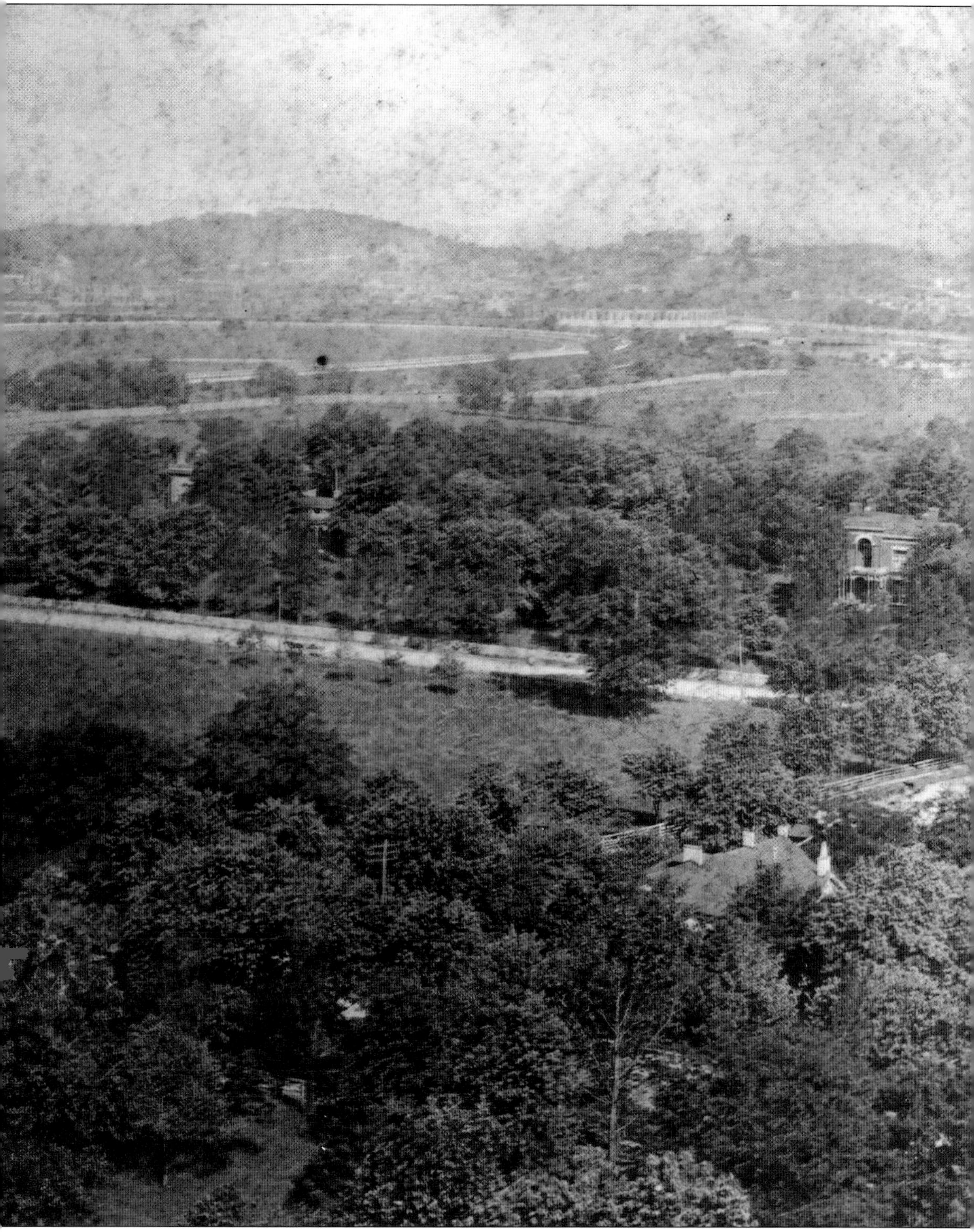

was called "By-Ma." At the top of the picture may be seen the racetrack at Centennial Park. In the foreground is the old gymnasium on Vanderbilt University campus.

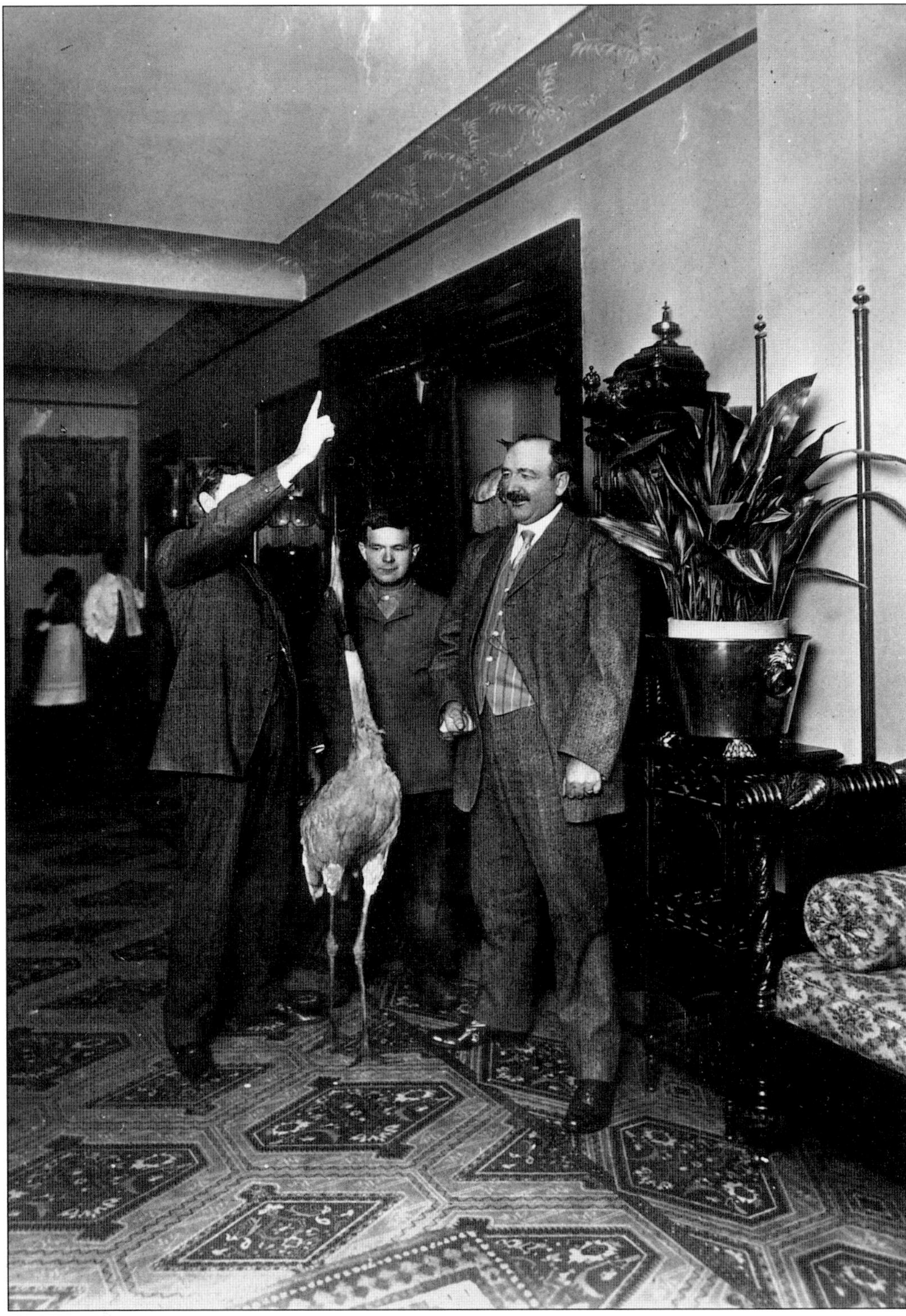

RENRAW

James C. Warner, a wealthy iron master, was living on North Spruce Street (Eighth Avenue North) in downtown Nashville when he purchased 60 acres and a small house on Gallatin Road for a summer home in 1880. In 1890, he made extensive additions to the house and occupied it as his permanent residence. Many Colonial Revival elements are evident in the architecture: columns with Ionic capitals, a hip roof, balustrades, a dentil cornice, and a triangular pediment crowning the entrance to the porch. One end of the porch terminates in a porte-cochere and the other in a circular gazebo-like seating area with a bell-shaped dome reminiscent of the schoolhouse in the upper garden at Mt. Vernon. The golf links at Renraw in the 1890s were probably the first in Nashville. This large house was home not only to James C. and Mary Tom Warner, but also their son, Percy Warner, and his family. After James C. Warner died in 1895, the family continued to live there until 1913, when they moved to Royal Oaks on Harding Road. Renraw still stands today on the corner of McClurken Avenue. It is the home of the Nashville Auto Diesel College. Renraw is "Warner" spelled backwards.

While only one interior view of Renraw exists, there are a number of interior views of Royal Oaks. Although the Warners were a family of means, we know from firsthand accounts that the furniture and decorative objects at Renraw were used at Royal Oaks. One case in point is the day bed shown in the photograph on the opposite page. It may also be seen in the entry hall at Royal Oaks. The wispy fern pattern in the wallpaper border is in stark contrast to the bold geometric pattern of the machine-loomed carpet with matching border. An aspidistra plant in a brass planter is seen behind Percy Warner. Others in the photograph are Clare Lovett, aviary keeper, and cartoonist Homer Davenport. Two servants are seen in the rear, standing under a family portrait. The crane, named Rufus, was Mr. Warner's pet.

These photographs may be dated between 1910 and 1913. The earlier date is when the photographer M.W. Wiles opened his studio. The later date is when the Warners left Renraw.

Photographer: M.W. Wiles
Photographed: c. 1912
From the collection of Margaret W. Greenlee, Tennessee State Library & Archives

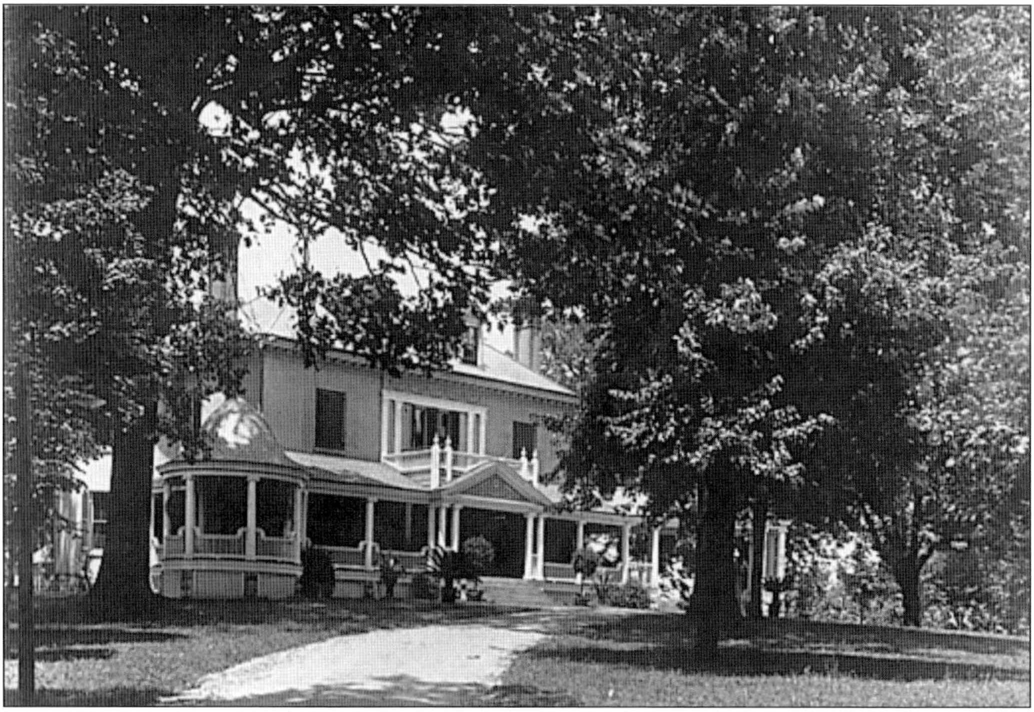

The wide shaded porch at Renraw was an outdoor living room in the summer months. It housed not only wicker chairs and tables but a large collection of ferns and other large plants. Two gas porch lights flank the doorway. Over the doorway, between the porch lights, there appears to be a hanging clock.

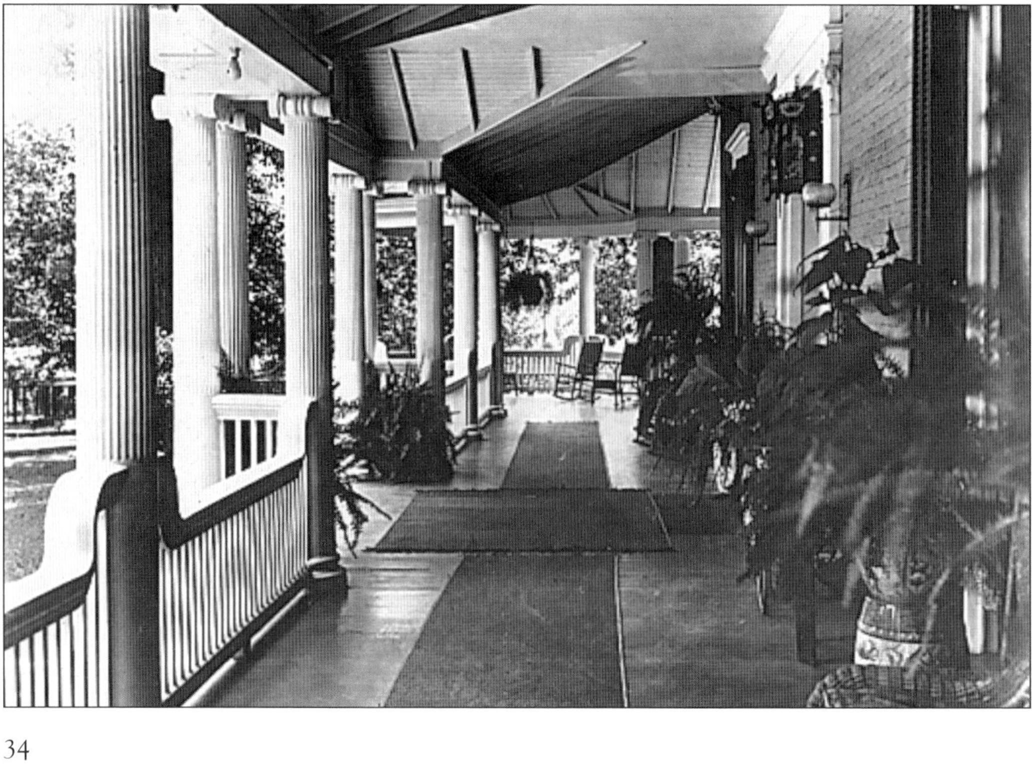

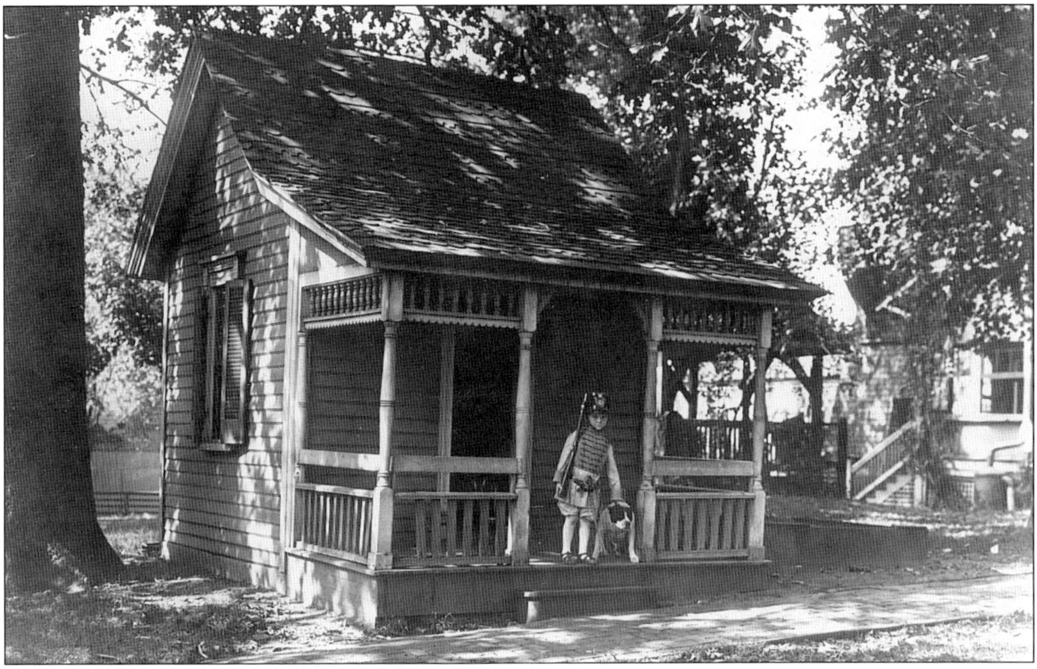

The present-day Warner descendants have been unable to positively identify the child on the playhouse front porch. His (or her) dress parade military uniform would have been suitable on The Plain at West Point. The soft water collected in the rain barrel on the right was highly prized by ladies of this era for shampoos and fine laundry.

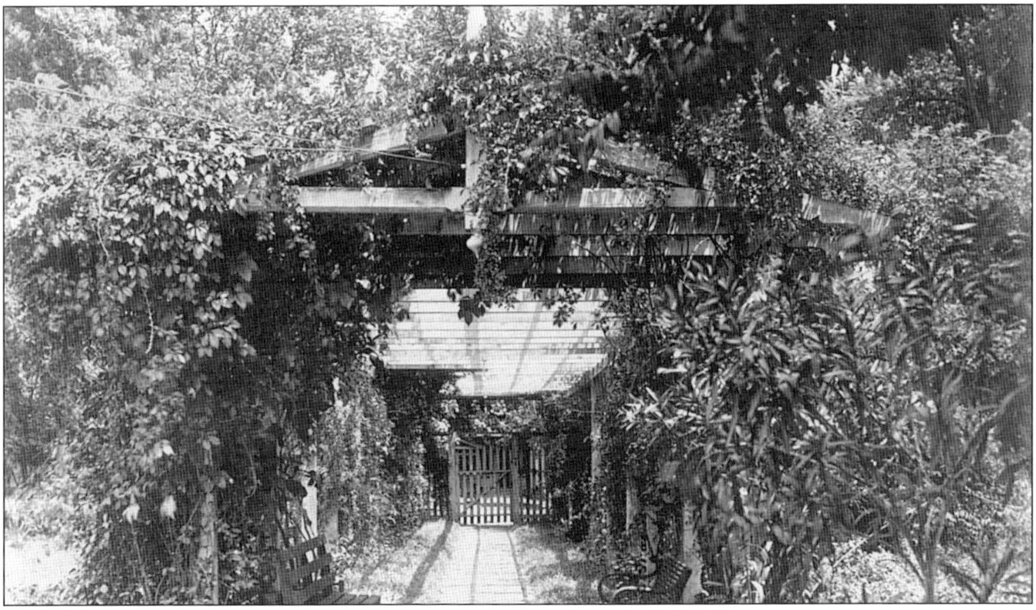

The many vine-covered arbors in the gardens at Renraw also provided outdoor living space in the early 1900s. There were numerous outdoor benches on the property under the giant trees that shaded the house and grounds. The Warner family's passion for nature could be seen here in the large plant and bird collection. The entire community benefited from this passion when the family donated the Percy Warner and Edwin Warner Parks to the city.

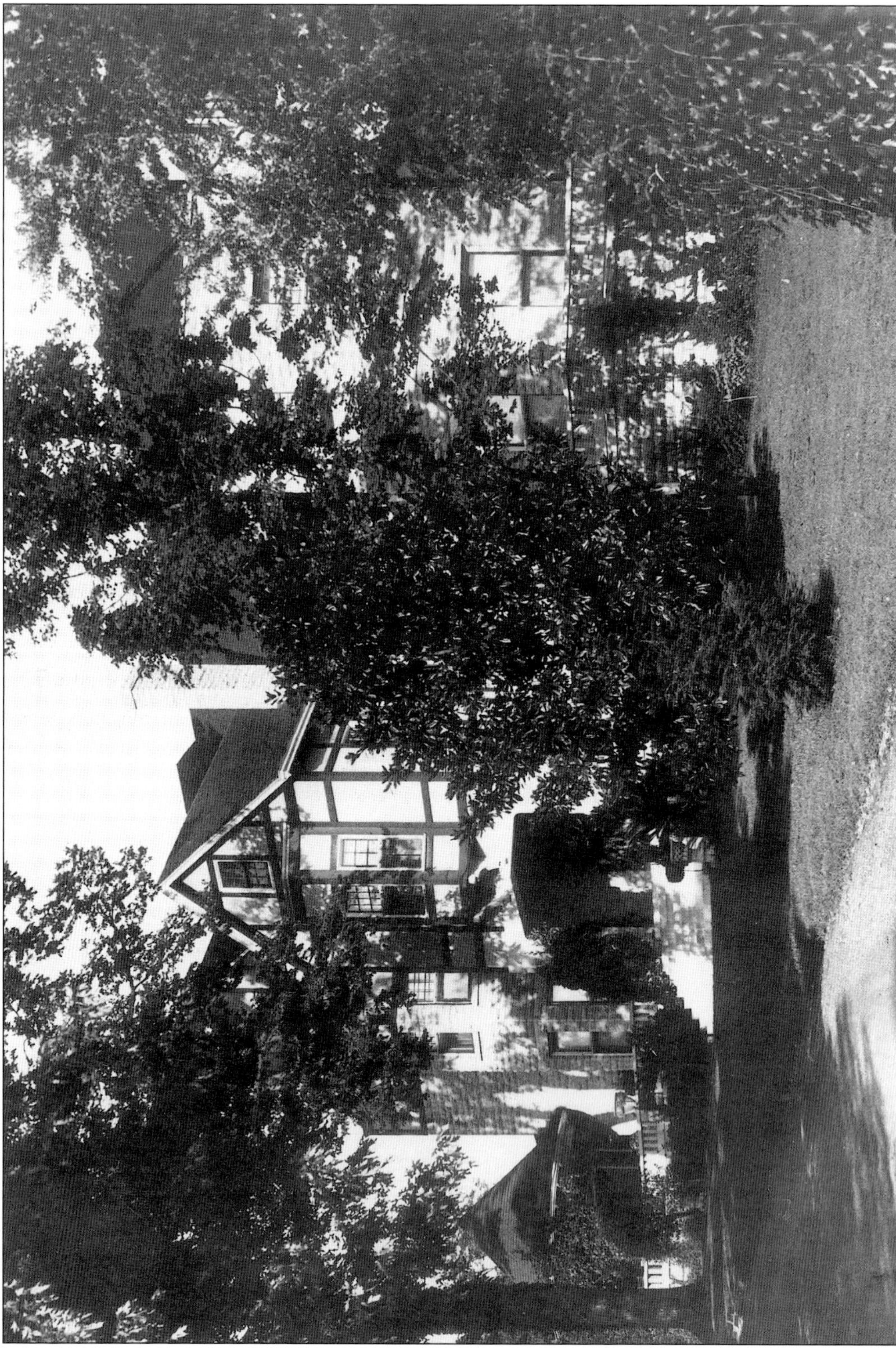

Royal Oaks

Percy Warner married Margaret L. Lindsley, his neighbor and daughter of educator John Berrien Lindsley, whose North Spruce Street (Eighth Avenue North) house interiors may also be seen in this volume. Percy and Margaret Warner lived first on North Spruce Street, then at Renraw with their children and the elder Warners until the family moved to Royal Oaks on Harding Road in 1913. By this time, Percy Warner's family consisted of he, his wife, and three unmarried daughters, Margaret L., Percie, and Mary Tom. His daughter Saidee had married George Frazer. Another daughter, Mary Louise, had married Luke Lea.

Royal Oaks had been built in the fashionable English Tudor style in the early 1900s by Mrs. John W. Baker on Harding Road. The estate consisted of 20 acres and a large house that was the scene of many lavish social events, including debutante balls and weddings. Although the location of Royal Oaks was still considered to be in the countryside in 1913, it was certainly not a farm. A suburban way of life had developed around the turn of the century due to the proliferation of motorcars.

The property was sold in 1940; the house was razed in the 1960s. Royal Oaks Apartments and Park Manor Presbyterian Retirement Home now occupy the site. The view on the opposite page of the front entrance shows the variety of plant material used in the foundation planting as well as in the gardens. Also visible is the gazebo porch feature similar to the one at the Warner's former home, Renraw.

Photographer: M.W. Wiles
Photographed: *c.* 1913
From the collection of Margaret W. Greenlee, Tennessee State Library and Archives

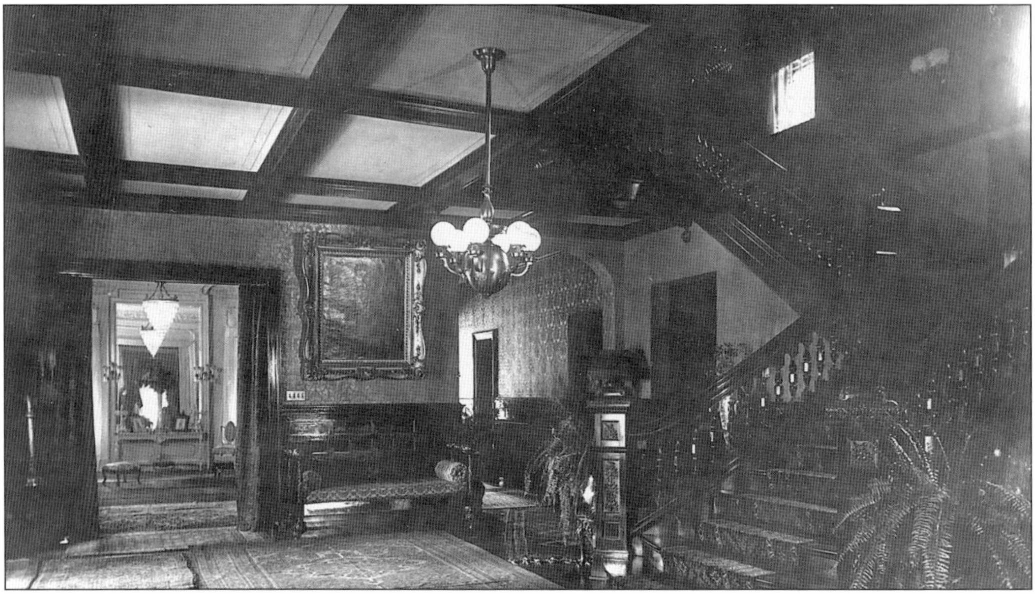

The spacious entry hall was dominated by a wide staircase that divided at a landing. In this photograph, we glimpse the drawing room and side hall. Under a portrait of Randall McGavock, a relative and former mayor of Nashville, was the day bed that was in the entry hall at Renraw. This painting, by Washington Cooper, now hangs in the Nashville Room at the Ben West Public Library.

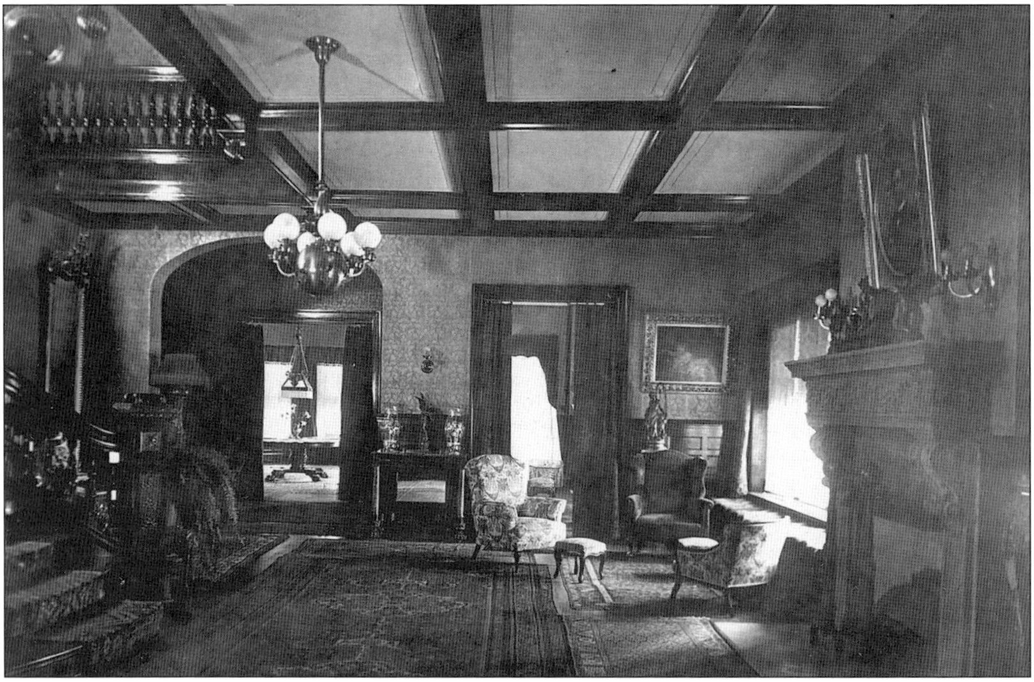

The opposite side of the large passageway was also used as a seating area. A number of handwoven Oriental rugs covered the polished floor. From this view, we see the dining room and the library. Heavy portières covered the doorways. Like the dining room and library, this room had dark wainscoting and a coffered ceiling.

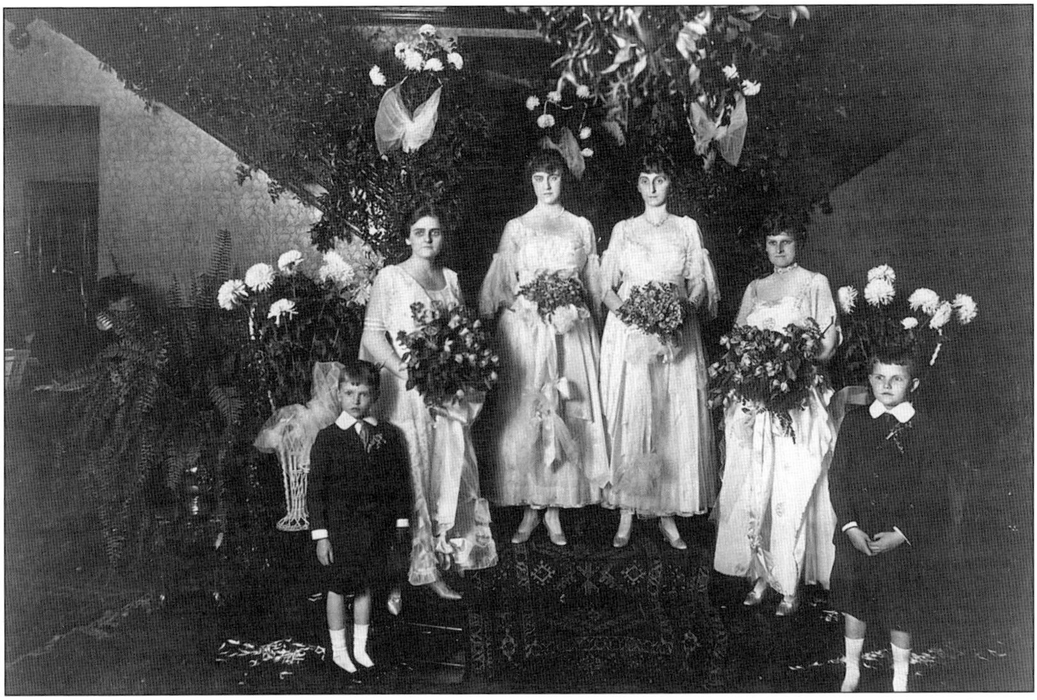

One of the many notable social events that took place at Royal Oaks was the wedding of Mary Tom Warner to W.T. Mallison on October 28, 1915. Pictured here from left to right are the following: Percy Lea, Jean Morgan Ewing, Percie Warner, Margaret L. Warner, ? Morgan, and Luke Lea Jr.

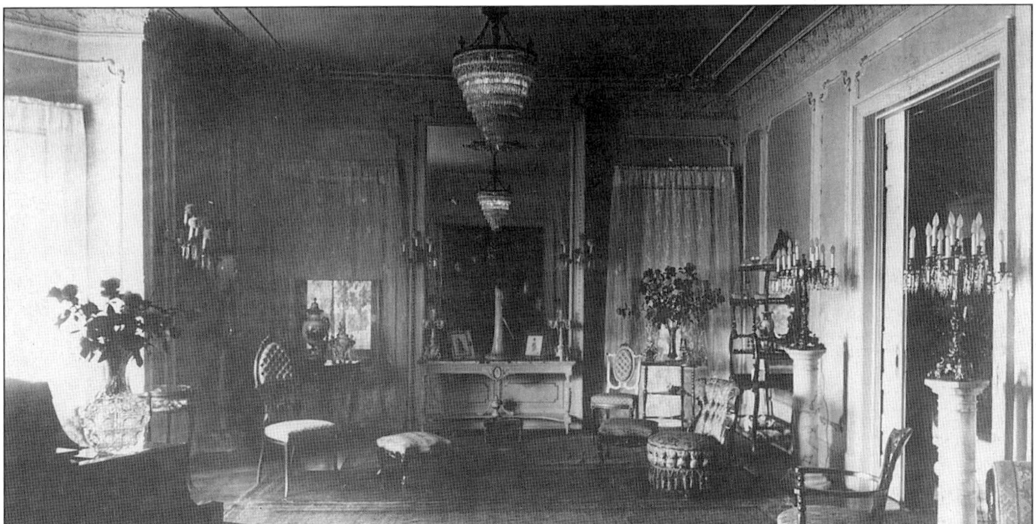

Without the authenticity of a museum, this room had the flavor of the French eighteenth century. The focal point was the ceiling-high mirror over a painted console table. Reflected in the mirror was a crystal cone-shaped chandelier. While the colors are not revealed in this black-and-white photograph, we know they were high values with subtle contrast. A classic frieze and the Rococo mouldings of the wall panels were reminiscent of the reigns of Louis 15th and Louis 16th.

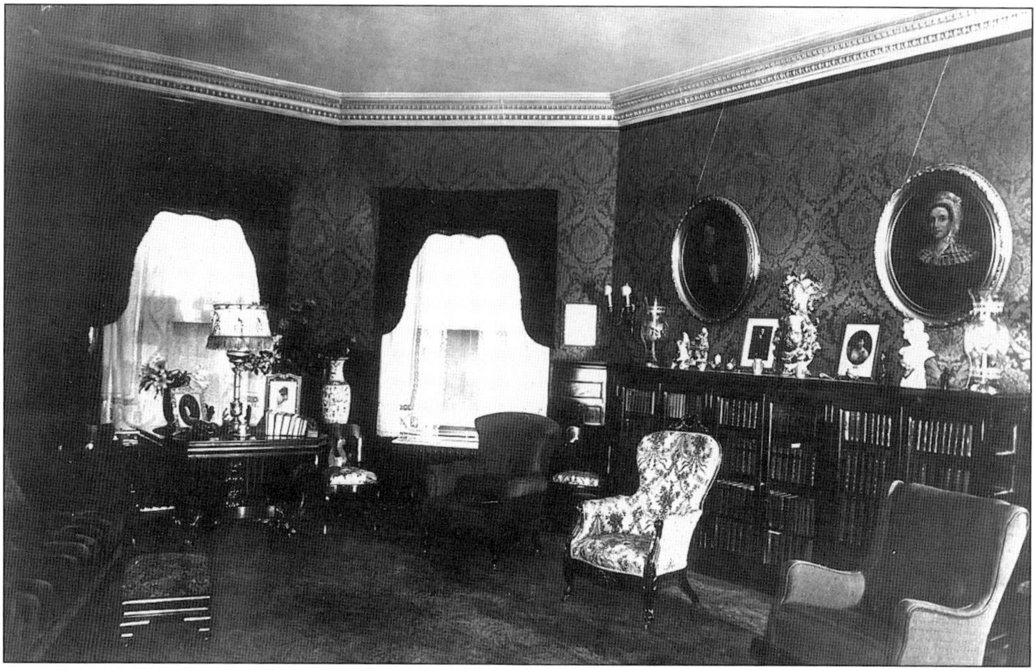

Comfort was the keynote in this room containing a tufted Turkish-style divan and upholstered chairs. The up-to-date lighting features an electrified candelabra on the mantel, a large table lamp that illuminates a library table, wall sconces that surround the room, and a large fringed shade that softens the glare of a light bulb suspended over the divan. Over the built-in bookcases were two portraits of Josiah Williams and his wife, parents of Mrs. James C. Warner (Mary Tom Williams). When the Warners left their Nashville home during the Civil War for safety reasons, Mary Tom cut these portraits out of their frames and took them with her to their Chattanooga refuge.

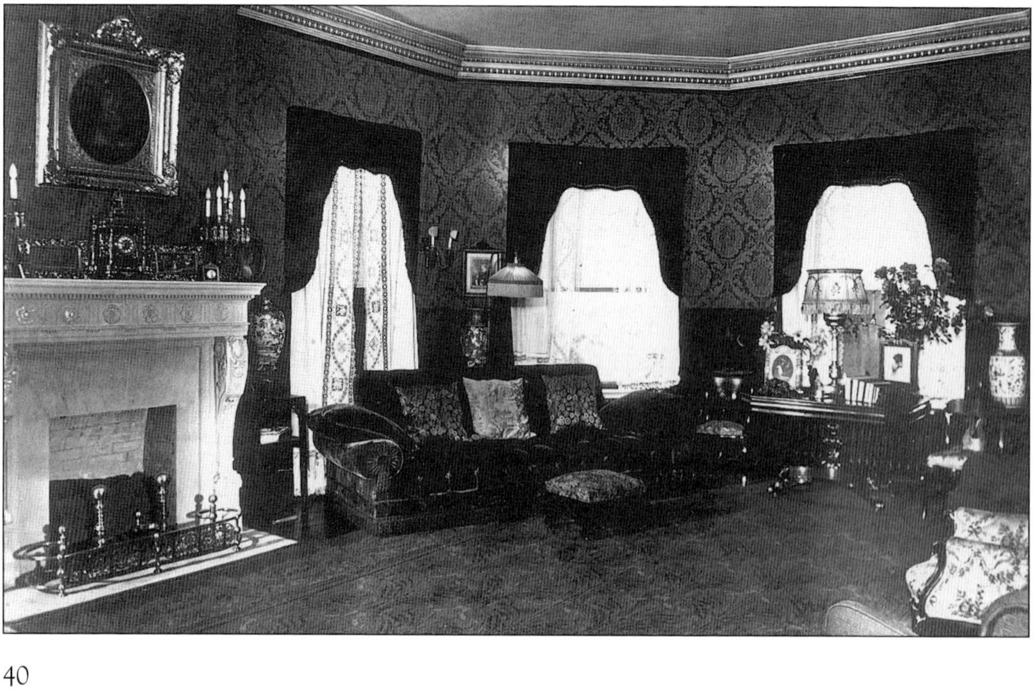

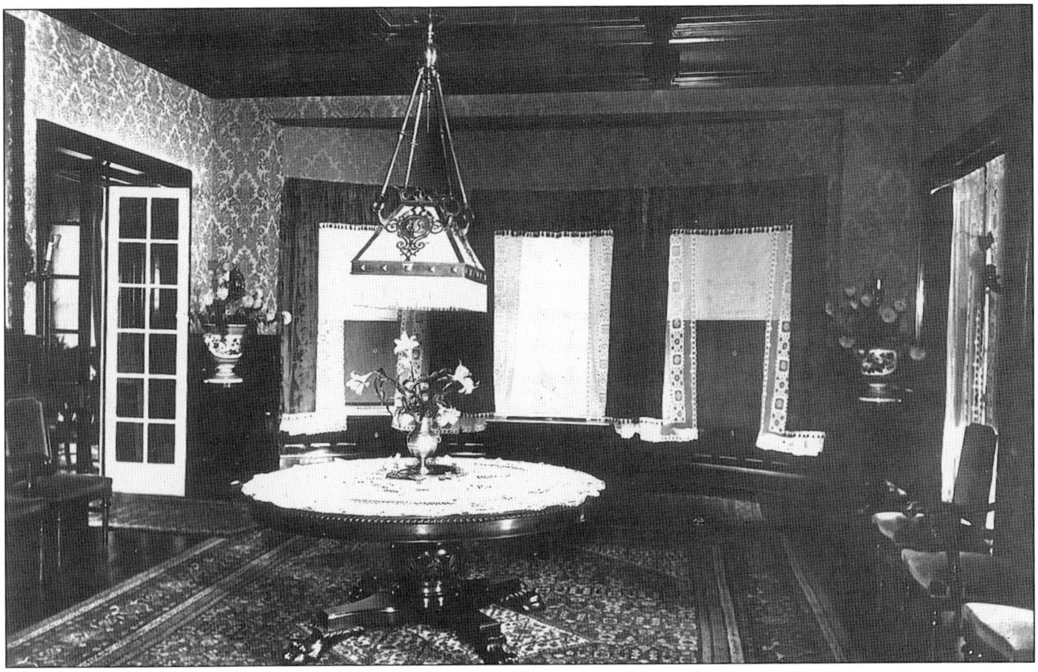

There were two dining areas at Royal Oaks. The top photograph shows the more formal of the two with a coffered ceiling and a traditional, damask-patterned wallpaper. Both have American Empire extension tables, simple window treatments, roller window shades, and machine-loomed, room-size rugs. Both center light fixtures were electrical. The one in the upper photograph was very modern with glass panels and silk fringe. The one in the lower photograph was a traditional candle-style fixture.

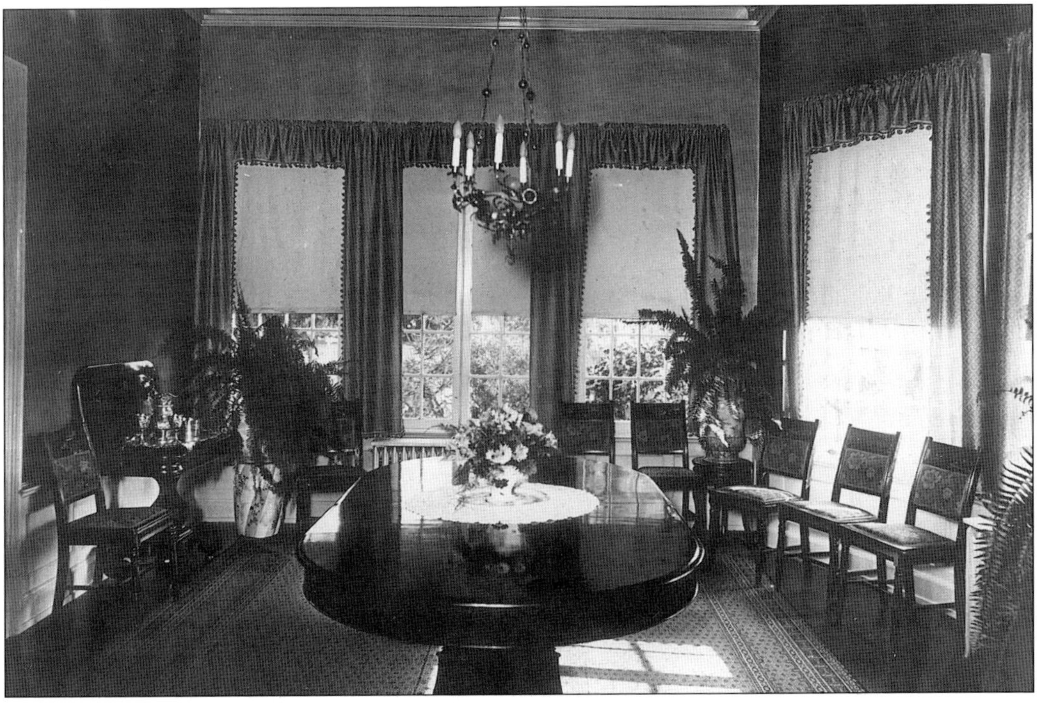

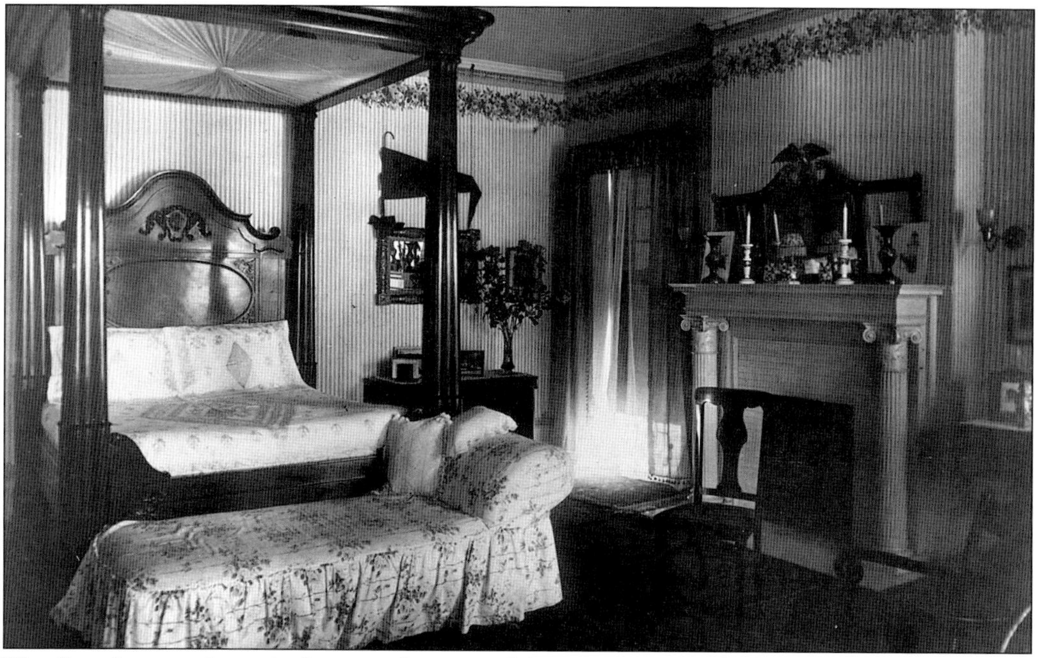

The fine cluster-column bed pictured in one of the seven upstairs bedrooms at Royal Oaks had once belonged to John Berrien Lindsley and his wife, Sarah McGavock Lindsley, who were the parents of Margaret (Mrs. Percy) Warner. The bed is now at Belmont Mansion, a gift of Margaret Lindsley Warden. By the time this picture was made by Marvin Wiles about 1915, the mantel and fireplace had become decorative features. The three radiators under the windows indicated that the house was heated by steam. Only the windows with radiators beneath them had short curtains; the others had proper floor-length window treatments. The striped wallpaper with its floral border and the slipcovered chaise indicate a lady occupied this room; the collegiate pendant on the wall infers it was a young lady.

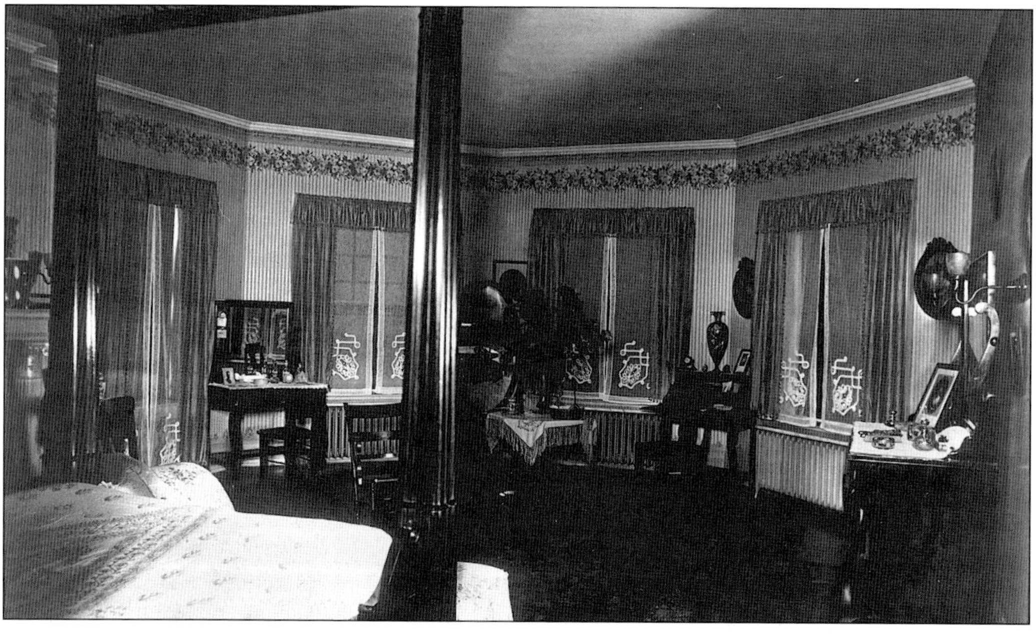

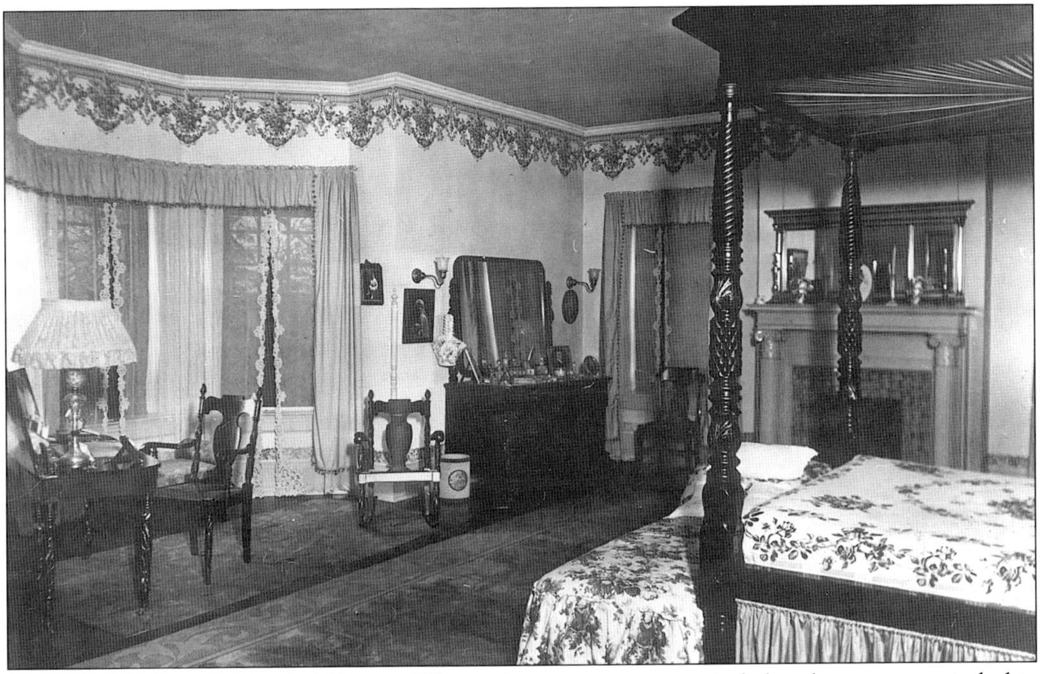

Margaret L. Warner, one of Percy Warner's younger unmarried daughters, occupied this room when it was photographed in 1915. It is decorated in the Colonial Revival style. While the intricately carved four-poster bed dates from an earlier period, the chairs, dresser, and desk were recent reproductions. For the first time, we see a waste basket in the house where working fireplaces were no longer available to burn old letters and papers. No ceiling chandeliers were used in any of the upstairs bedrooms. An electric lamp and wall sconces were used here for illumination.

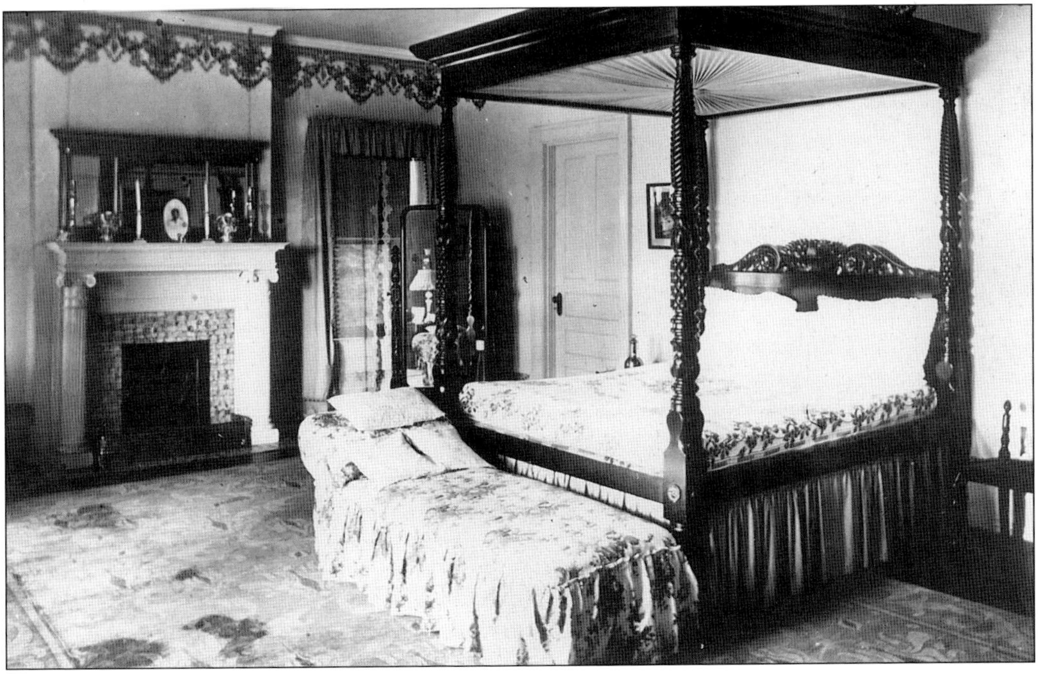

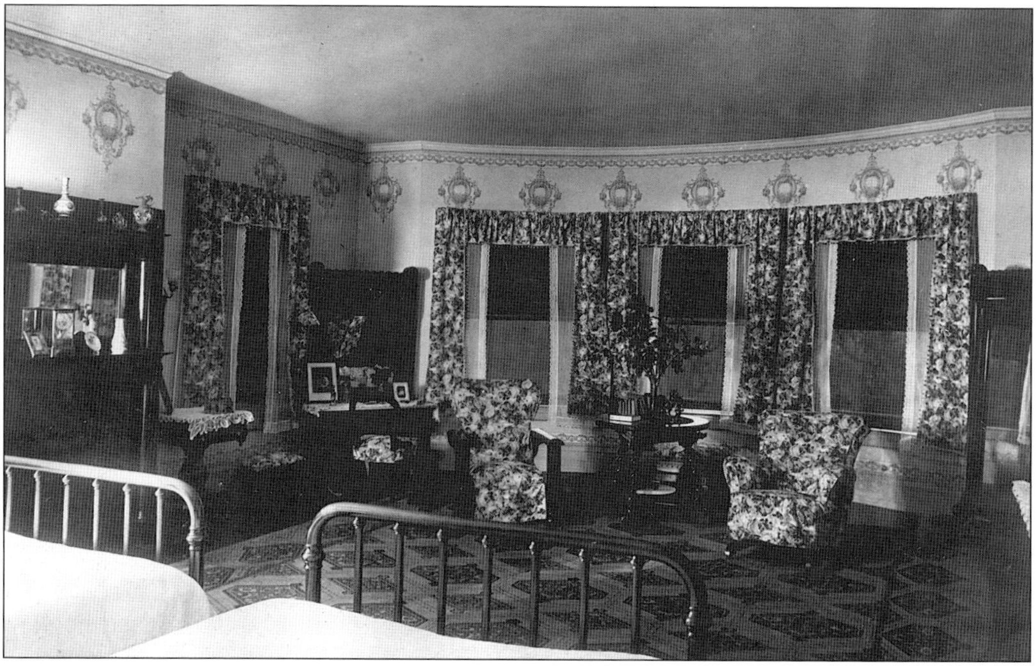

Comfort and tradition, rather than high style, were hallmarks at Royal Oaks. Here, a pair of brass twin beds rest on the stylized-patterned carpet that had covered the hallway at Renraw. A pair of comfortable chairs were slip-covered in the same patterned fabric as the curtains. Pairs of beds and chairs, as well as both masculine and feminine elements, indicate this may have been Mr. and Mrs. Percy Warner's bedroom.

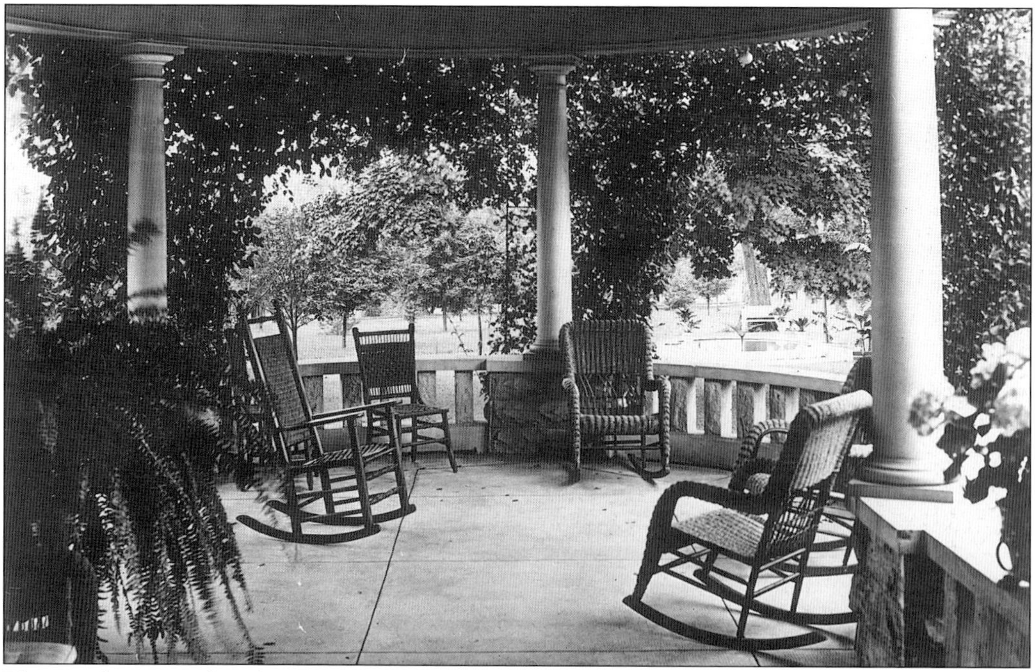

The porch at Royal Oaks terminated in a gazebo-style sitting area. This feature was similar to the porch at Renraw that the Warners had enjoyed on many a hot summer evening.

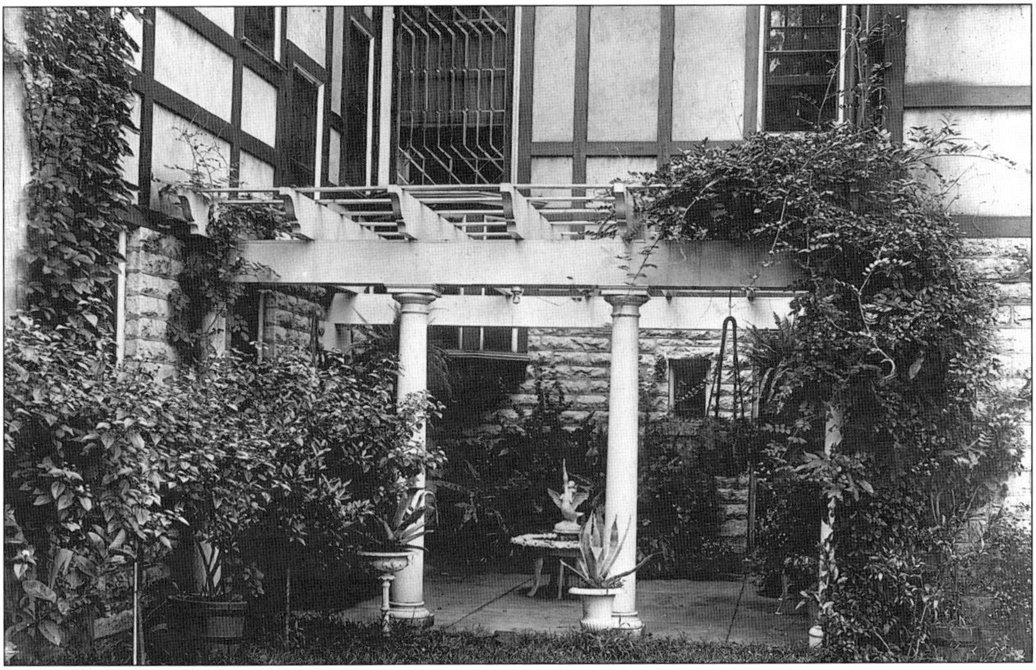

The vine-covered pergola at Royal Oaks offered yet another shady retreat in the days before houses were air-conditioned.

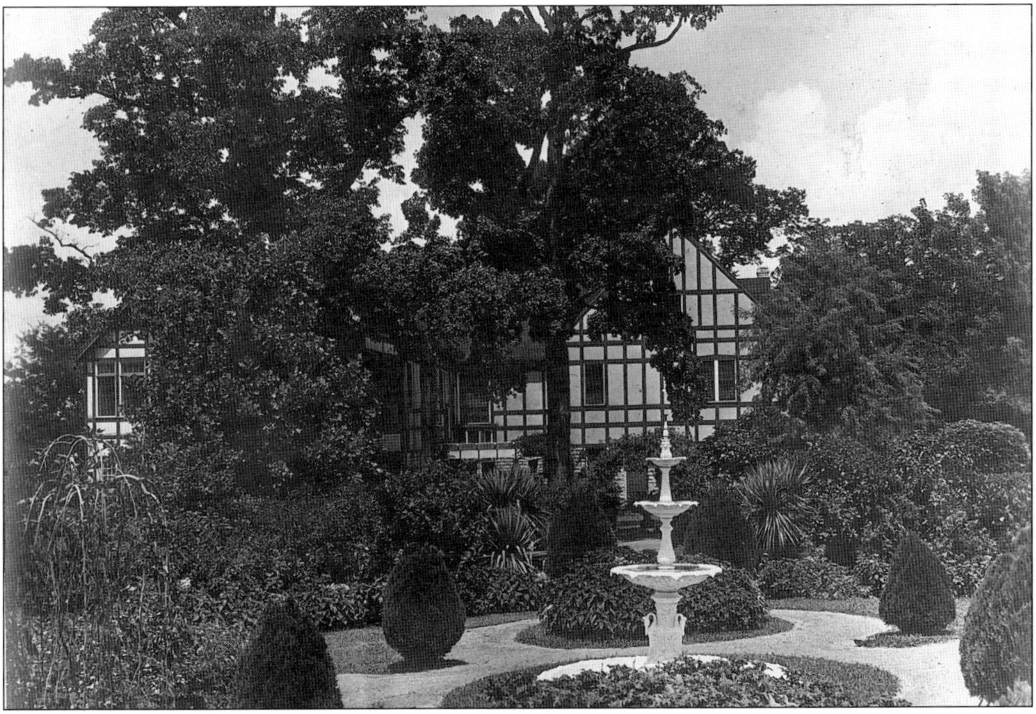

When the Warners moved to Royal Oaks in 1913, Margaret and Percy Warner, both avid gardeners, enlarged the existing gardens. Pictured here is one of several fountains that added beauty and sound for visitors to enjoy.

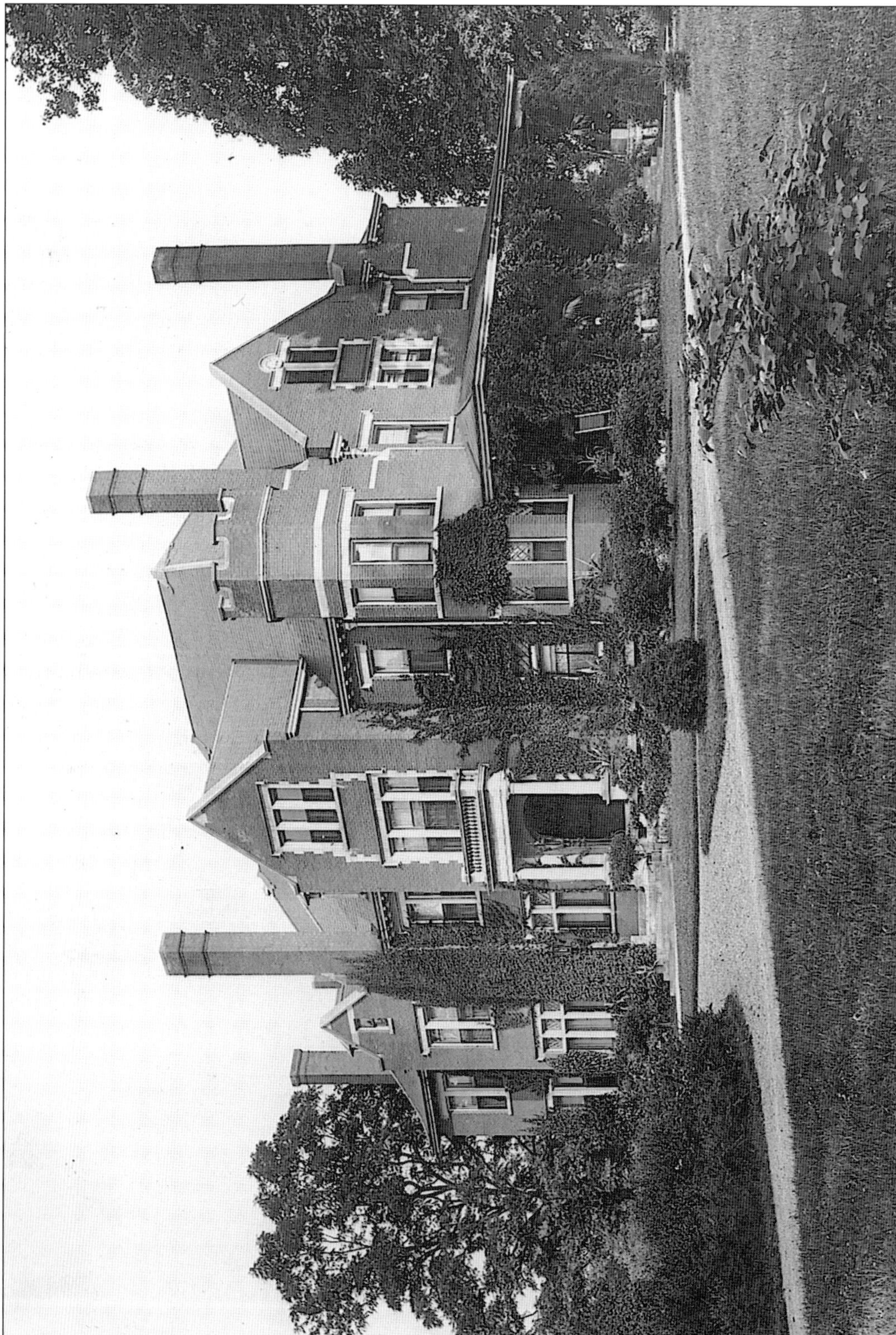

OVERTON HALL / CRIEVE HALL

Overton Hall was built in 1900 by Jesse Maxwell Overton and his wife, Saidee Williams Overton. It was located in a beautiful wooded area in the present-day Crieve Hall subdivision, on Stillwood Drive between Barrywood and Crieve Road. Contemporary accounts describe it as a Tudor-style house. The *c.* 1910 photographs shown here were made during the years that the Overtons occupied the house.

After Mr. Overton's death in 1922, the house was sold to Herbert Farrell and his wife, Ritchie Cheek Farrell. The Farrells changed the name of the house to Crieve Hall. They also engaged Charles Duveen (Charles of London), one of the world's best known interior decorators, to advise them on the decoration of the house. When Mr. Farrell died in 1947, the property was sold to developers, and the house was demolished. The area is now known as Crieve Hall.

Both the Jesse Overtons and the Herbert Farrells had close connections to other important houses in Nashville. Jesse Overton was the grandson of John Overton, who built Travellers Rest. Saidee Williams Overton was the daughter of John and Elizabeth Williams, and before her marriage, she lived at the old Governor's Mansion shown on page 50 of this book. Herbert Farrell was the brother of Norman Farrell, who married Josephine Elliston and lived at Burlington, which is shown on page 26. Ritchey Cheek Farrell was a second cousin of Leslie Cheek, who built Cheekwood, now Nashville's Home of Art and Gardens. Nashville is indeed a family town.

Photographer: Wiles
Photographed: *c.* 1910
From the collection of Ruth Robinson Warner

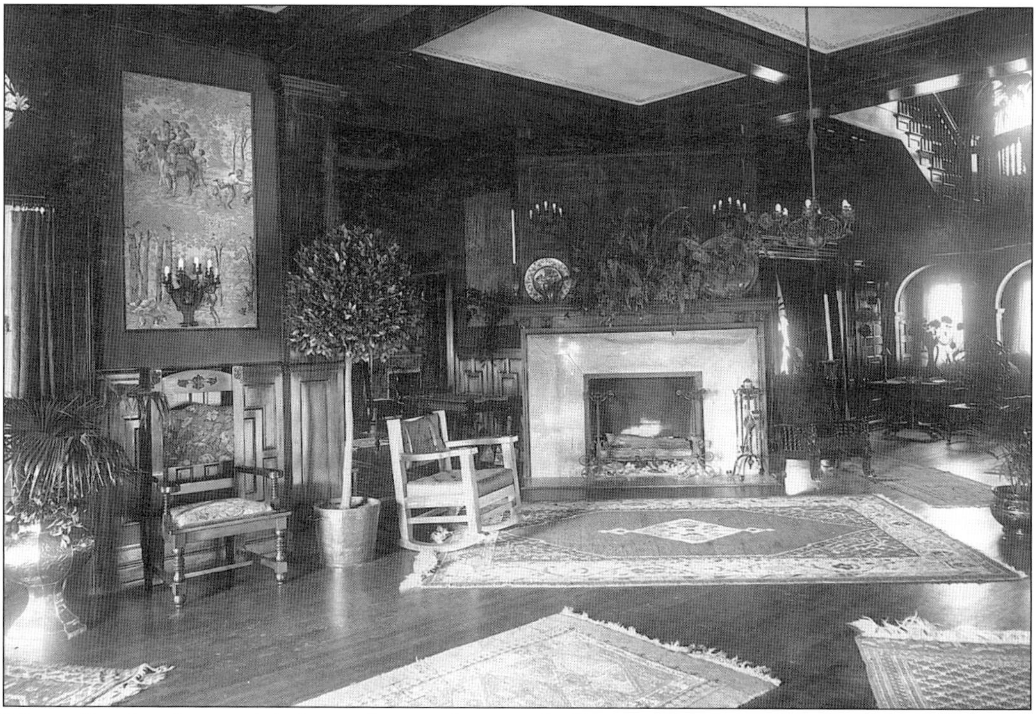

The coffered ceiling and dark paneling in the great hall suggest the strong influence of an English manor house design. The furniture appears to be new. It is adapted from English seventeenth-century styles with one exception; the rocker by the fireplace has its roots in the Arts & Crafts movement. Today, we call this style Mission furniture. The slab marble mantel facing is indeed avant-garde. It forecast the work of Art Deco designers 30 years later.

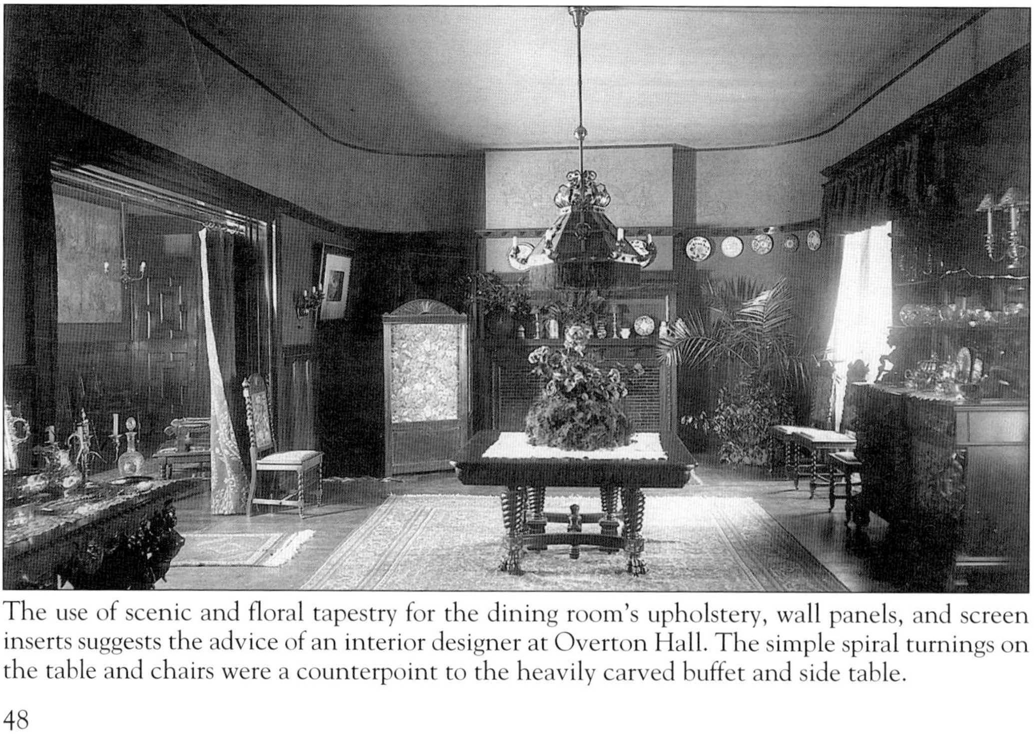

The use of scenic and floral tapestry for the dining room's upholstery, wall panels, and screen inserts suggests the advice of an interior designer at Overton Hall. The simple spiral turnings on the table and chairs were a counterpoint to the heavily carved buffet and side table.

Two

Urban and Suburban House Interiors

1. Williams/Gray/Governor's Mansion
2. J. Horton Fall Residence
3. Nathaniel Baxter Residence
4. McGavock/Lindsley Residence
5. Carter/Savage Residence
6. R.W. Turner Residence (I)
7. R.W. Turner Residence (II)
8. Elizabeth P. Elliott Residence
9. Dempsey Weaver Cantrell Residence
10. William A. Benson Residence
11. John T. Benson Residence

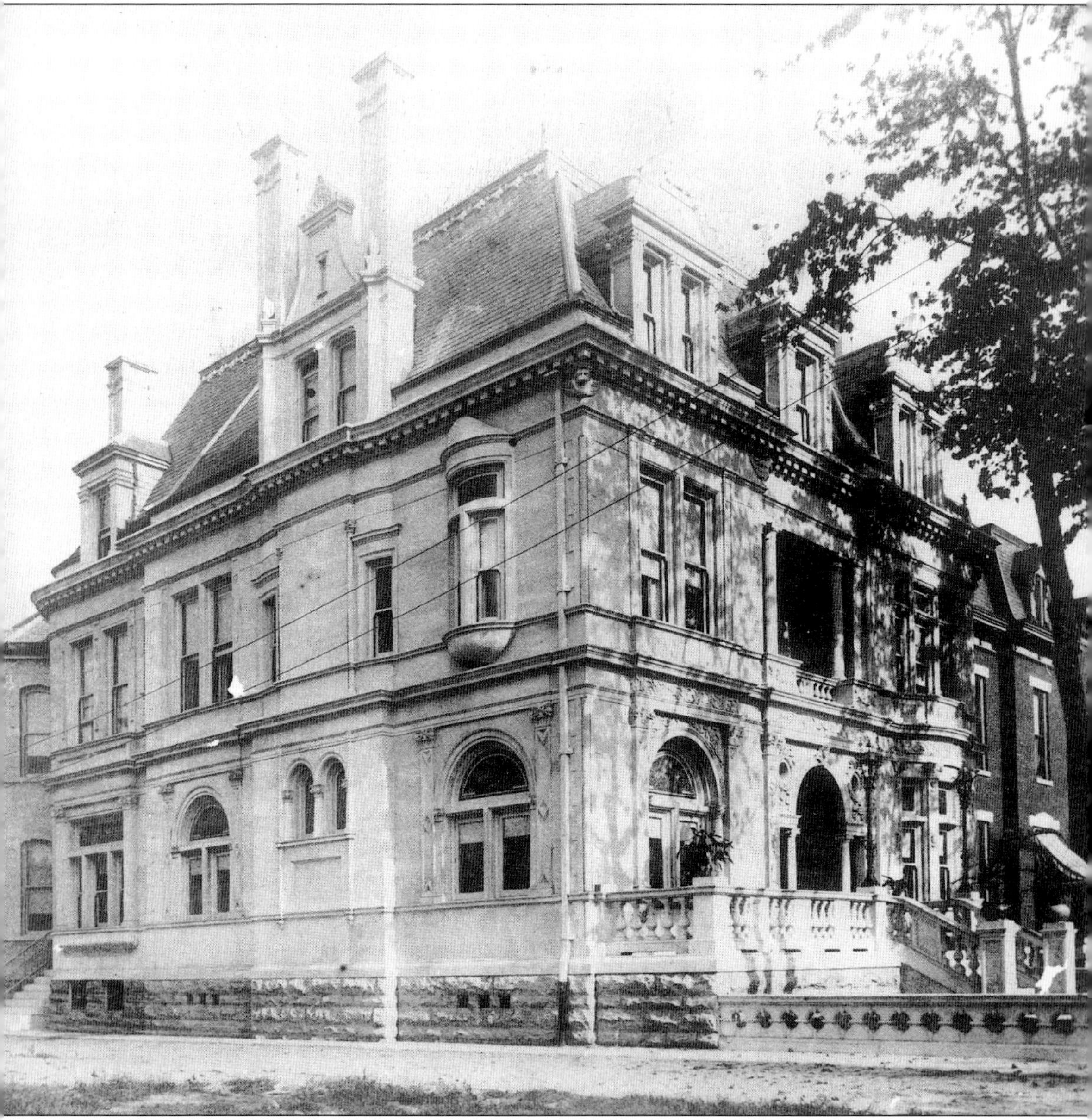

Williams / Gray / Governor's Mansion
314 Vine Street (Seventh Avenue North)

In 1890, banker John P. Williams and his wife, Elizabeth ("Lizzie"), employed the architectural firm of George W. Thompson and Henry Gibel to design a fine Second Empire–style house at 314 North Vine Street (Seventh Avenue North). This was a prime location in 1890 for an affluent family with a beautiful daughter whose debut party was in the offing. The house contained a large parlor, a conservatory, and a third-floor ballroom. The restrained classical decoration of the Williams house was unusual for the 1890s, when it is believed these photographs were made by an unknown photographer.

Since the original photographs are the property of a Williams descendant, it may be assumed they were made between 1890 and 1899, when the Williams family occupied the house. In 1899, the house was sold to Mr. and Mrs. John M. Gray. In 1907, it was sold to the State of Tennessee to be used as the first Governor's Mansion. In 1923, after serving as the home of six Tennessee governors, the house was demolished to make way for the War Memorial Building.

In addition to the grand debut ball of Saidee Williams (Mrs. Jesse Overton), the house was also the site of a reception given by Governor A.H. Roberts for war hero Sergeant Alvin C. York and his bride, Gracie, after World War I.

Architects: Thompson and Gibel
Photographed: *c.* 1895
From the collection of Ruth Robinson Warner, Tennessee State Library & Archives

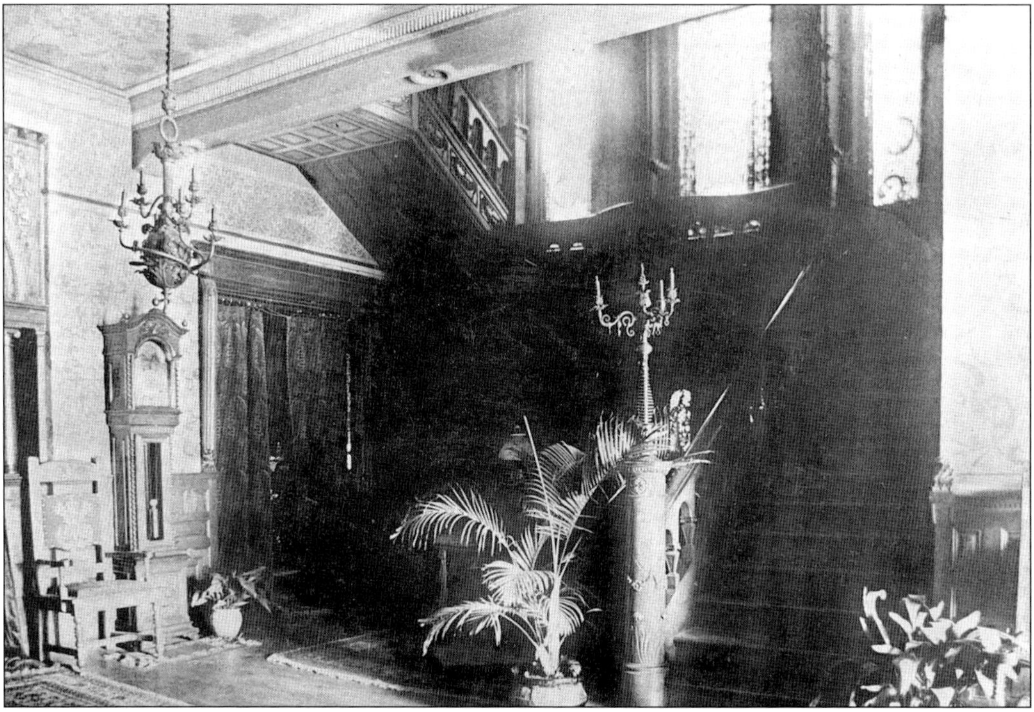

The architectural style of this house is sometimes referred to as "chateauesque." The great hallway shown here appears to merit this designation. The sophistication of the design, both exterior and interior, may be attributed to the European background of both architects; George W. Thompson was from England, and Henry Gibel was from Germany.

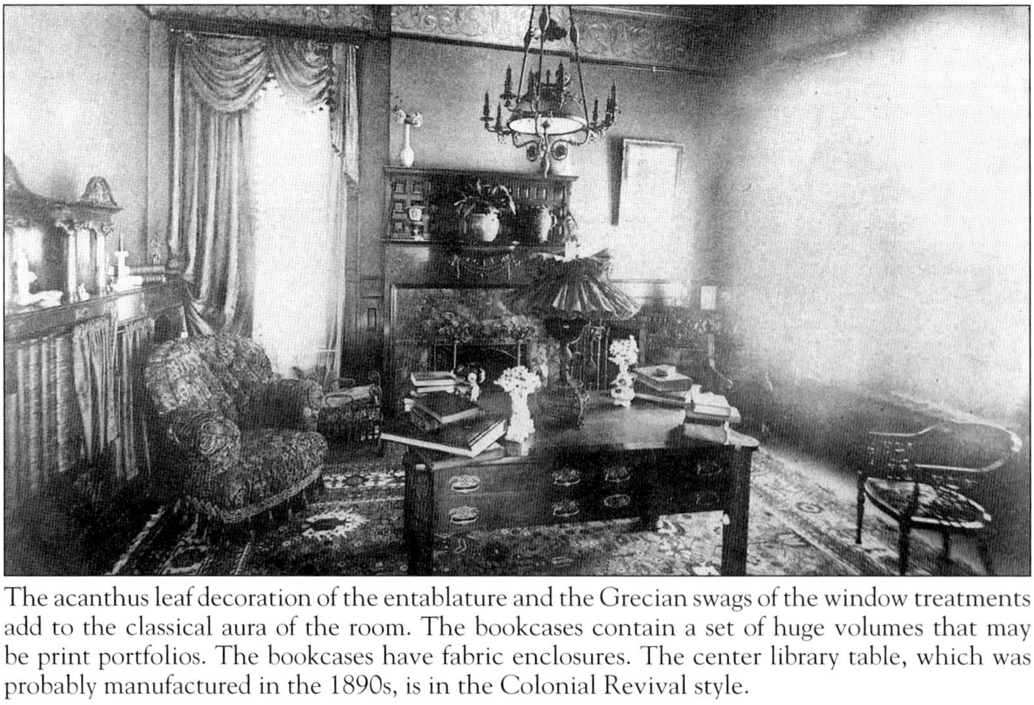

The acanthus leaf decoration of the entablature and the Grecian swags of the window treatments add to the classical aura of the room. The bookcases contain a set of huge volumes that may be print portfolios. The bookcases have fabric enclosures. The center library table, which was probably manufactured in the 1890s, is in the Colonial Revival style.

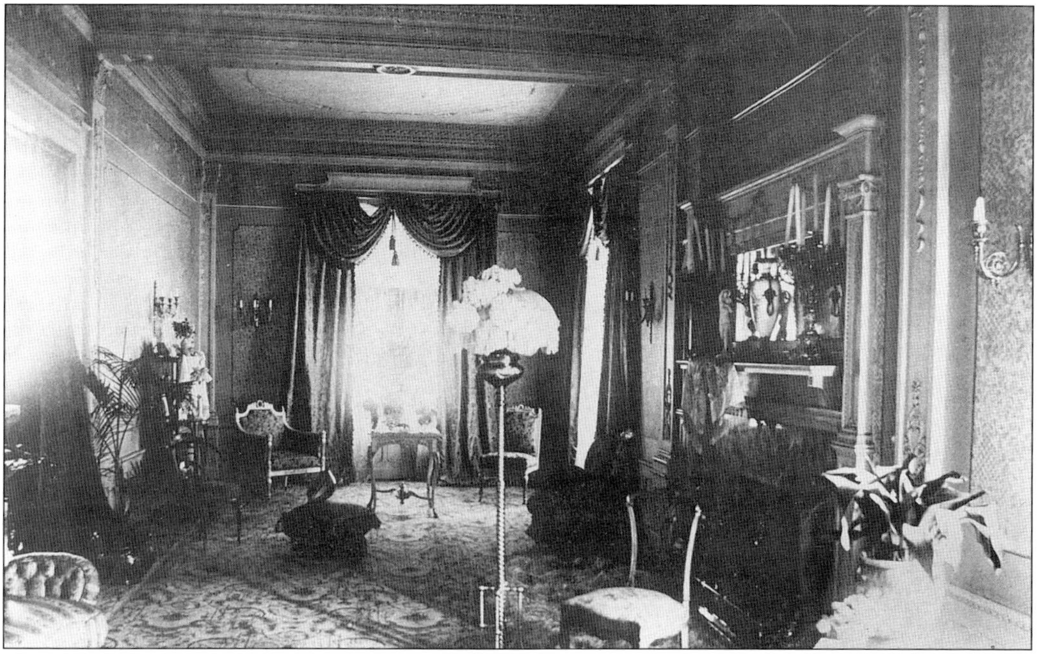

Harmony and balance were principals that were understood by the designer of this room. Carefully proportioned, damask-covered wall panels were separated by pilasters with raised plaster decoration; each panel is centered with a sconce. The room appears to be divided into three sections with the fireplace dominating the middle section. The Louis 15th and 16th furnishings, although probably replicas, were high style in the 1890s. The flamboyant floor lamp seems to be an intruder in this otherwise peaceful parlor.

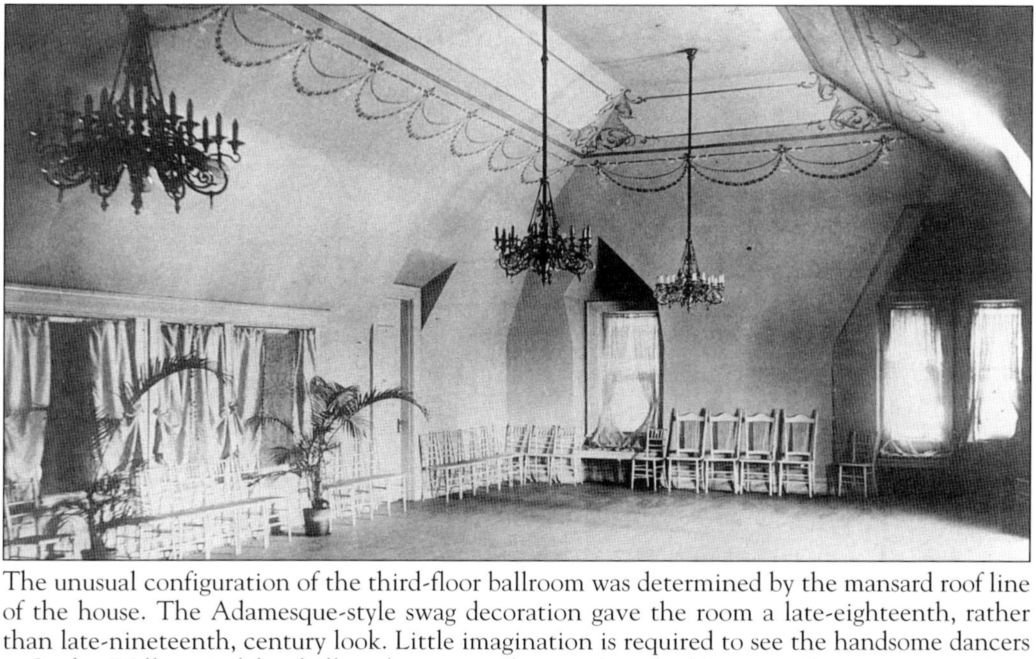

The unusual configuration of the third-floor ballroom was determined by the mansard roof line of the house. The Adamesque-style swag decoration gave the room a late-eighteenth, rather than late-nineteenth, century look. Little imagination is required to see the handsome dancers at Saidee Williams's debut ball in this room. She was described by one of her young neighbors on Vine Street as "a vision of loveliness."

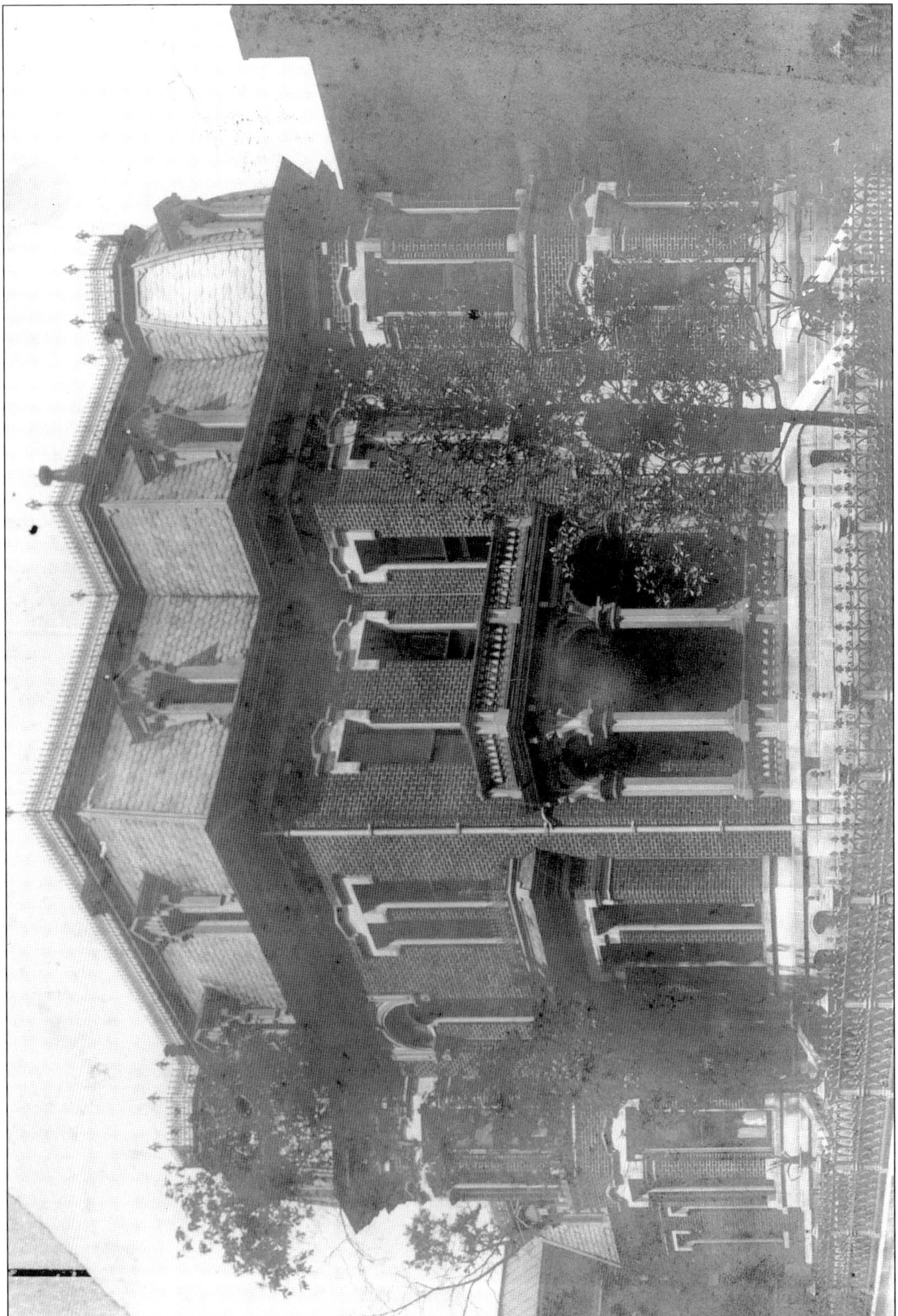

J. Horton Fall Residence 701 North Vine Street (Seventh Avenue North)

J. Horton Fall, a successful hardware dealer, built this handsome three-story, Second Empire–style house for his growing family in 1885. While the date of the photographs is unknown, the small tree in the front yard, when compared to a 1897 photograph, suggests a date in the early 1890s. Although the photographs only include rooms on the first floor, contemporary accounts relate that, while all the bedrooms were on the second floor, there was only one bathroom.

The house stood on the northwest corner of Union and North Vine (now Seventh Avenue North) across the street from Polk Place, home of the widow of President James K. Polk.

Most of the furnishings shown in these photographs are now in the summer home of Mrs. J. Horton Fall Handly in Mt. Eagle, Tennessee. The Fall house was razed in 1918. For many years, the site was occupied by the offices of National Life and Accident Insurance Company.

Photographed: c. 1890
From the collection of Opie C. Handly, Tennessee State Library & Archives

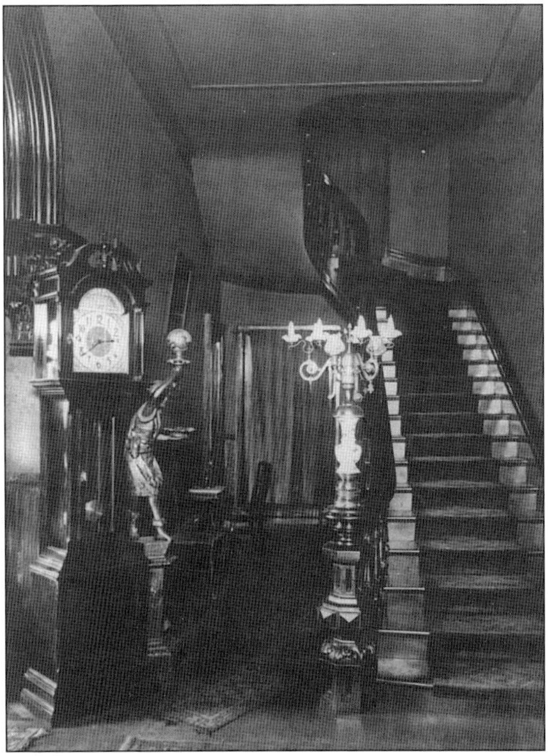

Technology prevails in this very traditional entry hall. Atop the newel post is a candelabrum-style electric fixture; beside the grandfather clock is a bronze statue holding an electric torch aloft. In the rear hall on a small table is a "newfangled" telephone. Communication of this sort was still something of a novelty, although the first telephone was installed in Nashville in 1877.

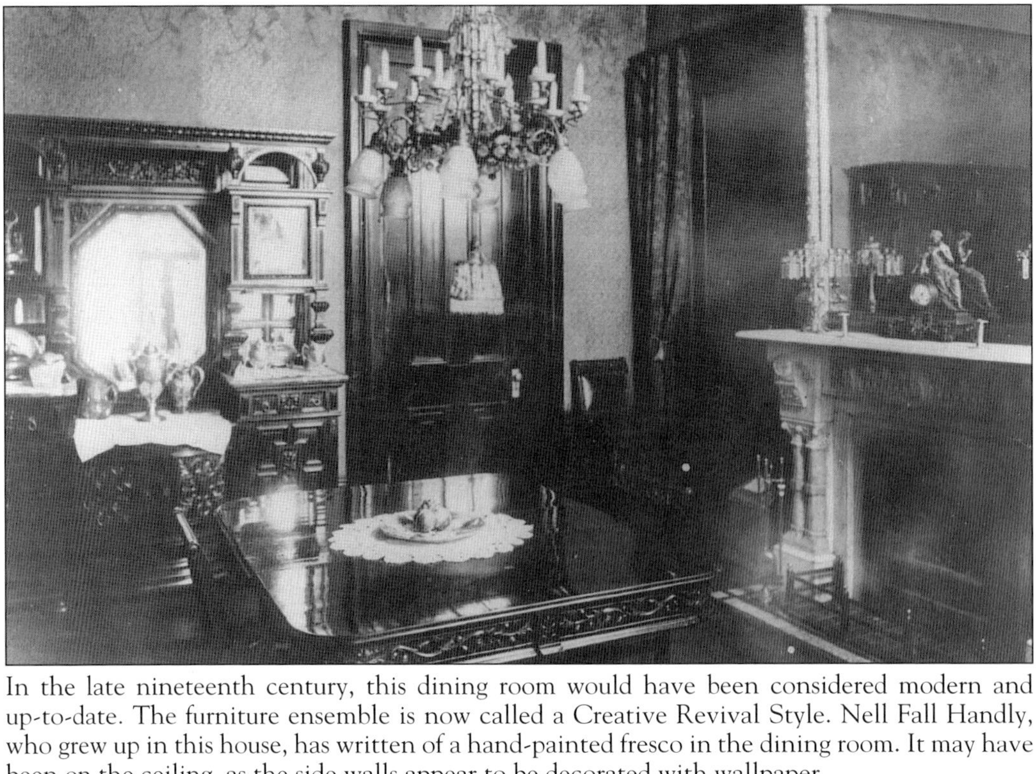

In the late nineteenth century, this dining room would have been considered modern and up-to-date. The furniture ensemble is now called a Creative Revival Style. Nell Fall Handly, who grew up in this house, has written of a hand-painted fresco in the dining room. It may have been on the ceiling, as the side walls appear to be decorated with wallpaper.

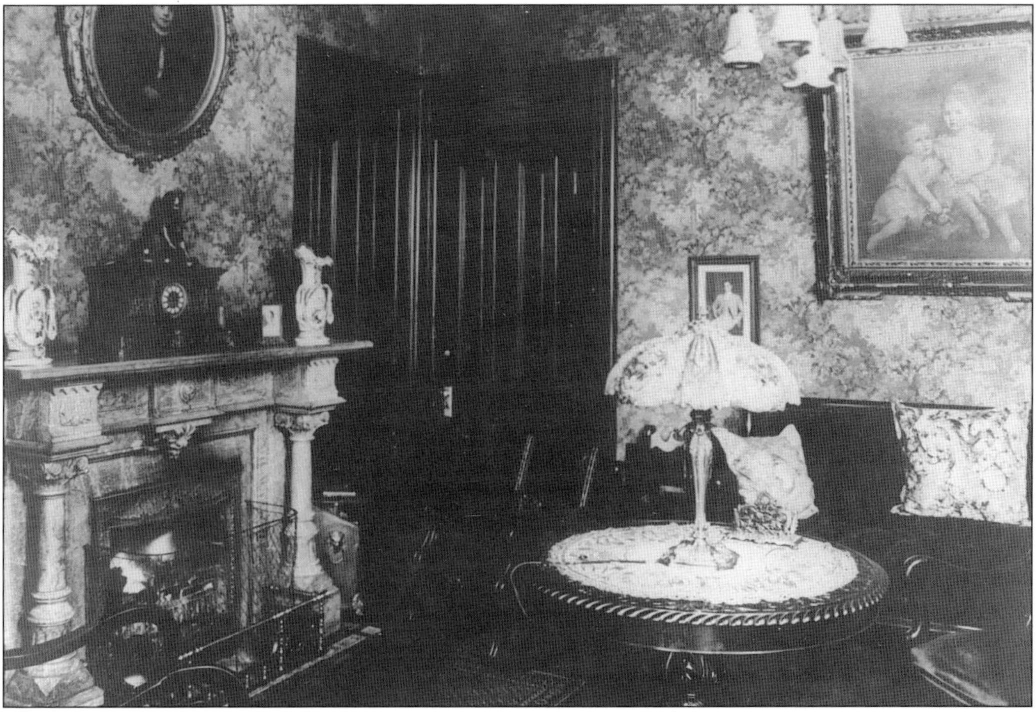

The densely-patterned, floral wallpaper in this room is typical of the 1880s. The mantelpiece is of fine Carrara marble. Although there was a furnace in the house, there was a working fireplace in each room. The coal scuttle is to the right of the fireplace. On the mantel shelf are a pair of French Sèvres vases and a bronze mantel clock. There is a lady's photograph on the mantel and one on the wall. While the electric wire from the lamp on the center table is visible, we can only wonder about the location of the outlet. Center lamps were sometimes connected into overhead chandeliers and disconnected when not in use.

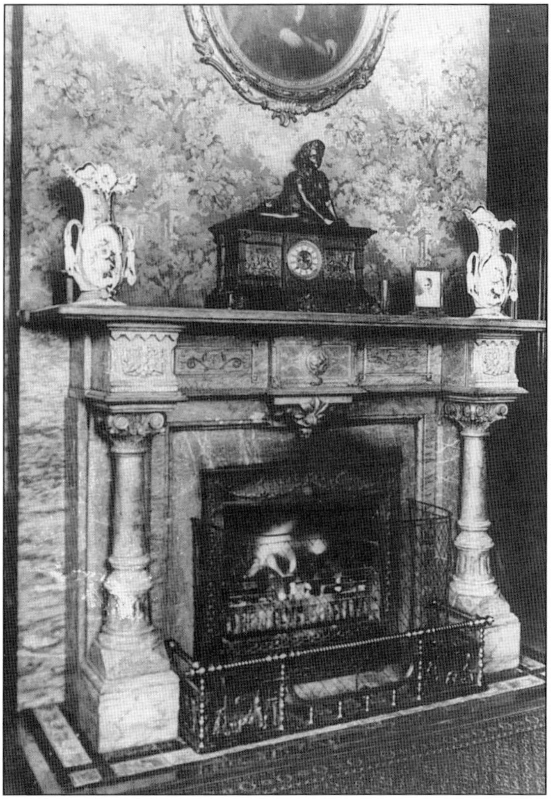

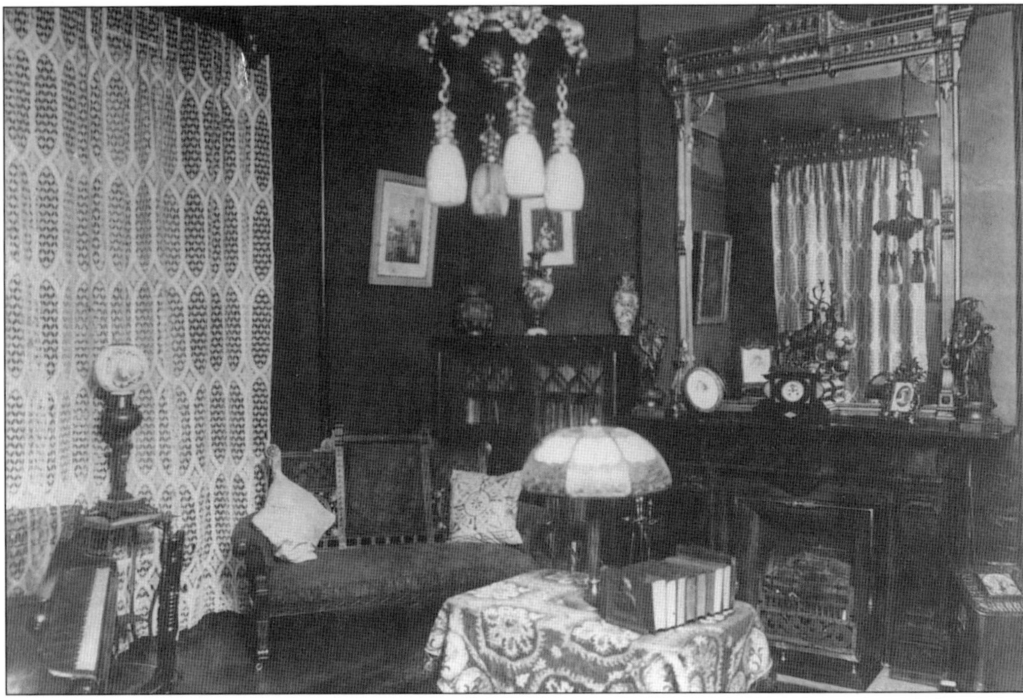

The library in this late-nineteenth-century house gives the viewer a preview of the move toward simplicity in decoration that was to characterize the twentieth century. The mantel mirror, stylish sofa, and center chair were American Eastlake styles with straight lines and incised carving friendly to machine production. The walls were plain and unadorned. The curtains were machine-made lace in an elongated hexagon pattern with metal cornices. In addition to the central chandelier, there were two table lamps and a floor lamp beside the baby grand piano.

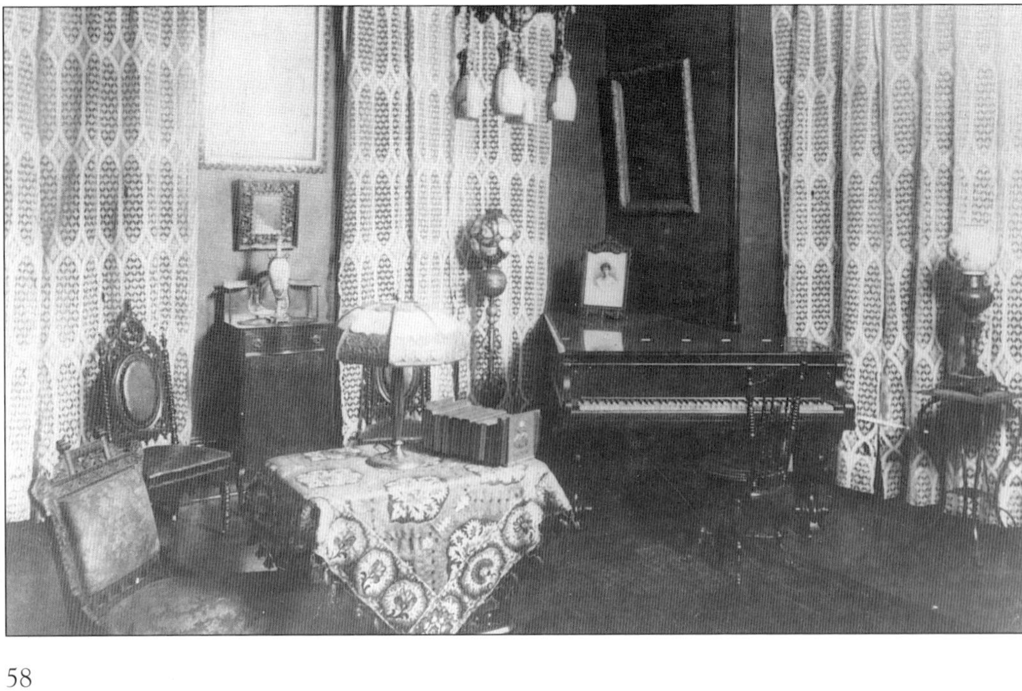

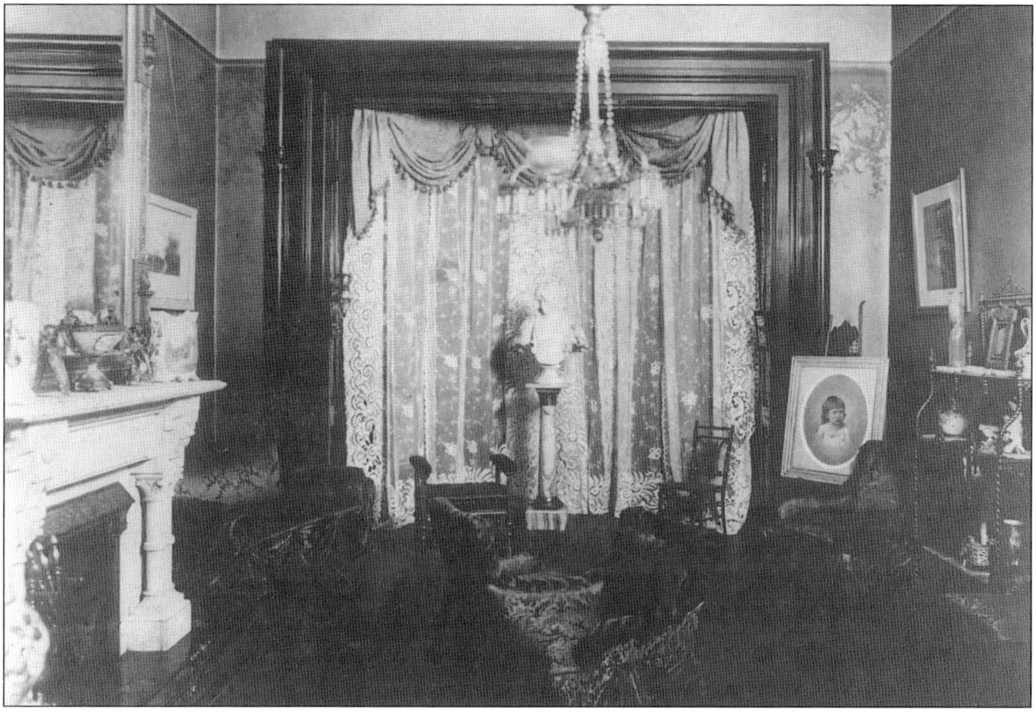

The drawing room was to the right of the entry hall and opened into the dining room. This high-fashioned room featured a balanced arrangement of architectural elements and furnishings. The front bay window is hung with Brussels lace curtains of the highest quality and topped with a swag. On the opposite wall is the double sliding door to the dining room. This opening is decorated with a "gingerbread" moulding on the dining room side and heavy portières on the drawing room side. The set of damask-covered seating pieces are in the French Second Empire style. The double chair under the chandelier is called a tête-à-tête.

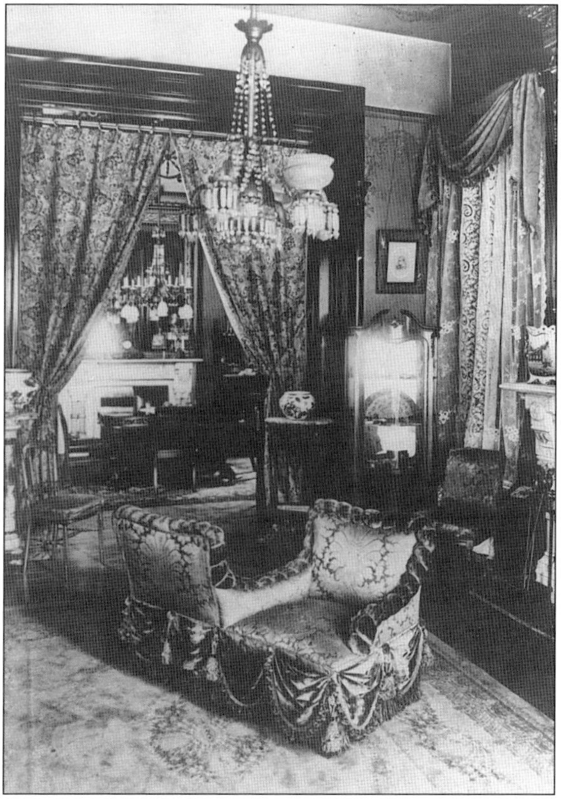

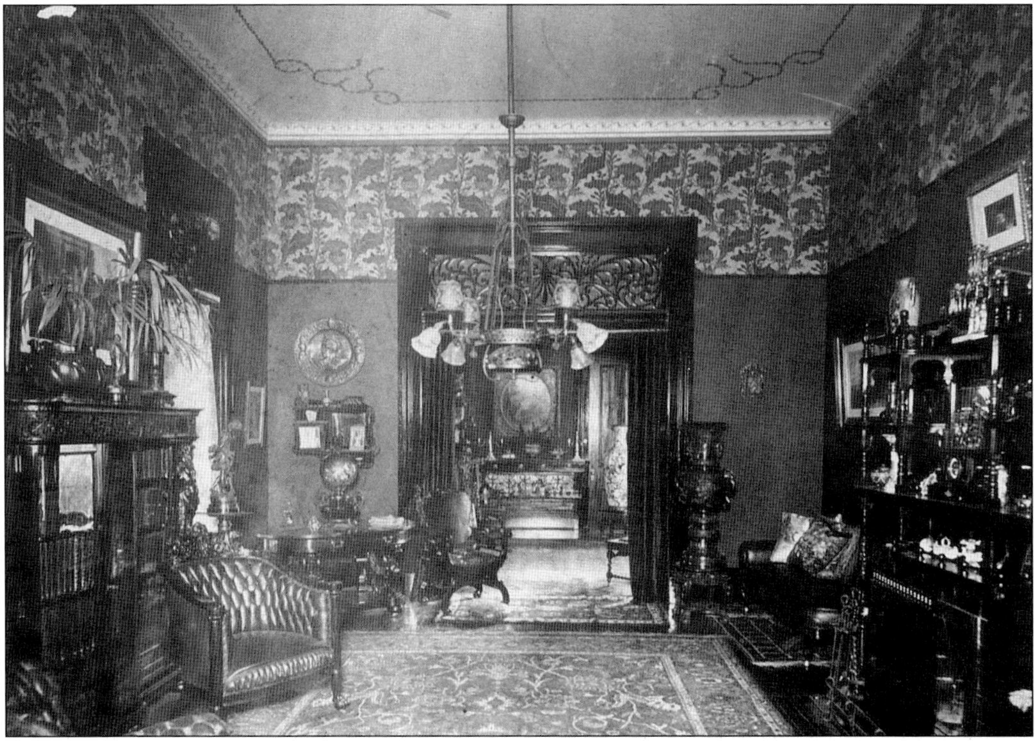

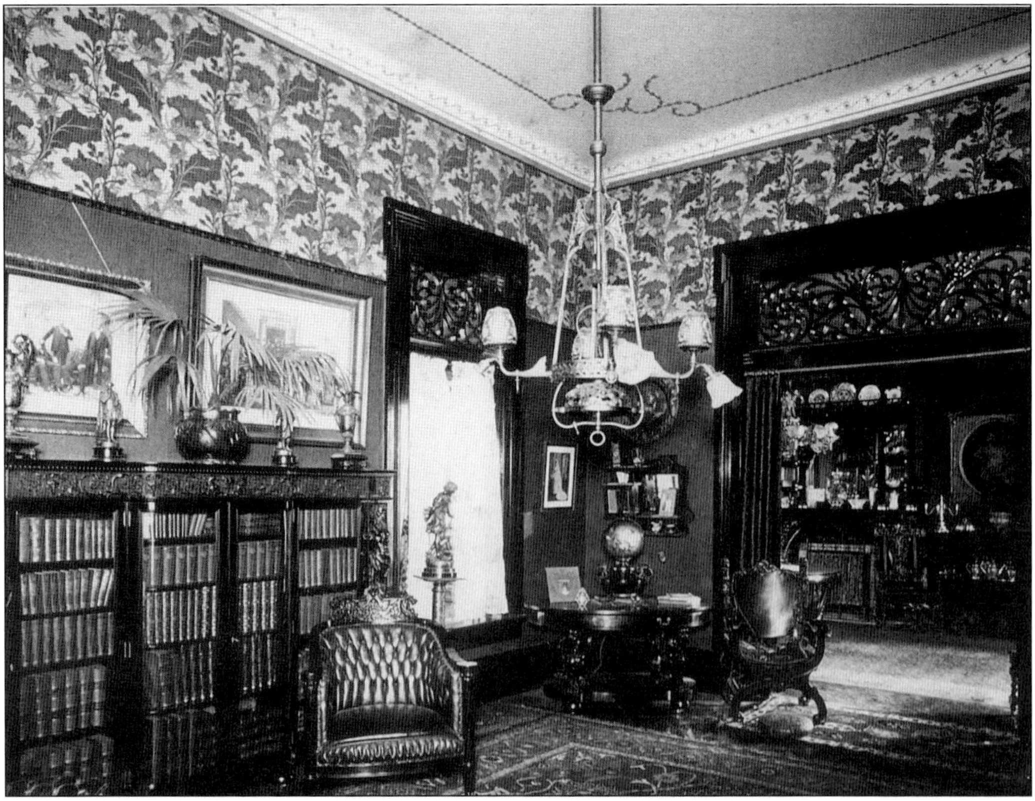

NATHANIEL BAXTER RESIDENCE
117 NORTH SPRUCE STREET

Nathaniel Baxter Jr. (1844–1913) and his wife, Laura Lavender Baxter, lived at 117 North Spruce Street (Eighth Avenue North) when two photographs were made of their library. Although the photographs are undated, they are identified as "library in the city residence of Nathaniel Baxter by Thuss."

The Baxters were a prominent Nashville family. Nathaniel Baxter Jr. was the son of Judge Nathaniel Baxter and the brother of Jere Baxter, a lawyer who owned the Tennessee Central Railroad Company. Nathaniel Baxter Jr. was a Civil War veteran and speaker of the state senate, in addition to his various business interests.

Mr. Baxter housed a collection of law books in a large ornate bookcase opposite the étagère-style mantelpiece in this room. One of the pictures over the bookcase was from a series of English jurist prints published in *Vanity Fair* magazine. The other picture was hidden by a potted palm. Both the rug and the wallpaper depict the high-style Art Nouveau patterns prevalent in Europe and America in the 1890s and early 1900s.

The upper lights of the chandelier appear to be Welsbach gas mantles. The lower lights may be gas or electric. Combination fixtures continued well into the first decade of the twentieth century even though electric lighting had been introduced at the Tennessee State Capitol Building in 1882 by Brush Electric Company. The lower portion of the chandelier seems to be a reflector shade lined with metal or mirrors for either gas or electric use.

Photographer: Thuss
From the collection of Ridley Wills II

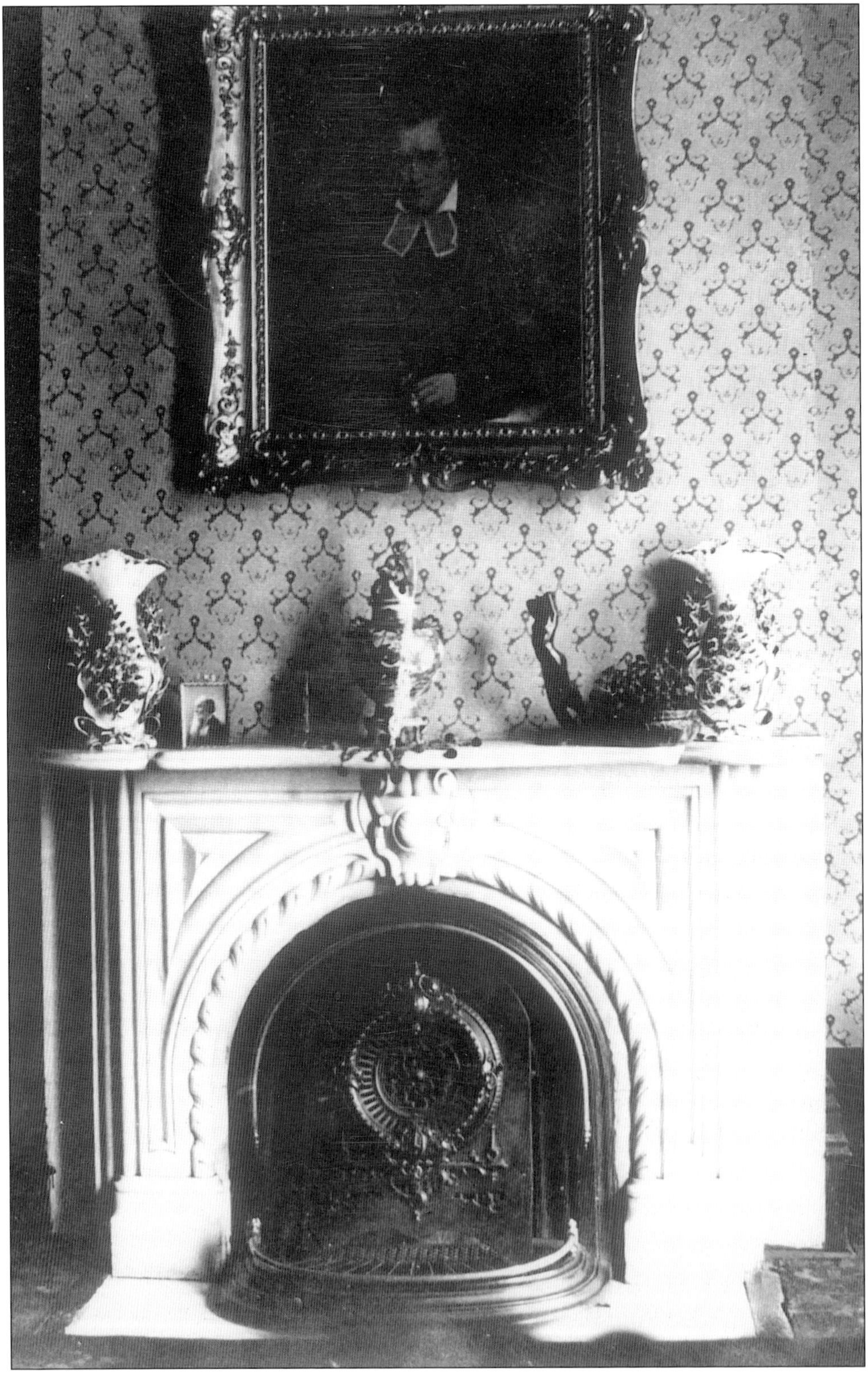

McGavock/Lindsley Residence
135 North Spruce Street

After the Civil War, in 1868, Jacob McGavock (1790–1878) and his wife, Louisa Grundy McGavock, bought a large house on fashionable North Spruce Street (now Eighth Avenue North). Their daughter, Sarah McGavock, had married educator Dr. John Berrien Lindsley, the "Benjamin Franklin of Nashville." The Lindsleys had three daughters: Margaret, Annie, and Louise. The McGavock and Lindsley families occupied the house until it was demolished in 1914.

Margaret Lindsley married Percy Warner, Annie Lindsley married Dr. Carl Warden, and Louise Lindsley, a Nashville civic leader, never married. An unknown photographer made the three photographs of the parlor sometime during the 50 years that the house sheltered this family.

In the photograph of the mantelpiece is a portrait of Phillip Lindsley, father of John Berrien Lindsley, painted by artist John Grimes. For many years, Dr. Lindsley was president of the University of Nashville. The painting is now on display at the Tennessee State Museum. On either end of the mantel shelf are a pair of fine Old Paris vases. These vases may now be seen in the staircase niches at Belmont Mansion. The small bronze statue is called *Hesperus, Goddess of the Dawn* by Pollet. It is now in the home of Margaret L. Warden.

Photographed: *c.* 1900
From the collection of Margaret Lindsley Warden, Tennessee State Library & Archives

Page 64: It appears that there was a fireplace at each end of the parlor as the mantel shelf in each picture had different ornaments. The sofa and arm chair were in the Rococo Revival style of the 1850s and 1860s. This furniture is now at the Tennessee State Museum. The Oriental screen and plate on the mantel shelf became stylish in the latter decades of the nineteenth century. The leather platform rocker was also much later than the Rococo Revival furniture.

Page 65: Hanging over the piano that dominated the other end of the room was a painting of Beatrice Cenci. Beatrice was a Roman lady made famous in an early-nineteenth-century drama by Percy Bysshe Shelley. The floor was covered in a Brussels carpet; the wallpaper pattern was conservative for this time period. The draperies were a dark yellow-green velour; the Rococo furniture was covered in a deep-maroon cut velvet. We know the colors because these textiles still exist in the collection of Belmont Mansion, a gift of a descendant, Margaret Lindsley Warden.

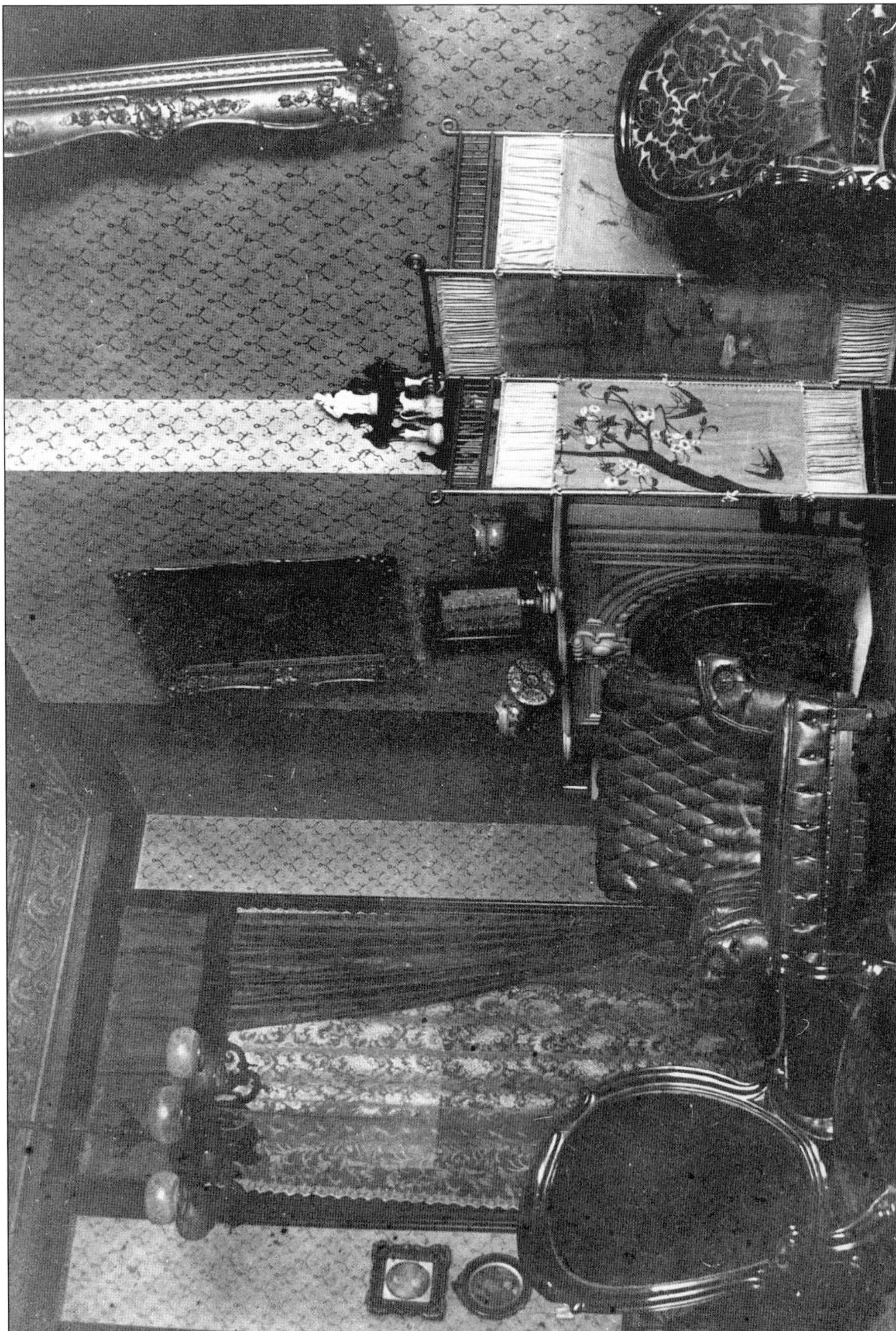

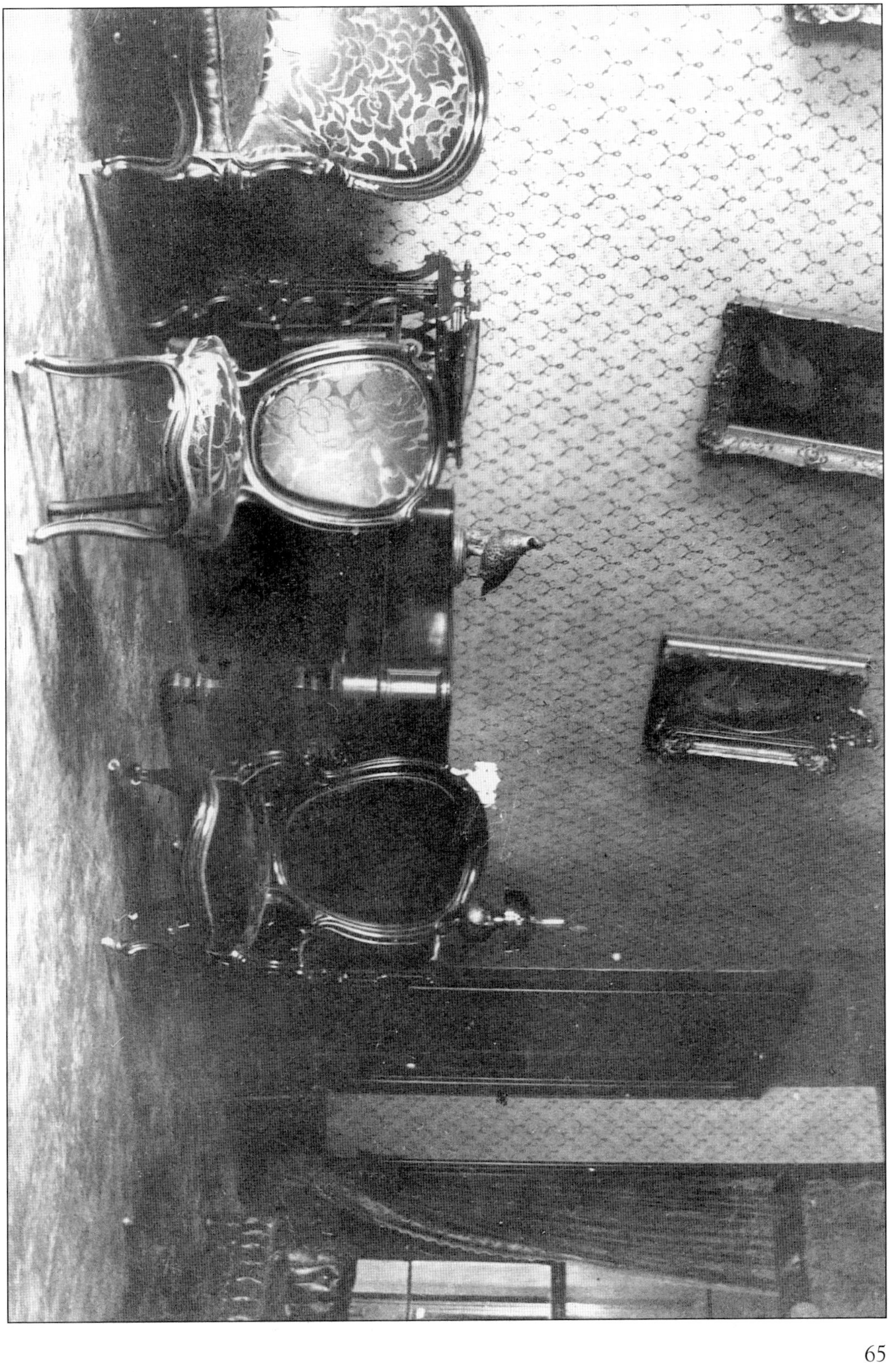

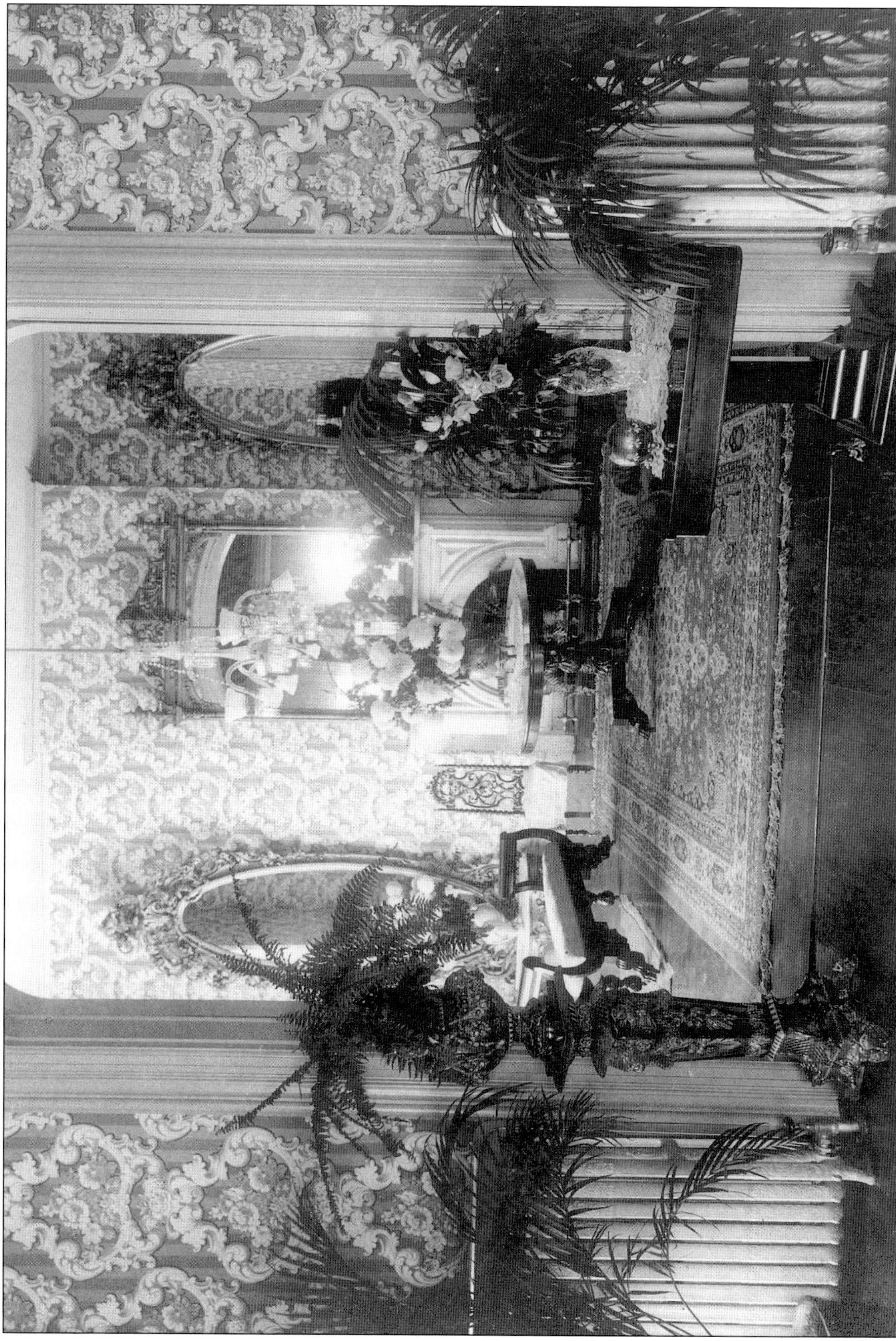

Carter-Savage Residence
117 Sixteenth Avenue South

Dr. Giles Savage and his wife, Leslie Alice Jones Savage, moved from their townhouse at 165 Eighth Avenue North (Spruce Street) in 1904 to this house at 117 Sixteenth Avenue South. Joel Carter, who manufactured shoes in Nashville, had built the house several years earlier. While the house on Eighth Avenue North is still standing and is now occupied by a restaurant, the Sixteenth Avenue South house was recently demolished. Although there is no known photograph of the exterior of this house, the following eight photographs are of the first-floor public rooms of Dr. Savage's new house while it was occupied as a residence.

The double parlors of the new house were wallpapered in a Baroque-patterned paper featuring scrolls that were dear to the heart of early-twentieth-century wallpaper designers. Despite the repetitive pattern of the wallpaper, the pair of elongated oval mirrors that flank the mantel give this room a strong Art Nouveau flavor. The chandelier is probably a combination gas and electric fixture. We see a wide range of furniture styles here: a Grecian Revival settee, an Empire center table, and a Gothic chair.

These double parlors have a sparseness seldom seen in late-nineteenth-century rooms. Homeowners were learning through experience the validity of the axiom followed by many later twentieth-century designers that "less is more." While the forms are still romantic, a more logical classical approach in room design is apparent.

Photographer: Thuss
Photographed: c. 1904
From the collection of Elizabeth Z. Fryer, Tennessee State Library & Archives

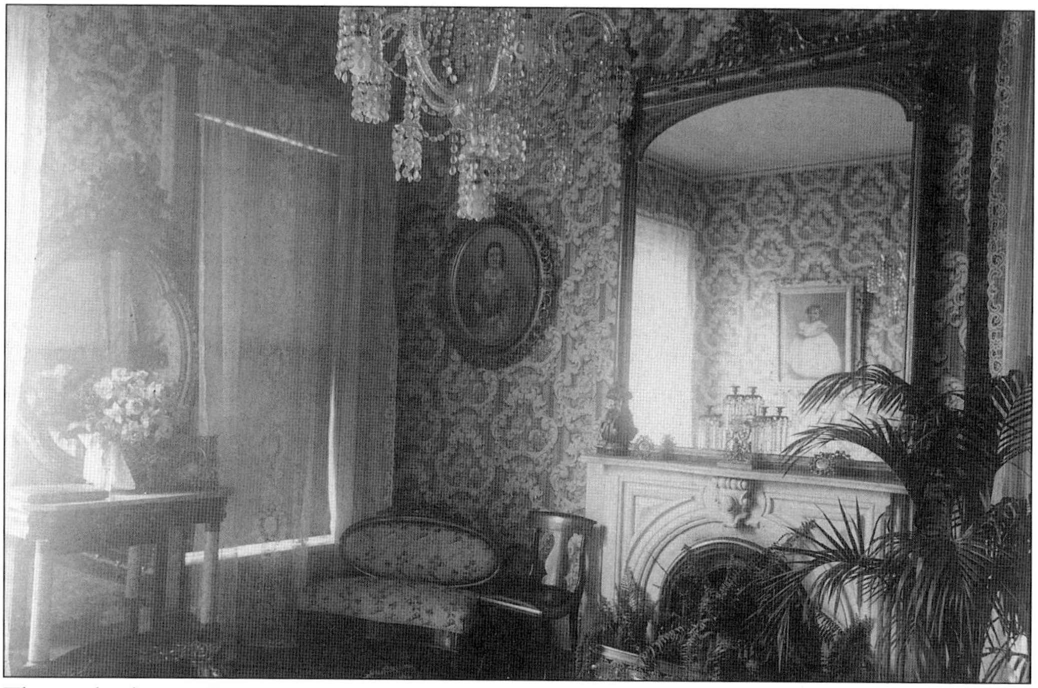

This parlor has an Empire "pier" table, a Colonial Revival chair, and a French Revival settee. Also in this room was a very fashionable electric crystal chandelier. The portrait beside the fireplace was of Mrs. Savage's mother called "Great Grandmother Jones" by her descendants. The wallpaper color was gray. We know this because it was copied and hung in the Stokes Lane residence of the late Dr. Kate Savage Zerfross and her husband, Dr. Tom Zerfross, in 1923.

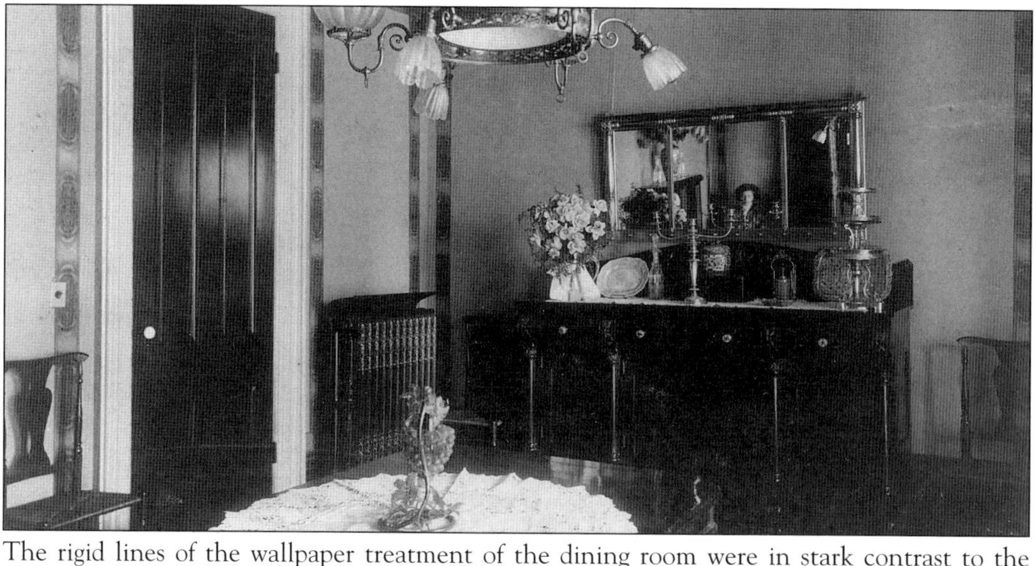

The rigid lines of the wallpaper treatment of the dining room were in stark contrast to the backgrounds of the hall and parlors. This treatment was a textbook example of a style called Japanesque or Anglo-Japanese. English designer Christopher Dresser played a major role in introducing the style to Americans shortly after the Centennial Exposition in Philadelphia in 1876.

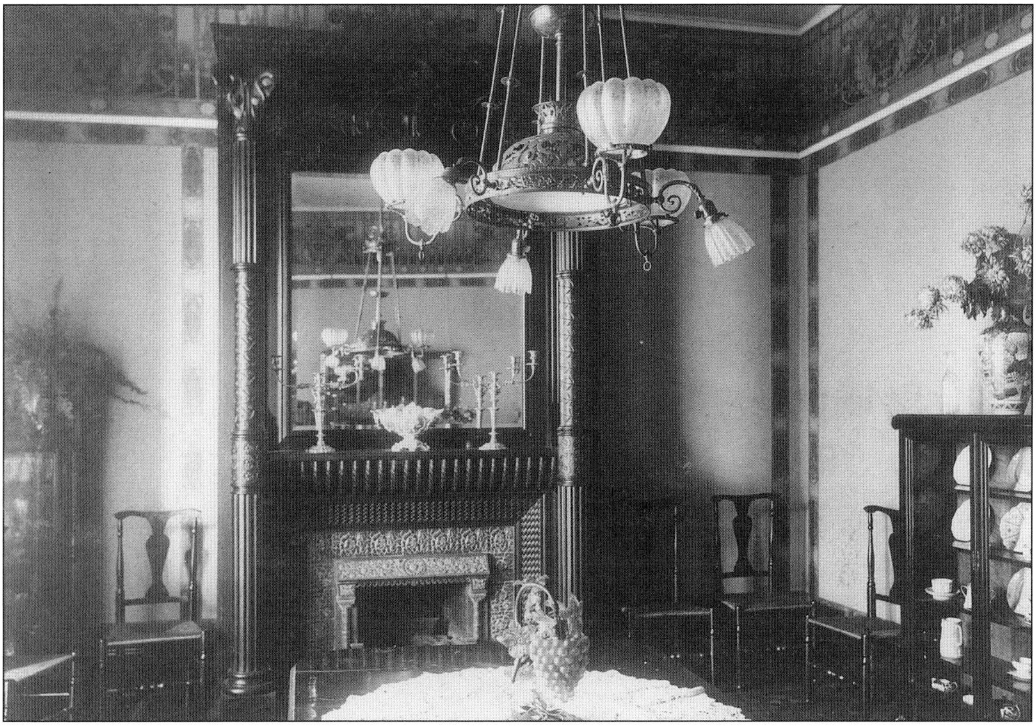

The stylized frieze and border panels give an updated look to the other elements of this room, especially the fine Empire sideboard and the multi-styled mantel. The dining chairs in the Colonial Revival style represent another trend Americans adopted after the Centennial Exposition.

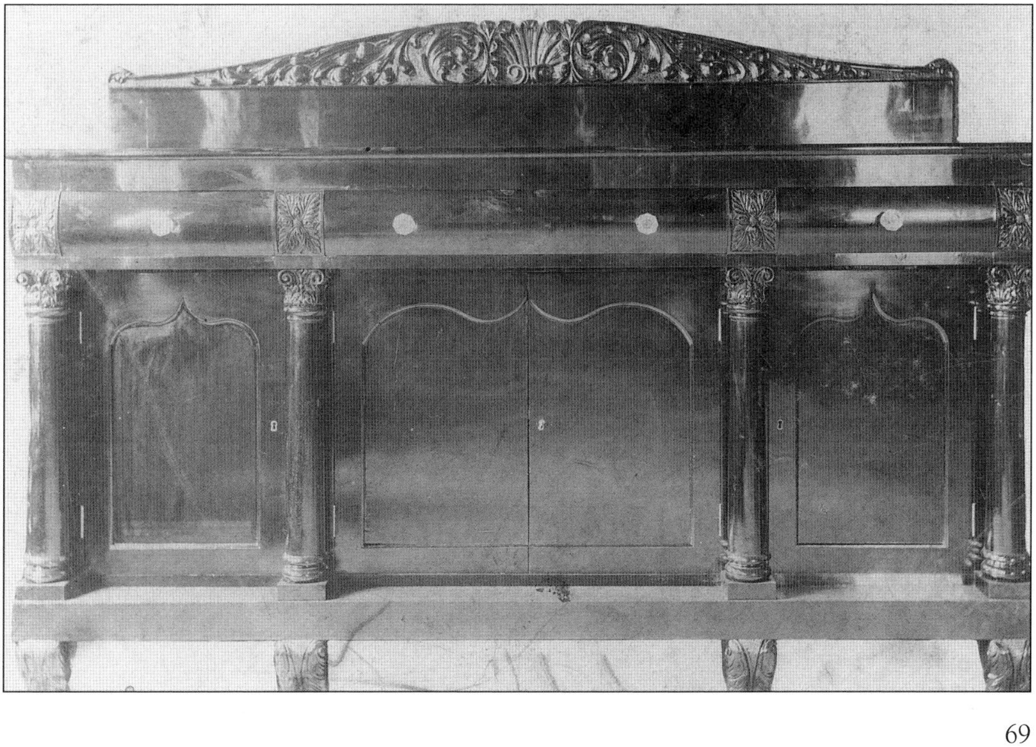

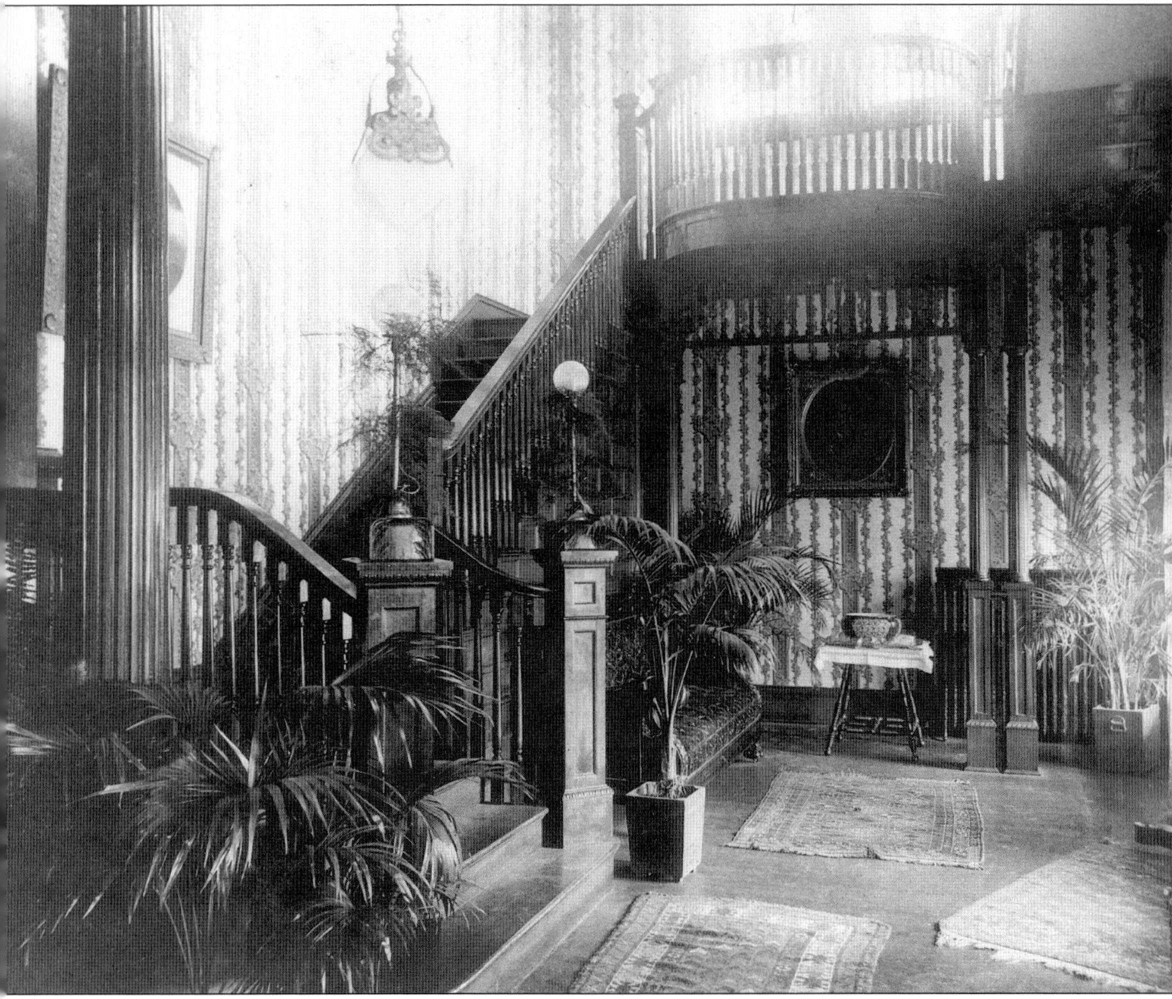

The entry hall was dominated by the elaborate, dark millwork of the staircase and the floral stripe wallpaper. This house, modern for its day, boasted electric light fixtures and steam heat delivered through the matching radiators at the end of the side hall and in the entry hall.

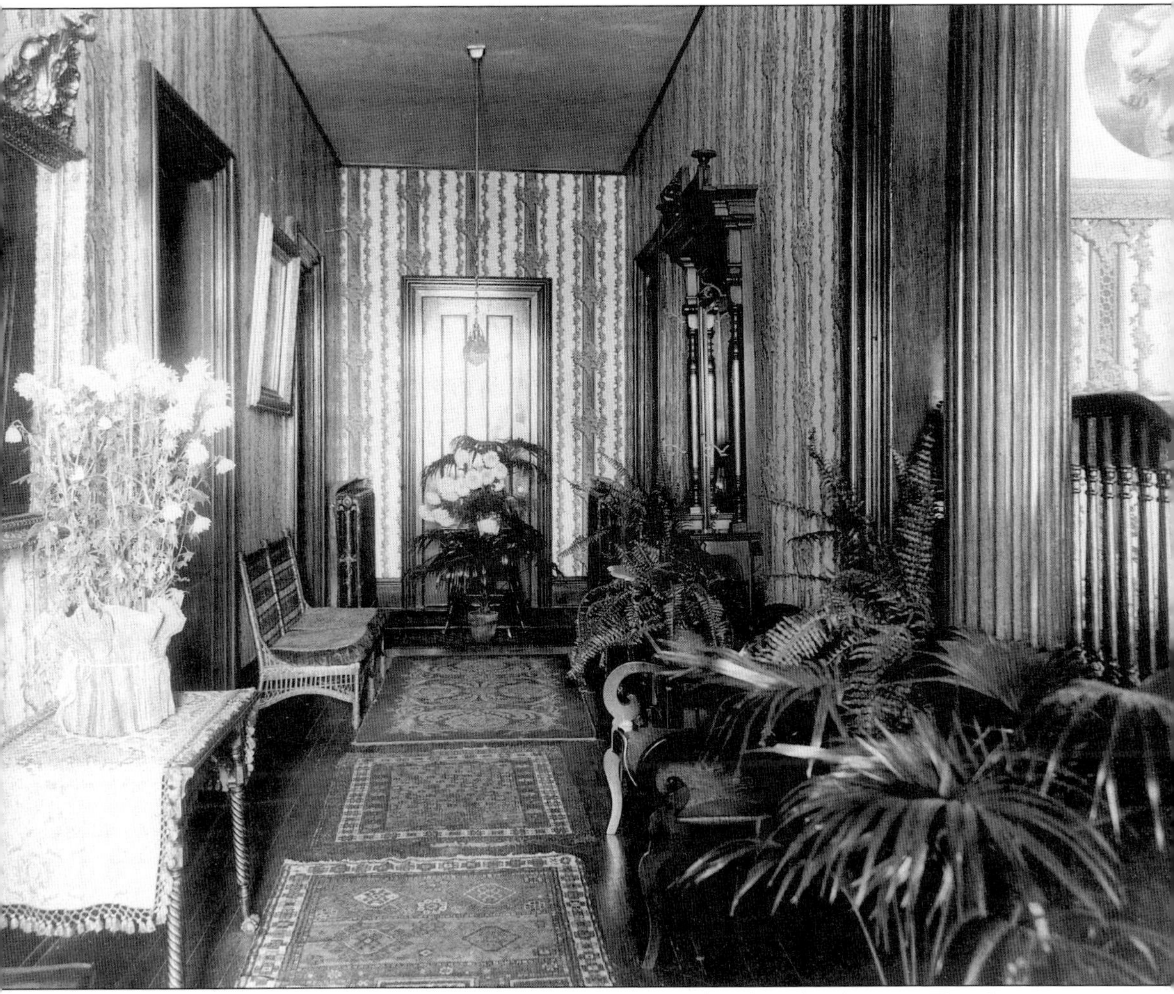

Classical features in this otherwise romantic space were the fluted columns. The furniture consisted of typical hallway benches and quaint tables covered in fringed scarves. The engraving of the double horse heads is an image used elsewhere in a nineteenth-century Nashville stable on Rutledge Hill as a terra cotta plaque. Gone were the carpeted floors of yesteryear. Here we see polished floors and Oriental throw rugs that were in high style between the turn of the century and World War I.

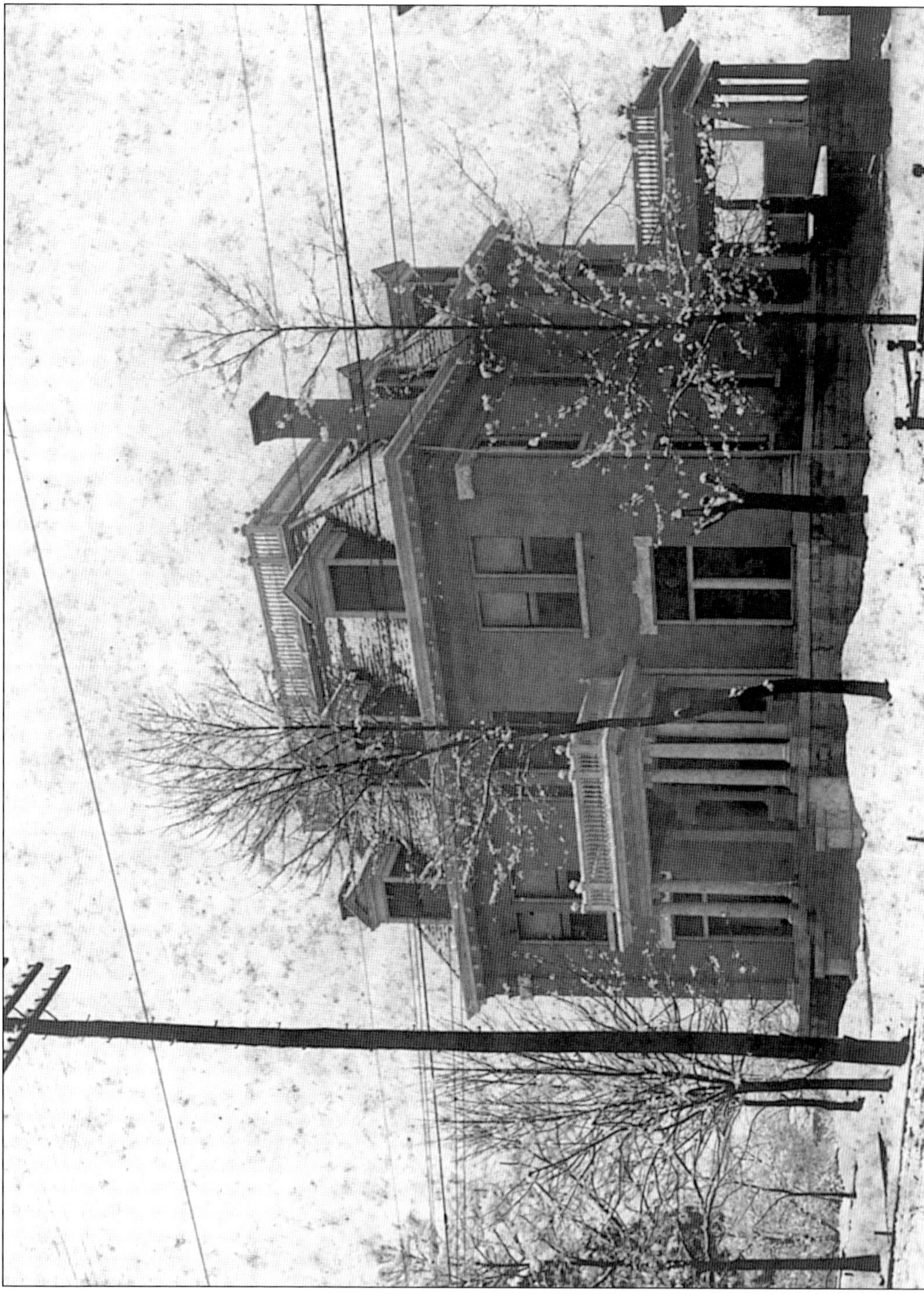

R.W. Turner Residence I
2122 West End Avenue

In the early 1900s, Robert Williamson Turner and his wife, Sally, built two fine houses near the Vanderbilt University campus. The first to be built was a Georgian Revival-style house at 2122 West End Avenue; the second is still standing on Kensington Avenue and may be described as a multi-styled house.

Turner's neighbor, at 2118 West End Avenue, was wholesale grocer C.T. Cheek. In 1923, the Cheek house became the Tennessee Governor's Mansion and remained so until 1949. Both Turner and Cheek selected a prime neighborhood. Although many fine houses and neighborhoods remained in north, east, and south Nashville before World War I, the trend was to move to the West End section for those with social aspirations.

The Georgian Revival style selected by the Turners was one adapted from eighteenth-century houses built by the colonists along the East Coast. The style was thus sometimes called Colonial Revival. Some of the classical earmarks of this style are a hip roof, triangular pediments, balustrades, and fluted columns with Ionic capitals. One outstanding feature of this house was the beveled-glass door and side lights. While stained glass of the late nineteenth century would have been inappropriate, in this Colonial Revival house the clear, beveled glass was equally decorative and sparkled like diamonds.

After the house was finished and furnished, professional photographer H.O. Fuller was commissioned to photograph the interior and exterior on a snowy December 7, 1904.

Photographer: H.O. Fuller
Photographed: *c.* 1903
From the collection of the late Suzanne G. Fassnacht, TSL&A

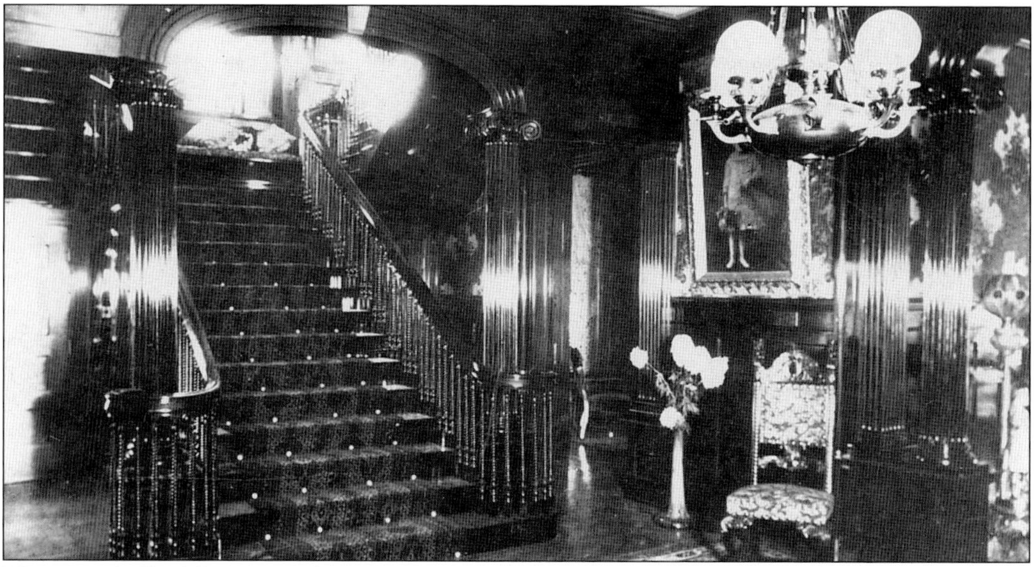

The entry hall of the Turner house on West End Avenue leaves no doubt that the Turners were a family of financial means. The staircase was reached through the grand elliptical arch with keystone, supported by classical Ionic order columns. The woodwork, paneling, mantelpieces, and floors are all of dark, highly-polished millwork here and throughout the house. The random-sized, Oriental-style rugs obscure much of the shiny floor in the entry hall. The portrait partially covered by the ceiling light fixture is of the Turner's daughter, Boneda, who was born in 1879. Edgefield artist William A. ClenDenning painted this portrait about 1890. It now hangs at the Turner cottage at Beersheba Springs, Tennessee, where the family spent their summers in order to escape the heat and epidemics of Nashville.

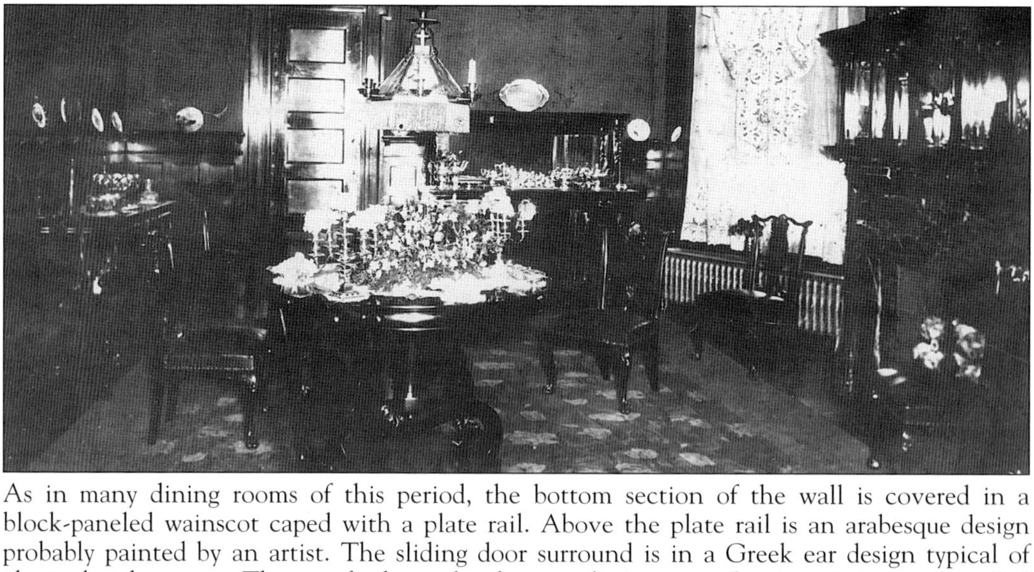

As in many dining rooms of this period, the bottom section of the wall is covered in a block-paneled wainscot caped with a plate rail. Above the plate rail is an arabesque design probably painted by an artist. The sliding door surround is in a Greek ear design typical of classical architecture. The matched set of mahogany dining room furniture is in a style called Chippendale that had been copied by both hand and machine since the eighteenth century. The ceiling treatment, with its oval of bare bulbs, is surrounded by a painted, undulating design in the Art Nouveau style. The candles (probably gas) are the only thing Colonial about the fringed light fixture.

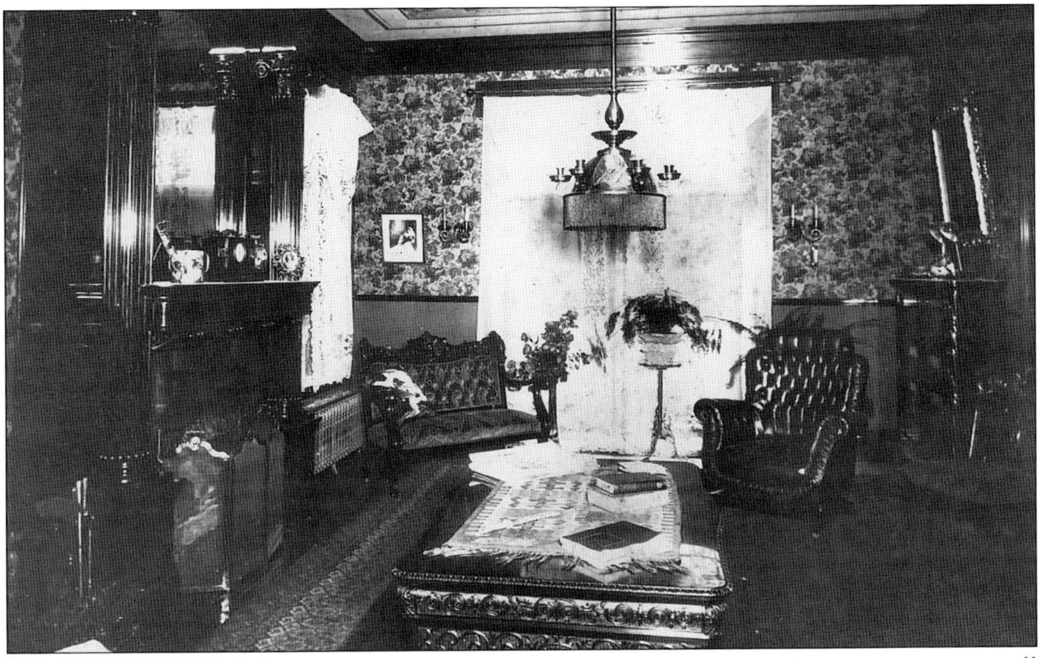

Since the only two bookcases visible in these photographs were in this room, it may well have been called the library. The heavily ornate table supports this theory. The table was in a different location in each photograph. This room could be entered through the great hallway arch or through the dining room. It had several features in common with the dining room, such as the window treatments and similar light fixtures. This room appeared to be more of a parlor for family gatherings after dinner than a guest parlor.

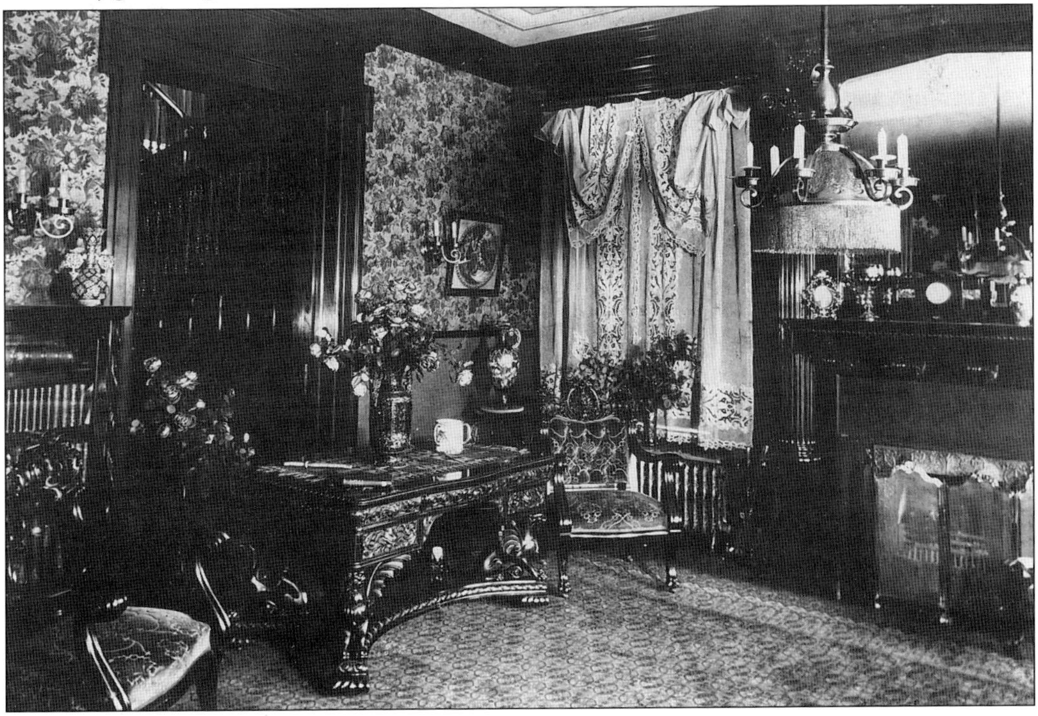

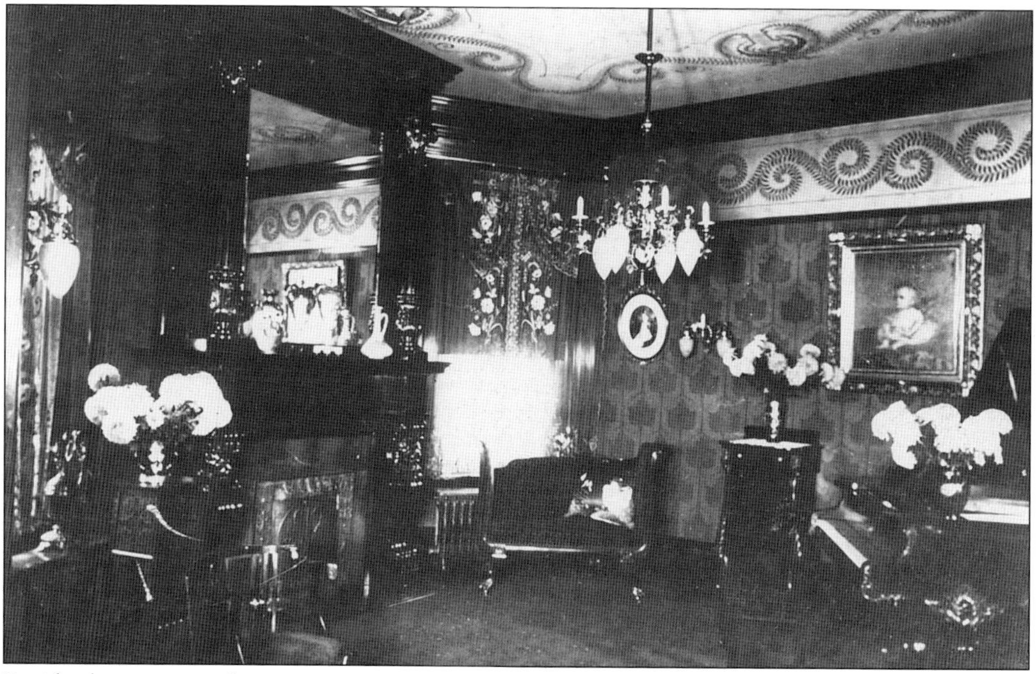

Beside the piano in the music room was a case piece that could possibly have housed an early record player or sheet music. There is no doubt that the undulating rhythm of the wave pattern used on the frieze and ceiling would have been appropriate for a room devoted to music. The portrait was of Henry Martin Turner, who died at age six months in 1882. It was painted by William ClenDenning and is now owned by the Tennessee State Museum.

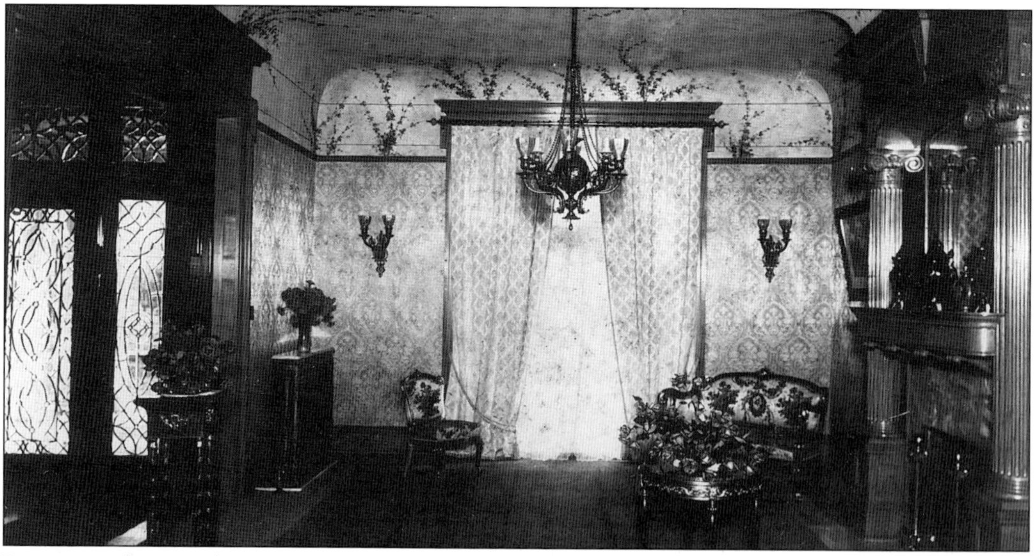

Rooms with French furniture, high values, and naturalistic designs are often considered feminine. While this room does not completely meet that definition, it is certainly the best candidate for a ladies' parlor in the Turner house. A traditional design frequently used in fabrics (especially damask) was used for the sidewalls. The dropped ceiling design could be described as light, gay, airy, and any other adjective that describes movement. The window hangings appear to have been in a trellis design supporting the garden feeling of the ceiling.

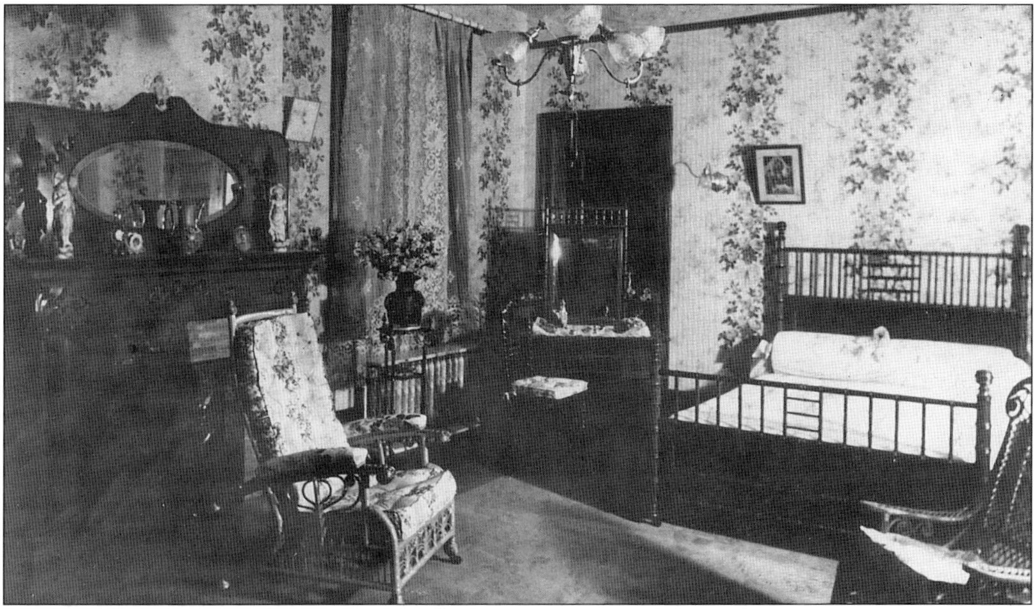

In two upstairs bedrooms, similar decorating devices were used: wallpaper, dropped ceilings, lace curtains, dark window shades, and similar lighting fixtures. In Room one, the furniture suite was in a style called Anglo-Japanese, which featured bamboo-turned spindles. The wicker chairs carried out the Oriental theme. In contrast, on the étagère-style mantelpiece are a pair of colonial figurines.

Room two was treated with a bold, striped wallpaper. The simple, marble-faced fireplace had an oval mirror hung horizontally above the mantel shelf. With a dressing table for her and a larger dresser for him, this was probably a master bedroom. Through the open door we see the ultimate in luxury for this time: an adjoining bathroom.

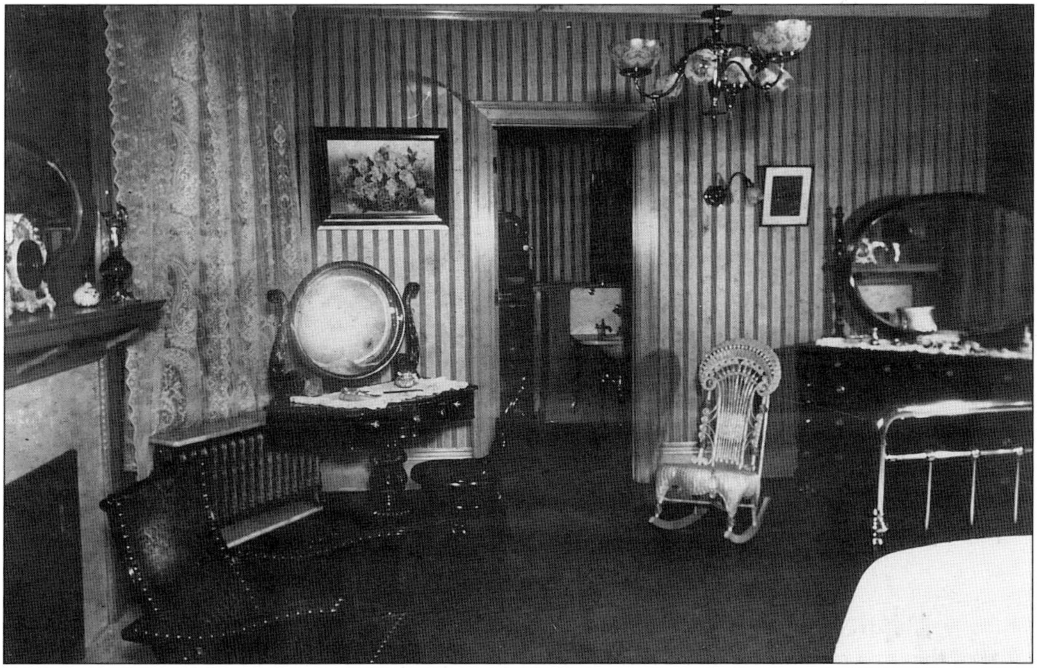

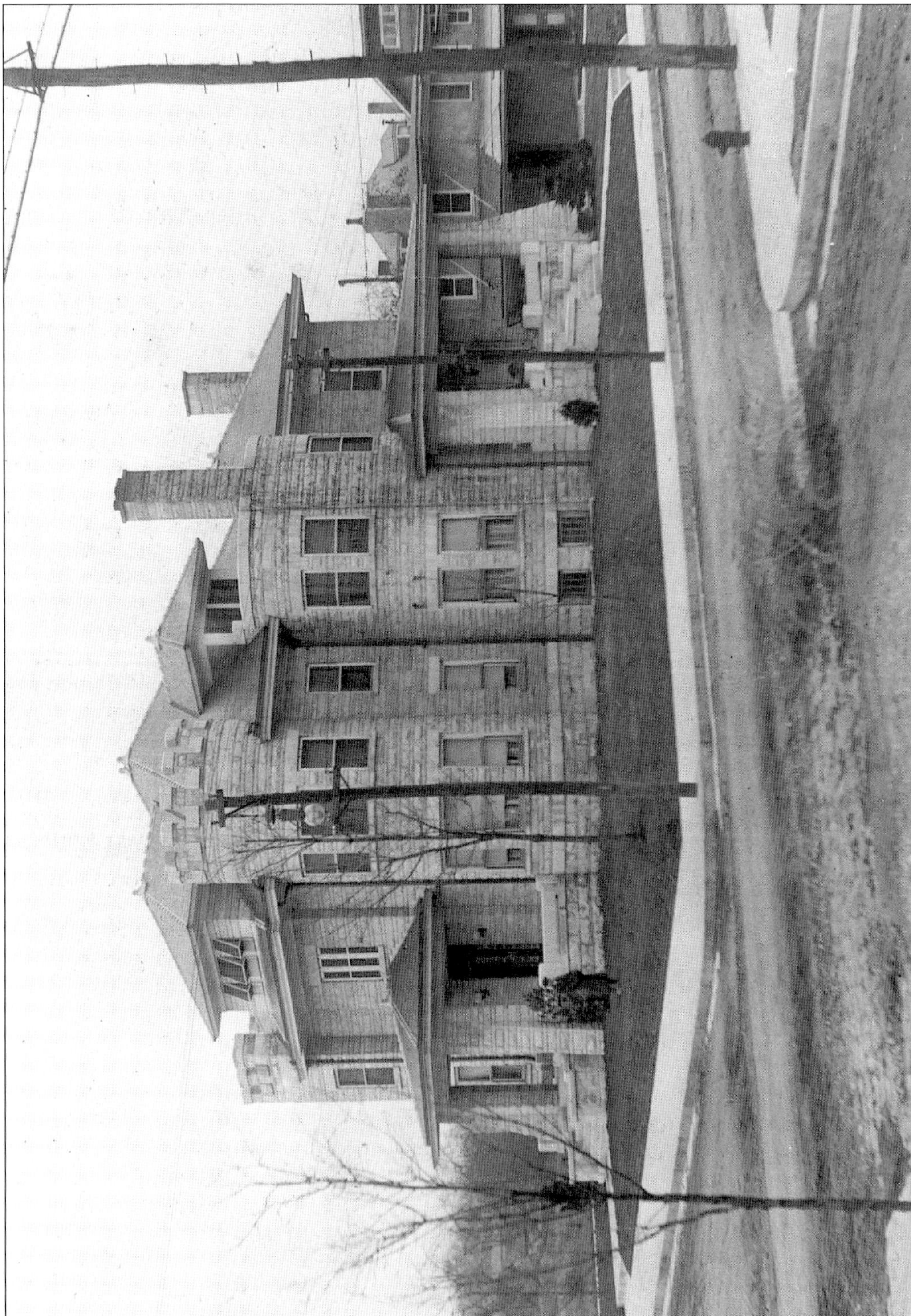

R.W. Turner Residence II
2500 Kensington Place

One of the most unique houses in Nashville was built by Sally Wright and Robert W. Turner at 2500 Kensington Place in 1910. The three-story house built of Bowling Green stone still stands today. It is on the Vanderbilt University campus where, until recently, it served as the Sigma Alpha Epsilon Chapter House.

Both inside and out, the house incorporates many stylish trends. The center section of the house has a tapered porch post and a gently pitched hip roof that terminates in a point. Both round and square crenelated turrets flank the main body of the house. This combination of bungalow and Gothic Revival features was the product of an architect whose identity has been lost in time. The only clue is that Nashville architect James Yeaman (who also designed Judge A.G. Merritt's house and Charles Mitchell's store) was employed by the Turners in the 1890s to remodel and enlarge their summer house at Beersheba Springs, Tennessee, known as the Turner Cottage.

R.W. Turner had a successful real estate business in downtown Nashville. In the 1909 City Directory, he is listed as selling real estate and fire insurance. One of his partners was A.G. Merritt Jr., who married his daughter, Boneda. Turner's office was at 304 Third Avenue North. In 1911, his son, R.W. Turner Jr., listed his business as Wright Bros. & Turner; his address was listed as 2500 Kensington Place.

Being in the real estate business, the Turners were constantly on the move. They first lived in south Nashville on College Street and on Market Street near Rutledge Hill. They then moved to West End Avenue and finally to Kensington Place. In addition to these moves, they spent three months every summer in their house in Beersheba Springs.

Photographer: R.S. Patterson
Photographed: *c.* 1911
From the collection of the late Suzanne G. Fassnacht, TSL&A

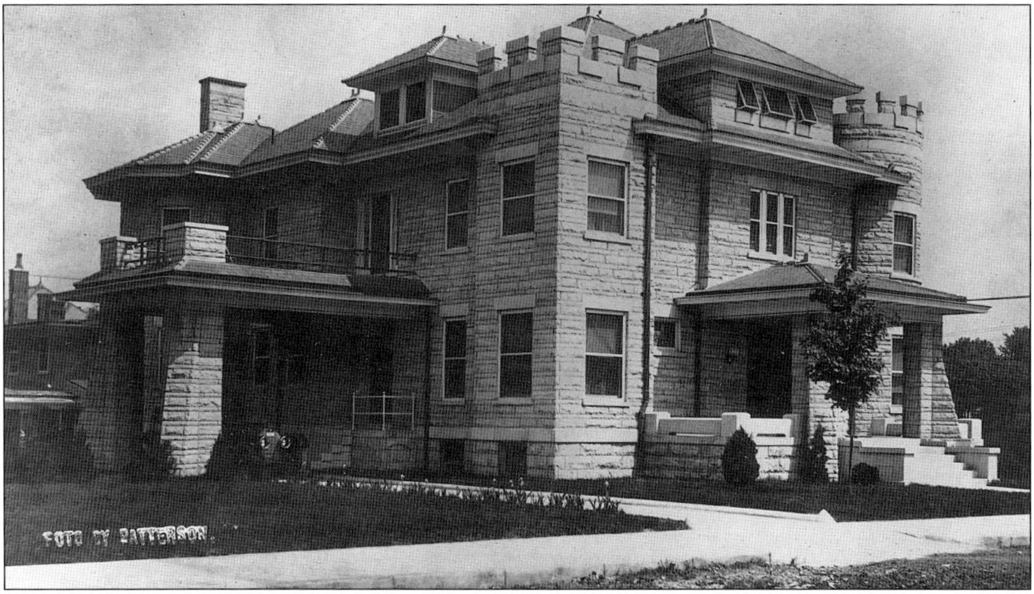

Photographer R.S. Patterson made several exterior views of this unusual house. One view shows the family automobile parked under the overhang, the servants' quarters in the rear, and the square turret. The view below shows the round turrets on the opposite side of the house.

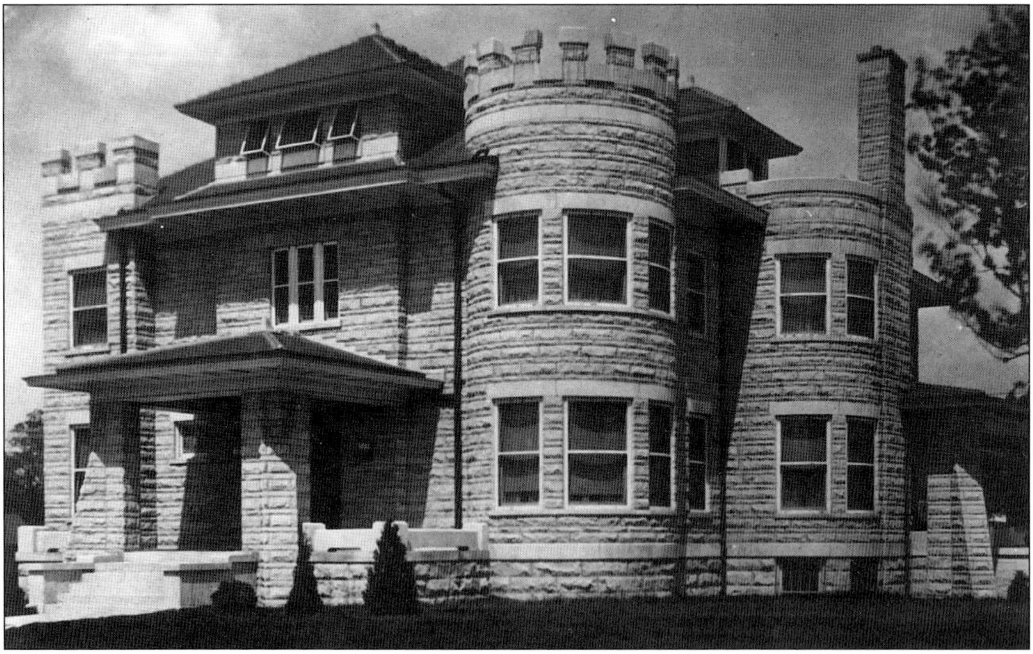

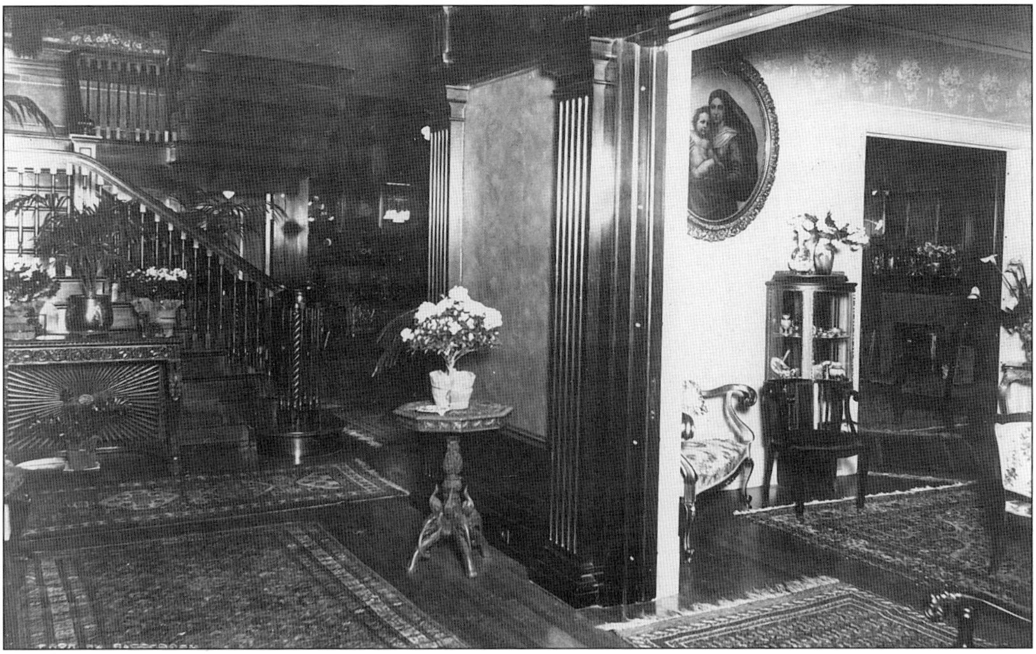

The same heavy millwork was used for the staircase and hallways on Kensington Place as was used in the Turner's former house on West End Avenue. The Doric-style pilasters blend with the elongated pattern of the stained-glass doors. Both the music room and the parlor may be seen from the hallway. In the music room was a copy of Raphael's *Sistine Madonna*.

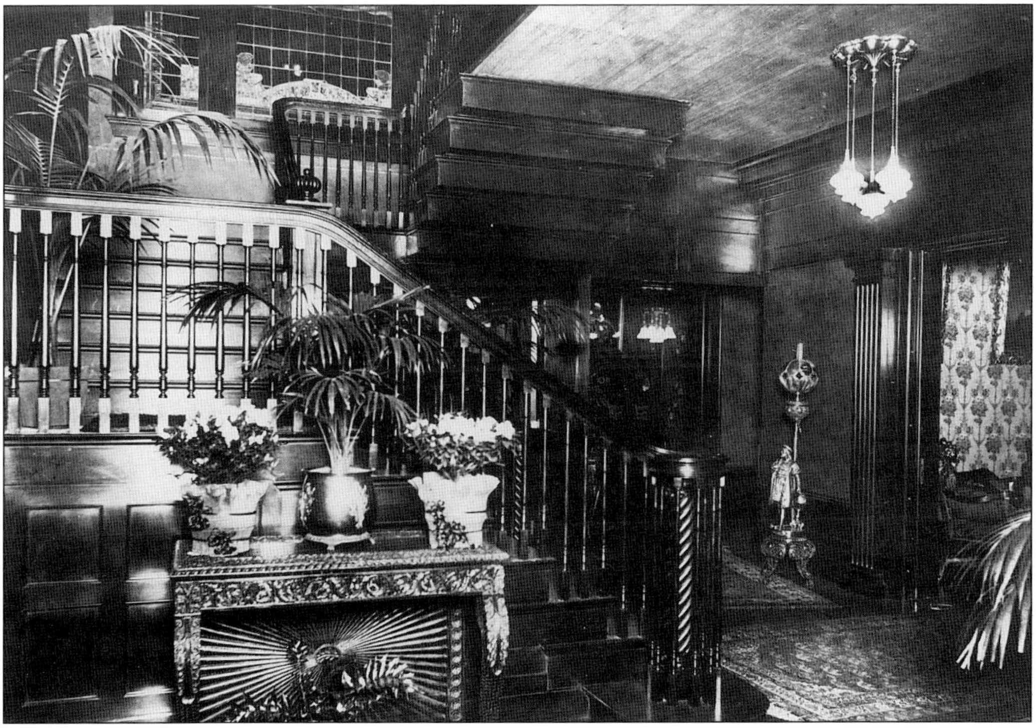

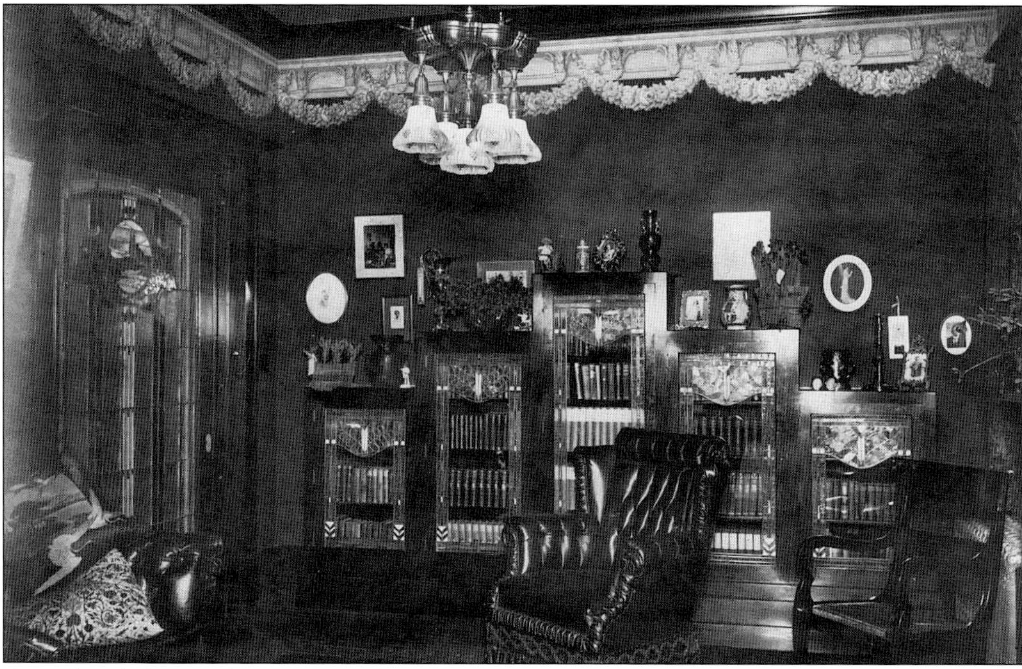

Over the tiled mantelpiece in the library hung the portrait of an infant by William ClenDenning that hung in the former house on West End Avenue. The design of the glass entry doors, as well as the bookcase doors, was in the style of Scottish architect and designer Charles Rennie Mackintosh. The repeat of the chevron pattern is a clue that the same artist fashioned all of the stylized glass doors. The flowered lace curtain and garlanded wallpaper border add a realistic design element.

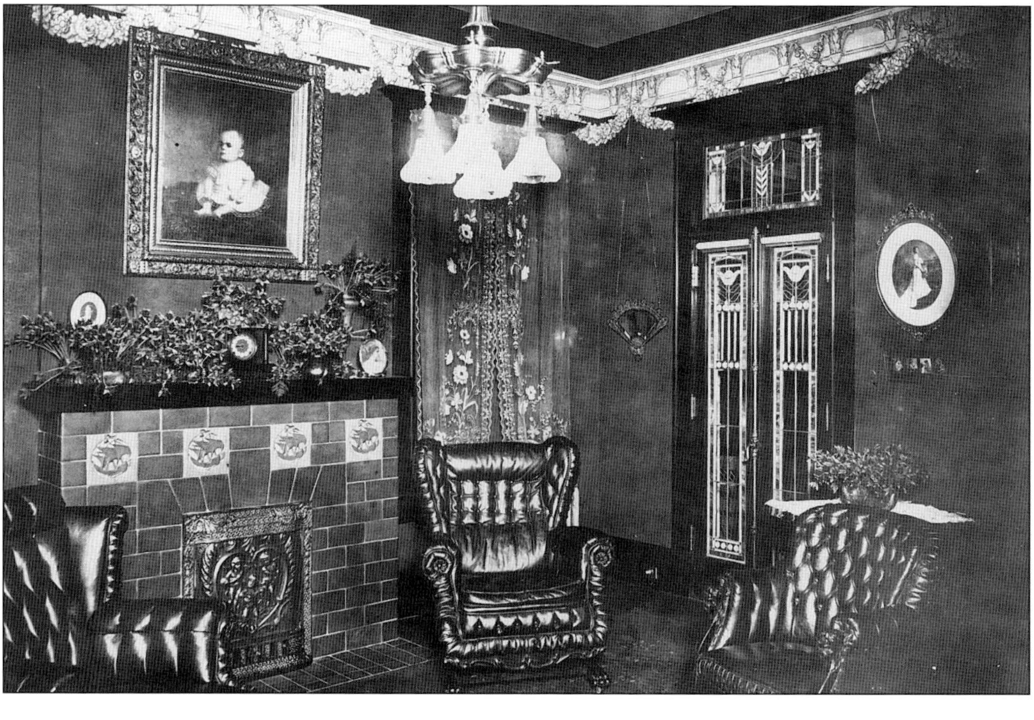

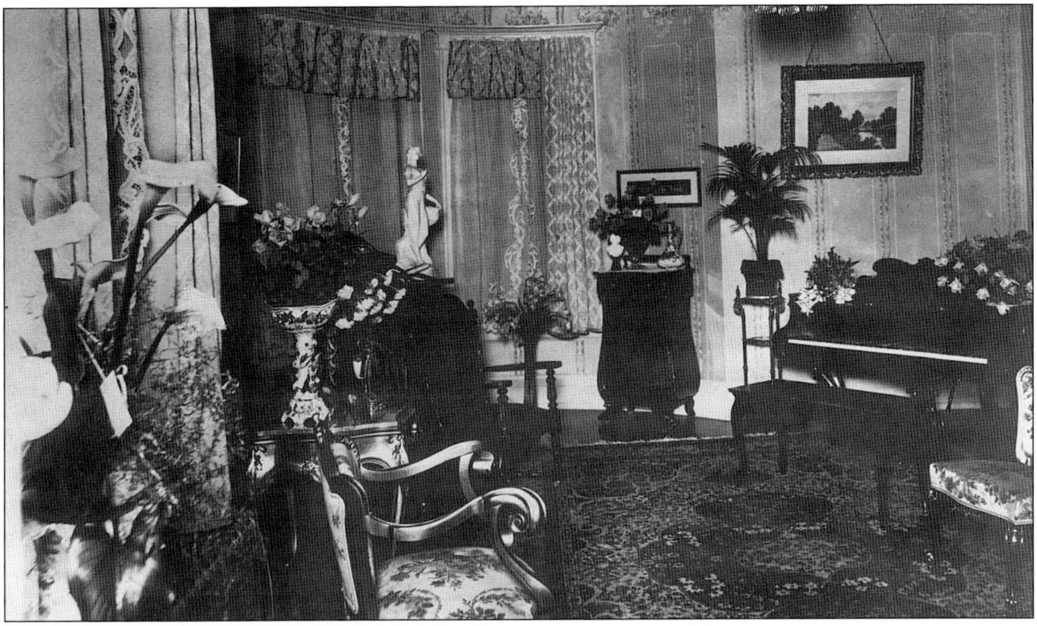

On Kensington Place the ladies' parlor appeared to also serve as the music room. In this house, the walls were covered with a paper that was inspired by French panels. The same lattice-patterned side draperies were moved to the new house and reworked to fit the new windows.

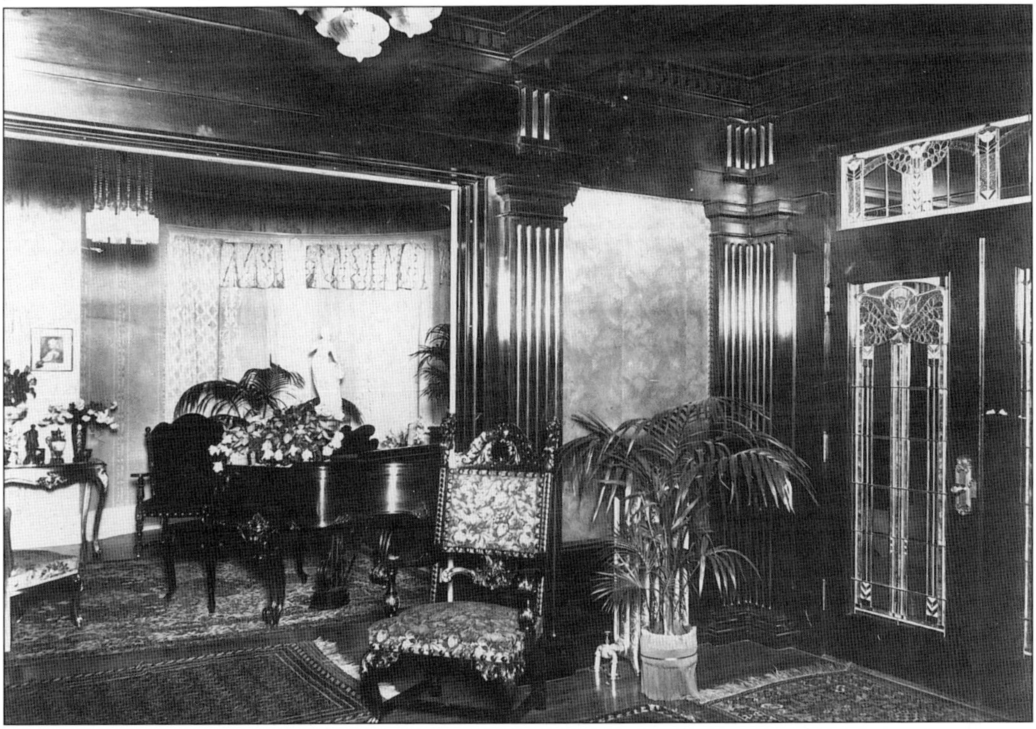

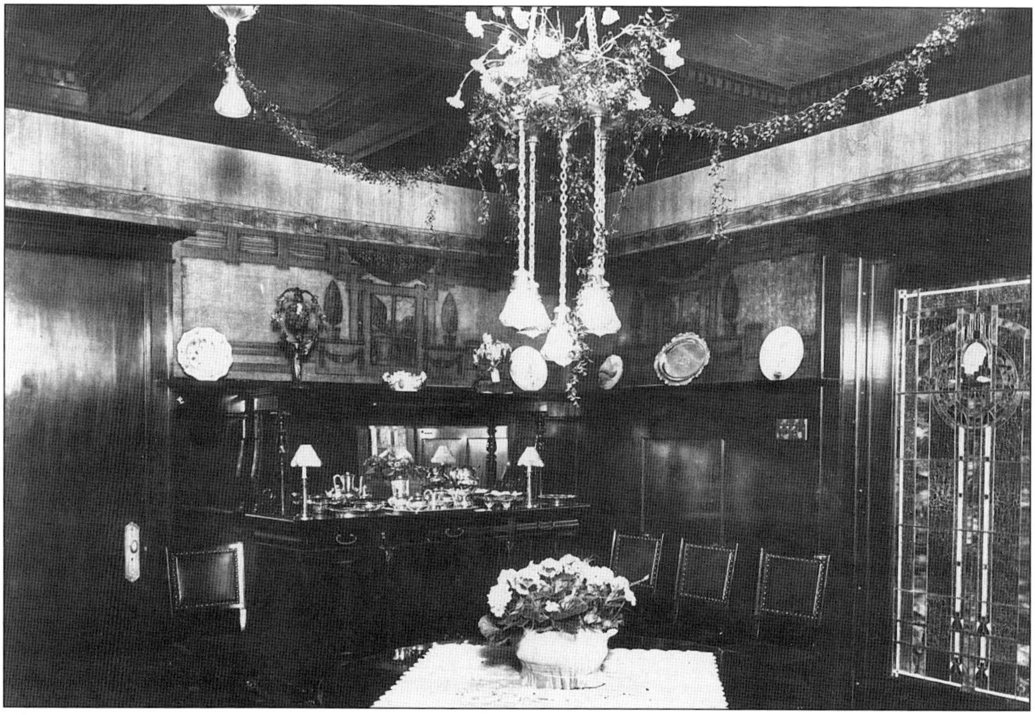

These two photographs of the dining room were taken after the room had been decorated for some special occasion—perhaps a wedding or debut ball. The furniture pieces, except for the chairs, were the same pieces used in the West End Avenue house. The new Renaissance Revival-style chairs have much straighter lines than the former chairs. The wainscot was topped by a plate rail and a stylized wallpaper pattern in the manner of English designer Walter Crane. In addition to the electric lights on the ceiling, there were tapers with little silk shades on the table and side board. According to contemporary accounts, these were quite a fire hazard.

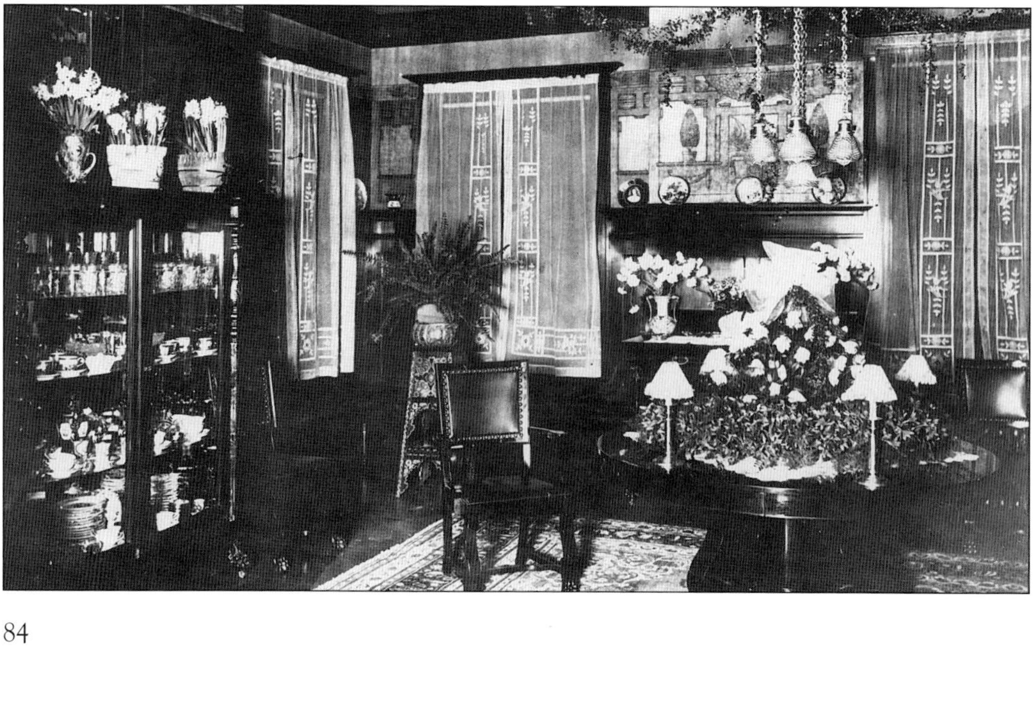

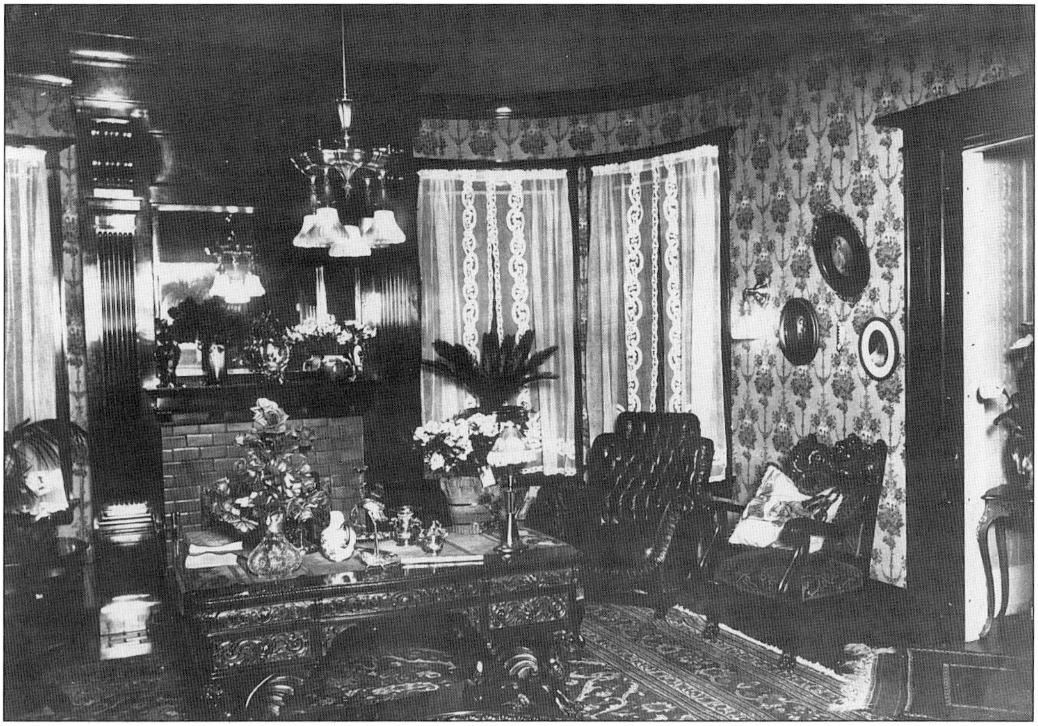

The comfortable chairs and homey decoration of this room indicate that it may have been the family parlor used for after-dinner gatherings.

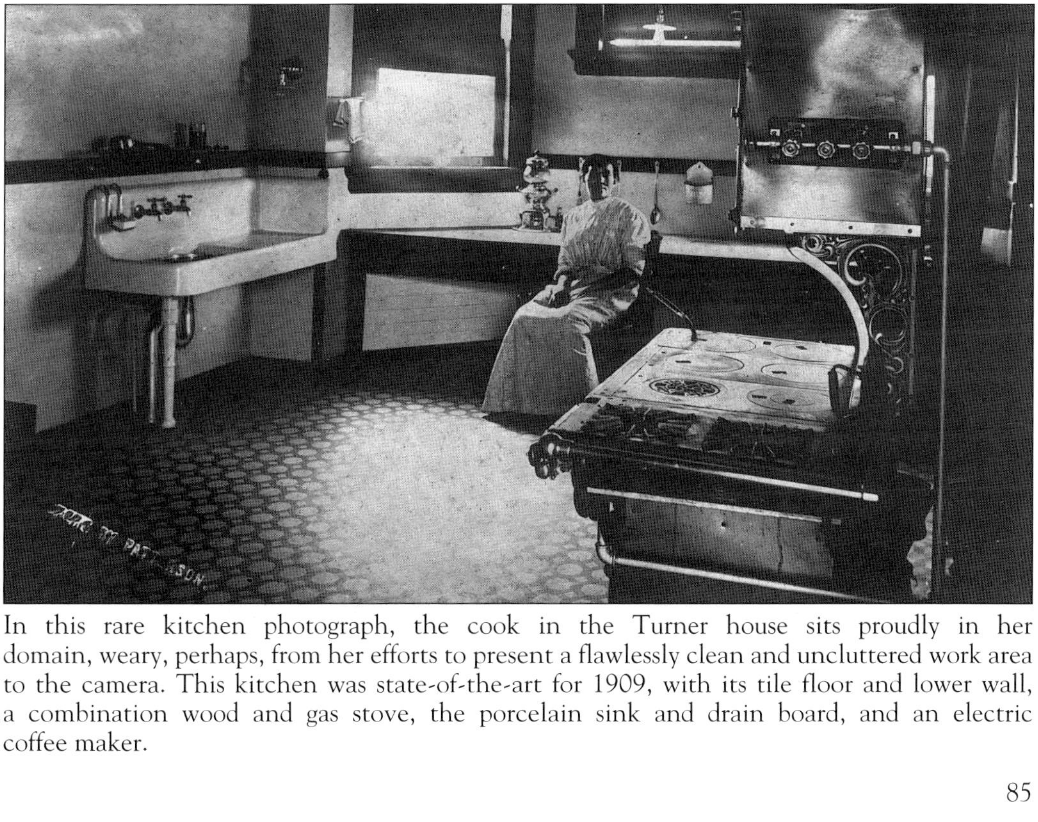

In this rare kitchen photograph, the cook in the Turner house sits proudly in her domain, weary, perhaps, from her efforts to present a flawlessly clean and uncluttered work area to the camera. This kitchen was state-of-the-art for 1909, with its tile floor and lower wall, a combination wood and gas stove, the porcelain sink and drain board, and an electric coffee maker.

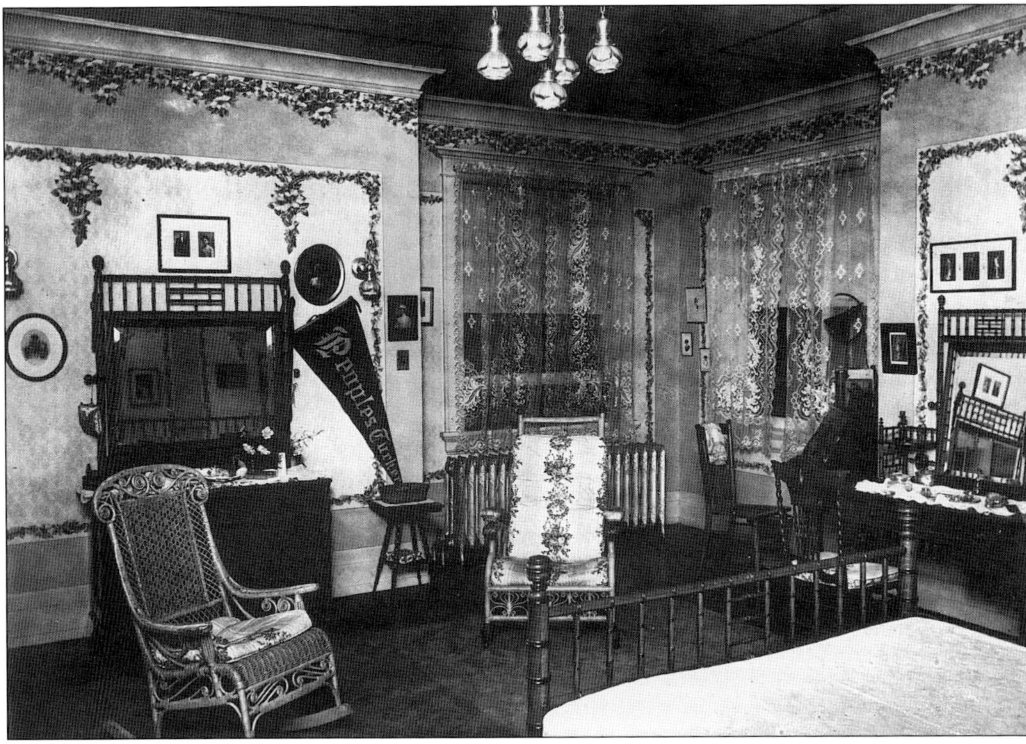

The same Anglo-Japanesque bedroom furniture was used on Kensington Place as was used on West End Avenue by the Turner family; even the lace curtains appear to be the same. The wallpaper panels are bordered in a rose pattern similar to the border under the crown moulding.

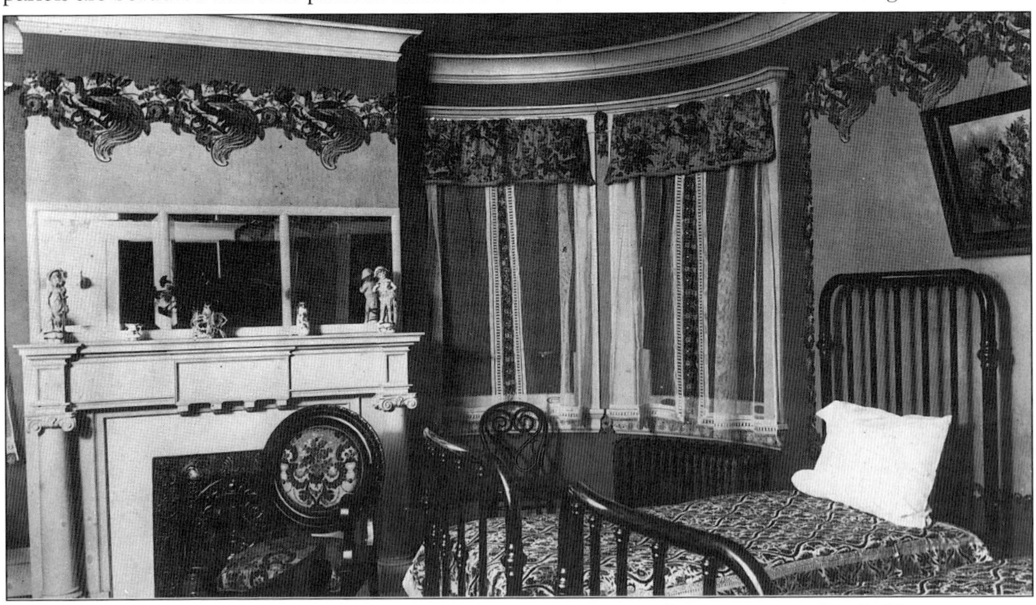

It seems that the furniture in one of the bedrooms on West End Avenue was divided between two bedrooms on Kensington Place. This room has the brass twin beds with India print bedspreads. Since only one side of the room is shown in this photograph, the other furnishings used here must forever remain a mystery.

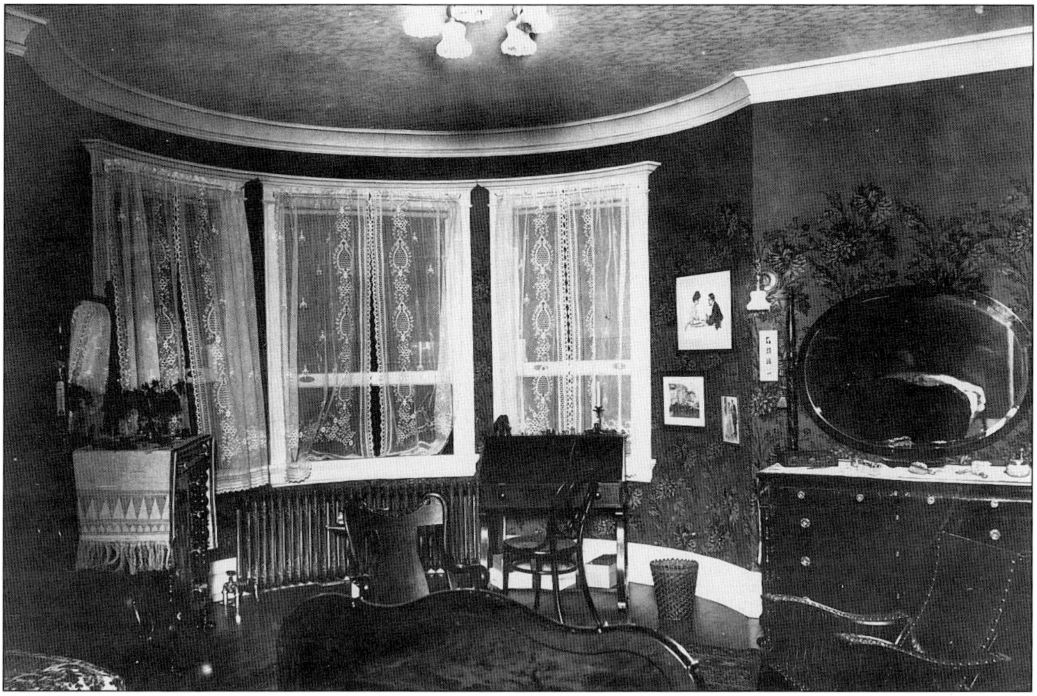

This bedroom, located in the upstairs turret room, has a patterned ceiling and side wallpaper that appears to "grow up" from the baseboard. There are new twin beds and a large dresser and chair from the furniture division of the former bedroom. A waste basket and a Charles Dana Gibson print are visible here.

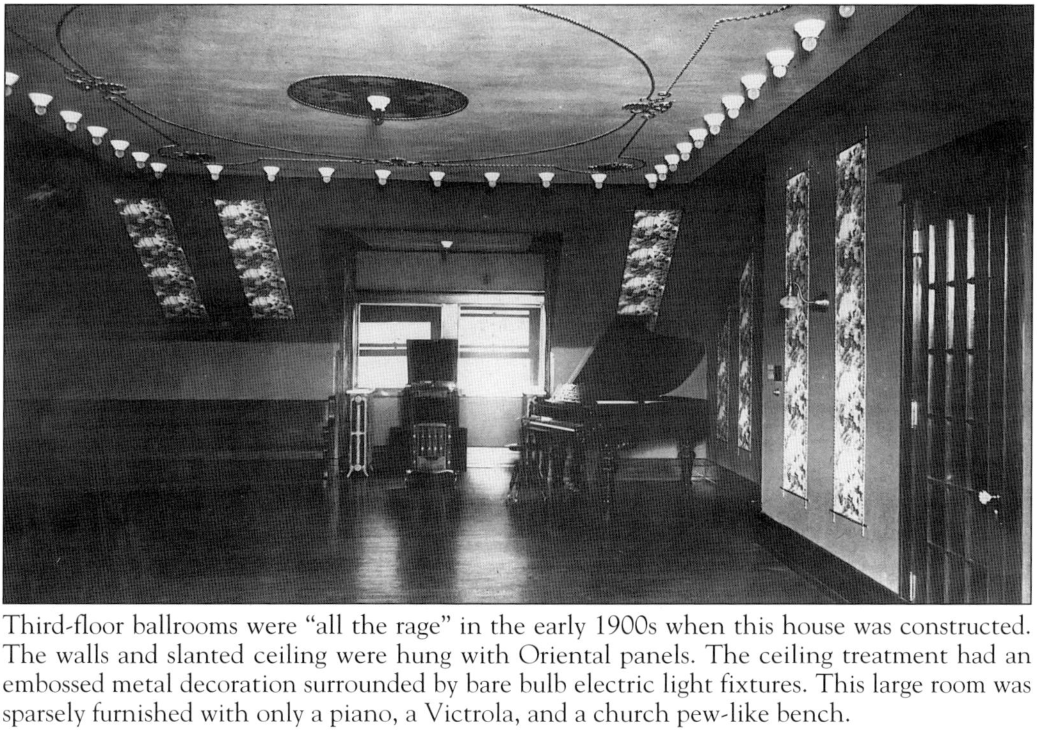

Third-floor ballrooms were "all the rage" in the early 1900s when this house was constructed. The walls and slanted ceiling were hung with Oriental panels. The ceiling treatment had an embossed metal decoration surrounded by bare bulb electric light fixtures. This large room was sparsely furnished with only a piano, a Victrola, and a church pew-like bench.

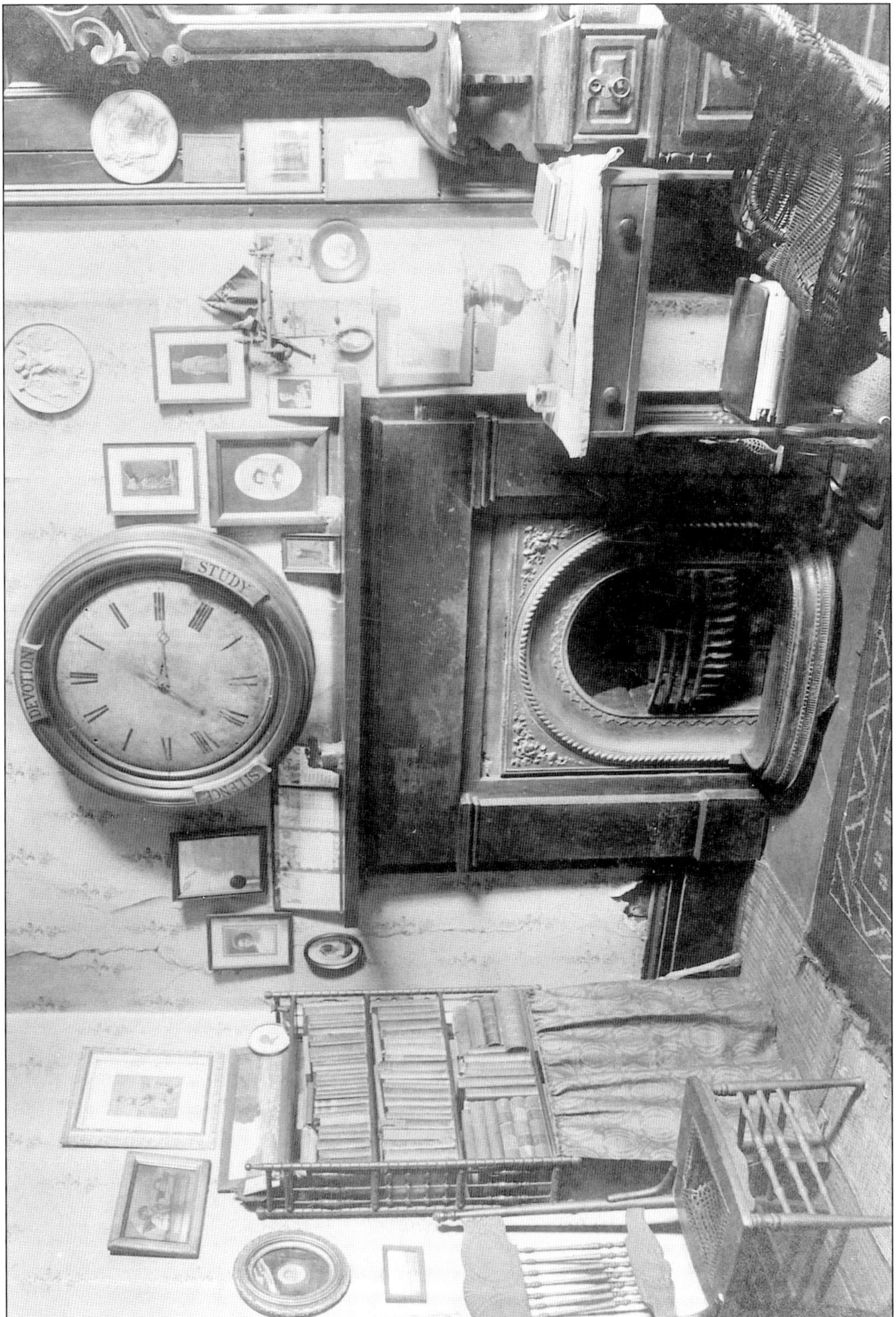
STUDY
DEVOTION
SILENCE

Elizabeth P. Elliott Residence
Spruce Street at Lea Avenue

The fireside scene pictured here was the living room of Elizabeth Porterfield Elliott (1860–1932), best known to Nashvillians as Miss Lizzie, teacher and author of *The Early History of Nashville*. Miss Lizzie, the daughter of Collins D. Elliott and Elizabeth Porterfield Elliott, grew up at Boscobel, a country home located at the intersection of the present Acklen and Elliott Avenues. The old house was for many years occupied by the Tennessee Children's Home. Since the house was razed, the site has been occupied by Mt. Gilead Baptist Church.

Miss Lizzie, whose father was the headmaster of the Nashville Female Academy before the Civil War, taught in the Nashville public schools for 50 years, 30 years at Howard Elementary School. In her last years she lived at 704 Demonbreun Street in the Norvell-Simpson House with her niece, Mrs. William Simpson. Nashvillians will remember this house as the site of the Nashville Union Mission in the 1970s and 1980s. Miss Lizzie died in 1932.

The old academy clock hanging over Miss Lizzie's mantelpiece is believed to have hung in the Nashville Female Academy at one time. She gave the clock to Peabody College, her alma mater. In her will, however, she requested the Tennessee Historical Society retrieve the clock from Peabody.

Her random arrangement of pictures and plaques contains photographs of her father, mother, and siblings. Raphael's angelic cherubs are a detail from *The Sistine Madonna*. We also see the *Nike of Samothrace*, or *Winged Victory*, as well as bas-relief classical plaques. Not only does her dresser block the doorway, but the pictures and plaques are hung on the door and door frame as well.

Photographed: *c.* 1916
From the collection of the late Norvell Rose, Tennessee State Library & Archives

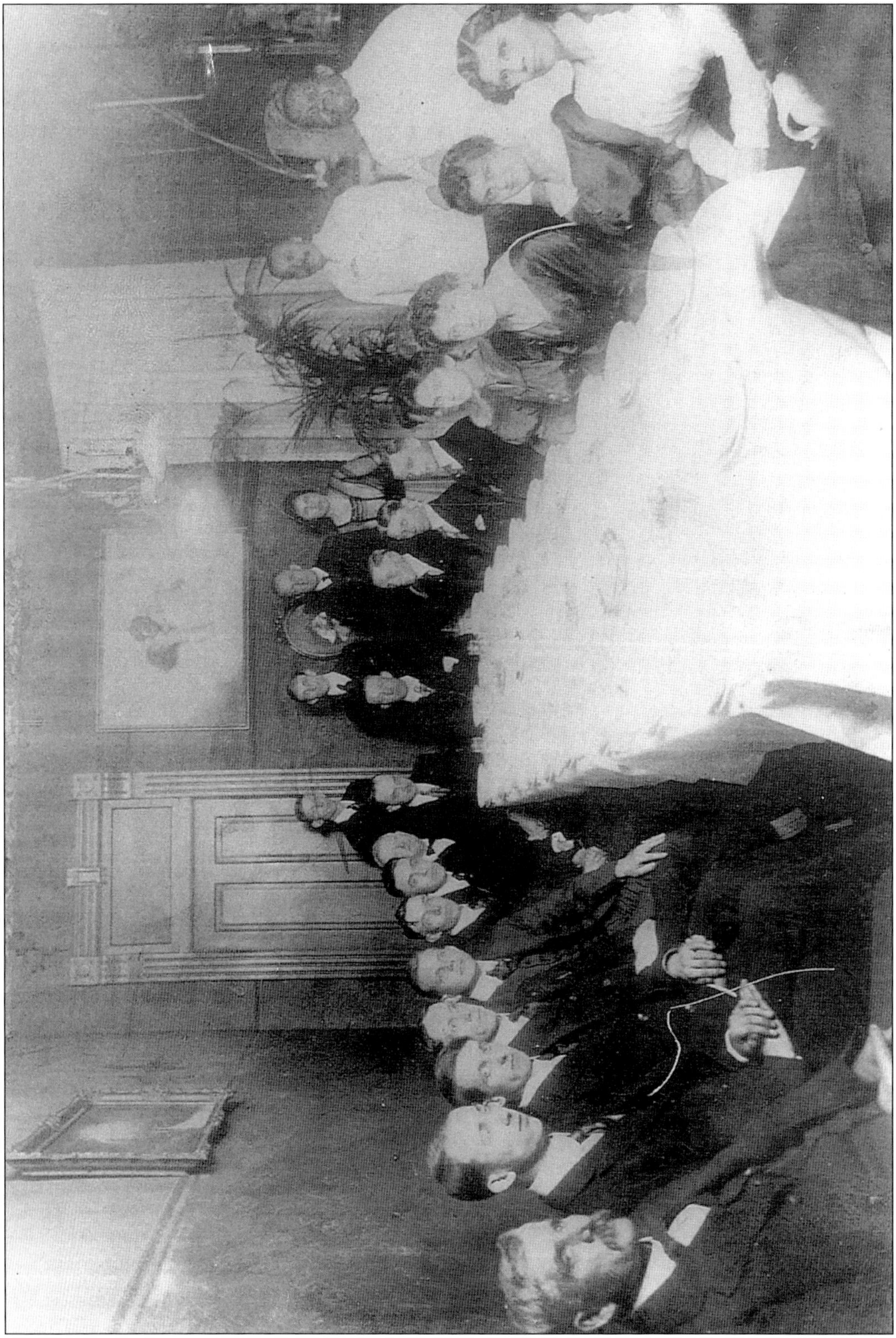

Dempsy Weaver Cantrell Residence
419 Russell Street

The host and hostess for this dinner party were Dempsy Weaver Cantrell and his wife, Nora Johnson Cantrell, seen standing in the rear on the right. Their home was in Edgefield, at 419 Russell Street. The time was *c.* 1915. Other than Mr. and Mrs. Cantrell and the two waiters, there are 6 ladies and 15 gentlemen at the table; all unidentified except for Mrs. Cantrell's father, J.J. Johnson, first gentleman on the left, and her sister, Myra Perry, the first lady on the right.

Above the moulding in the room was a wide-striped wallpaper capped with a scenic border. The lower wall was painted in a textured pattern. On the back wall was a romanticized painting of a mother and child. Underneath this painting in an oval frame was a photograph of Mrs. Cantrell and her daughter, Angie Fields Cantrell, now Mrs. DeWitt Ezell Sr. of Donelson.

Mr. and Mrs. Cantrell lived in Edgefield only a short while. Most of their married life was spent in the Donelson area, near Clover Bottom Mansion. Just across the Stones River on the bluff, where the early settlers had built half-faced shelters, the Cantrells built their house called Stone Hall. On the bank of the river they also built a three-story log lodge that was called Eversong. It was here that Mrs. Cantrell entertained her friends in the Lebanon Road Garden Club and the Tennessee Press and Authors Club. Both she and Mr. Cantrell were active members of the Donelson First Baptist Church.

Photographed: *c.* 1915
From the collection of Historic Edgefield, Inc.

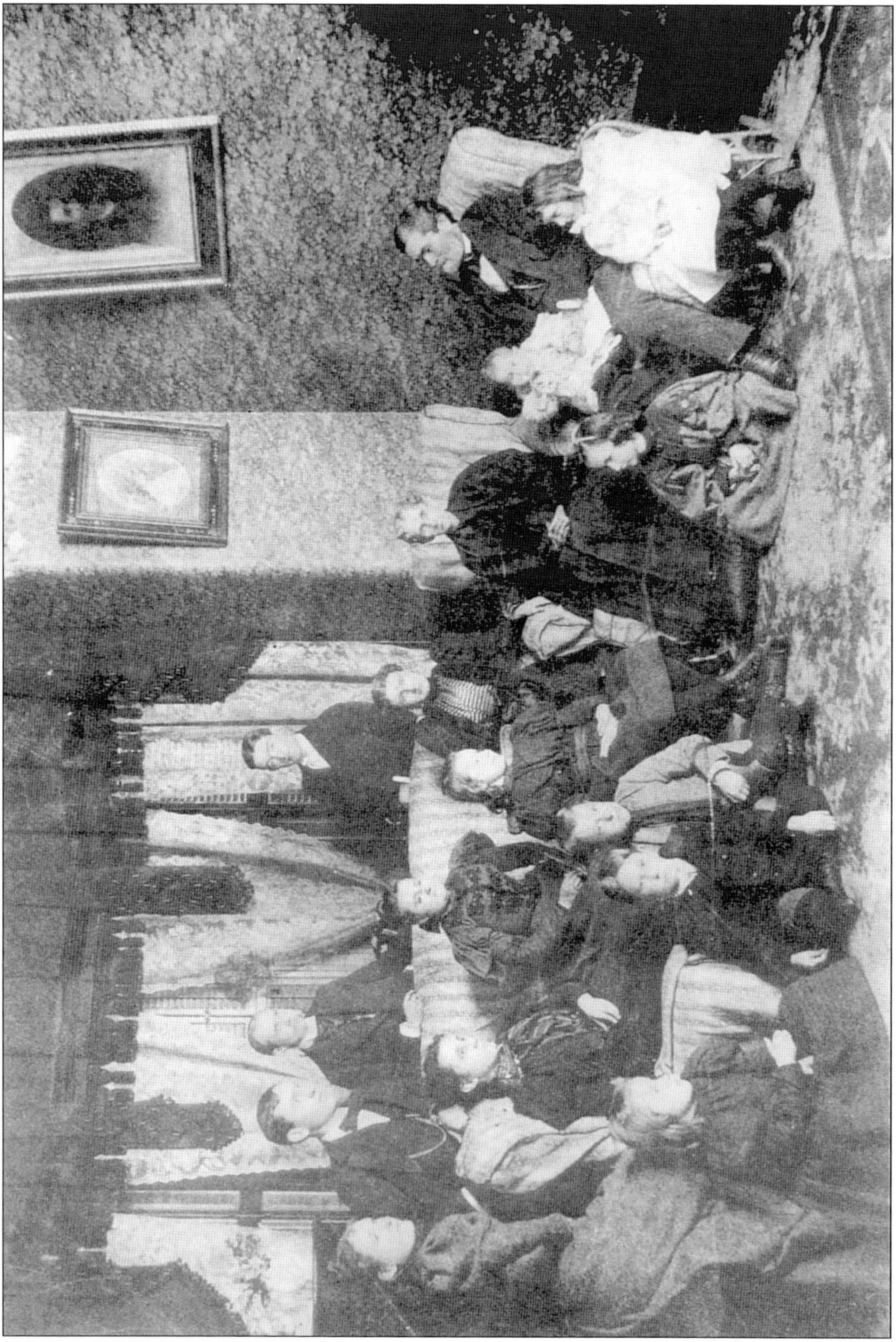

William A. Benson Residence
613 Woodland Street

On Christmas Day, 1897, the Benson family was photographed at the home of their father and mother, William A. and Mary Wherry Benson, at 613 Woodland Street in Edgefield. The elaborate treatment of the bay window consisted not only of custom-made cornice boards with fringed swags but also was treated with interior shutters and lace panels. The over-stuffed seating pieces were slip covered in a sturdy, striped fabric.

William A. Benson was in the home furnishings business at several locations in downtown Nashville. The younger family members formed Benson Printing Company around the turn of the century. Family members, from left to right, are as follows: (front row, seated on the floor) Mary Sue Cummins, Robert Green Benson, William A. Benson, and Lena Cummins; (middle row) Eva Green Benson, Mattie L. Benson Crockett, Emma Mai Benson Cummins, Shirley Cummins, Lillie Benson, Mary G. Wherry Benson, Mary Lee Crockett, William A. Benson, and Medora Shepherd Benson; (back row) John T. Benson Sr., Watkins Crockett, and William J. Cummins.

The Benson house on the north side of Woodland Street in Edgefield burned in the Great Fire of 1916, along with the other houses in this block.

Photographed: Christmas, 1897
From the collection of Laura Benson Davis

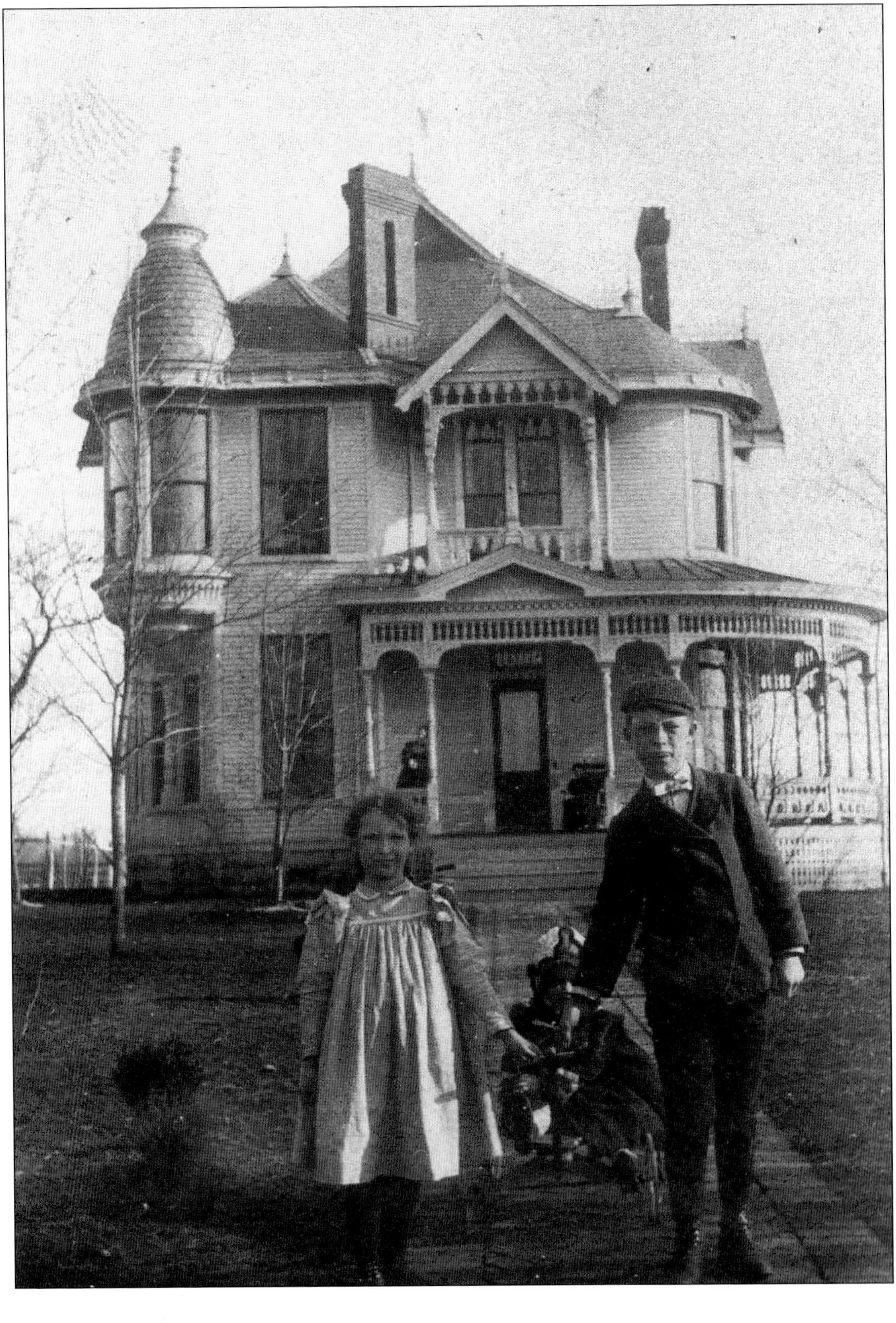

JOHN T. BENSON RESIDENCE
113 EASTLAND AVENUE

John T. Benson was the only son of W.A. and Mary Benson. When he married Eva Green in 1885, the young couple lived with his parents on 613 Woodland Street and later with her father at 712 Russell Street. In 1891, they built a large frame house at 1613 Eastland Avenue on a 5-acre tract where they raised four sons and two daughters.

The exterior photograph is dated *c.* 1898. The children are Medora, Robert, and W.A., who were students at the Sprout Springs School also on Vaughns Pike, later known as Eastland Avenue. The house, considered modern in the 1890s, was heated by a fireplace in each room. The family depended on a cistern and a well with a pump for water. The ice man came every day during the summer months. Housewives would place a sign in their window to let him know if they needed 25 pounds or 50 pounds of ice delivered.

John and Eva Benson were both born during the Civil War and grew up in the Edgefield community. Both families attended Tulip Street Methodist Church when it was located on Russell Street at the corner of Fifth Street.

At the time of his marriage, John T. Benson was employed in his father's carpet and drapery business on Union Street. When his father retired, John T. was connected with several other businesses. In 1909, he and his two older sons, shown in the exterior view of his house, formed Benson Printing company. This business venture was quite successful. It finally closed its doors in 1978 as younger family members pursued other business interests.

Photographed: *c.* 1910
From the collection of Laura Benson Davis

Page 96: The child at the piano may be one of the Benson's sons or a piano student of Eva Green Benson. The Colonial Revival arm chairs were new. The plant table was a much older piece in the Rococo Revival style. The Bokhara-style rug could have been machine-made or hand-woven in the Near East. The wallpaper was printed in a clover leaf pattern.

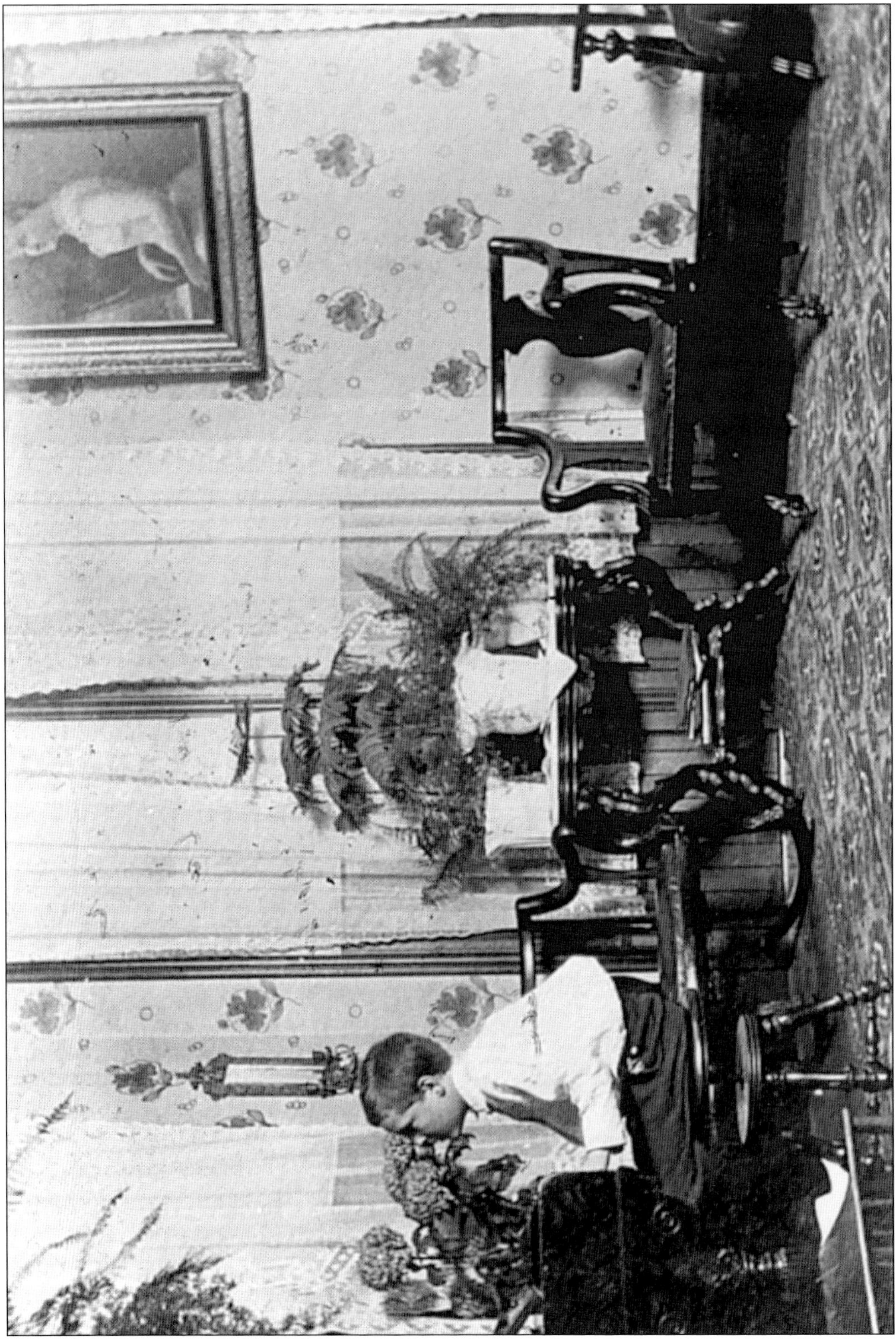

Three

Boarding Schools and Hotels

1. Buford College

2. Maxwell House Hotel

3. Belmont College for Young Women / Ward-Belmont School

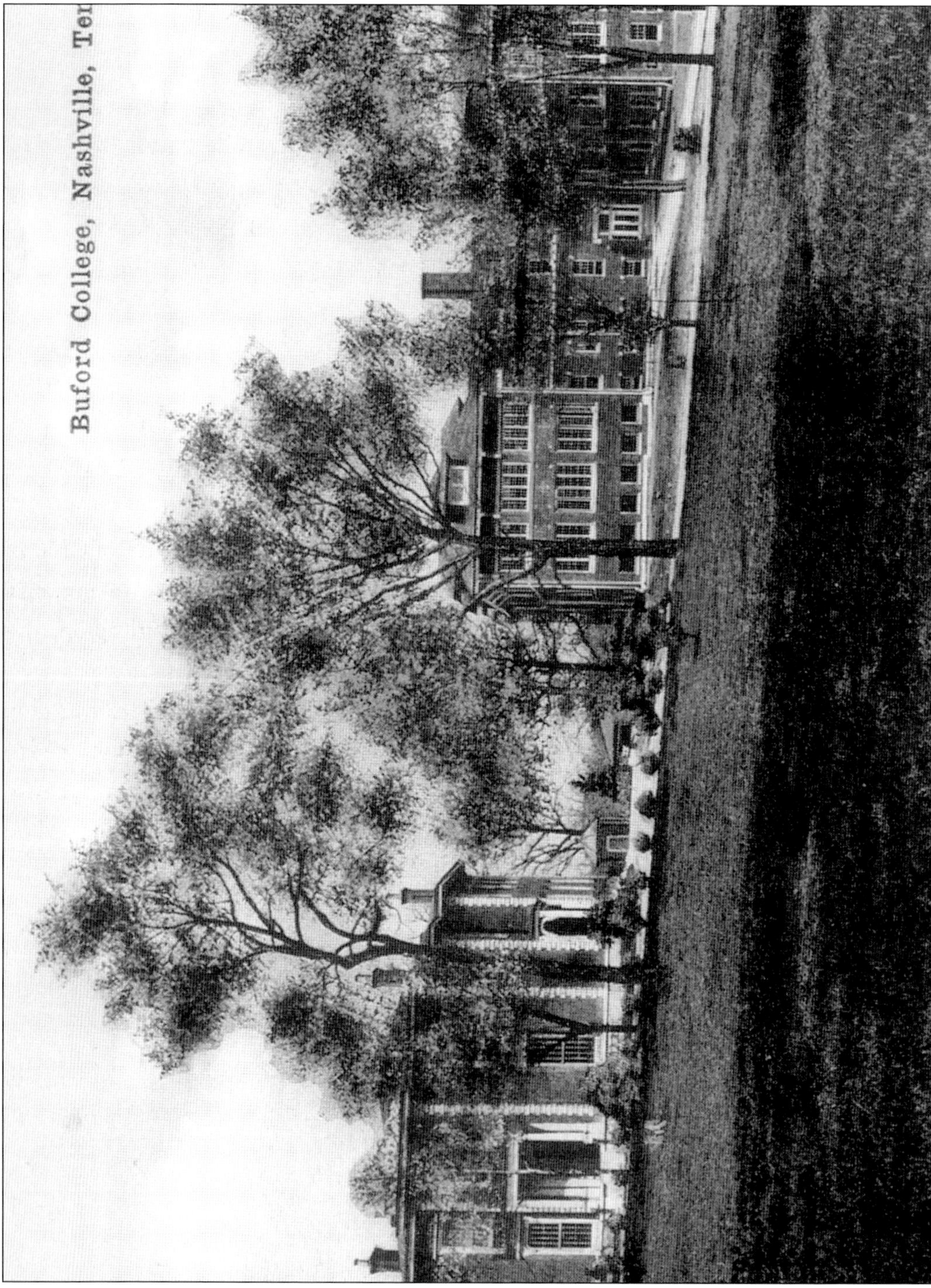
Buford College, Nashville, Te

BUFORD COLLEGE
CHURCH STREET

As a young woman, Mrs. E.G. Buford taught at Martin College in Pulaski, Tennessee, under Miss Hood and Miss Heron, who later founded Belmont College for Young Women and Ward-Belmont. Mrs. Buford also taught at Dr. Price's School in Nashville. In 1901, Buford College was moved from Clarksville to a site in the Glendale section of Nashville.

The location pictured here was on Church Street, between Twentieth and Twenty-first Avenues South. Mrs. Buford purchased the property in 1911 from the heirs of Samuel and Anna Hayes Murphy, who had acquired the property in 1869. In addition to the large brick Victorian house on the property, Mrs. Buford constructed a separate school building.

Samuel Murphy, who was said to be a millionaire, married the daughter of Charles M. Hayes, a Nashville merchant, in 1868. The following year, he bought the property on Church Street and began construction of his large house near Burlington, the Elliston estate.

Many stories have survived concerning the eccentricities of Mr. and Mrs. Murphy. He is said to have been in the whiskey business and to have been very fond of his product. One story is that he paid a Nashville plumber his regular plumbing fees to stay and drink with him. Another story concerns his thrifty nature: although he owned many fine horses, he chose to ride in an ordinary street hack. Since he always paid the driver well, there was a great rivalry among the hack men for his business.

Mr. Murphy died in 1900. The day his will was probated, Mrs. Murphy filed a petition to adopt Tom and Nettie Smith Felder, since she was alone and childless. The Felders went to Paris, France, to live and took Mrs. Murphy with them.

The house was then sold to Mrs. Buford for a school. In 1917, she moved the school to the old Bransford mansion on Gallatin Road. The school closed when she died a short time later.

Photographed: c. 1914
Interiors: from the collection at Tennessee State Library & Archives
Exterior: from the collection of Mike Slate

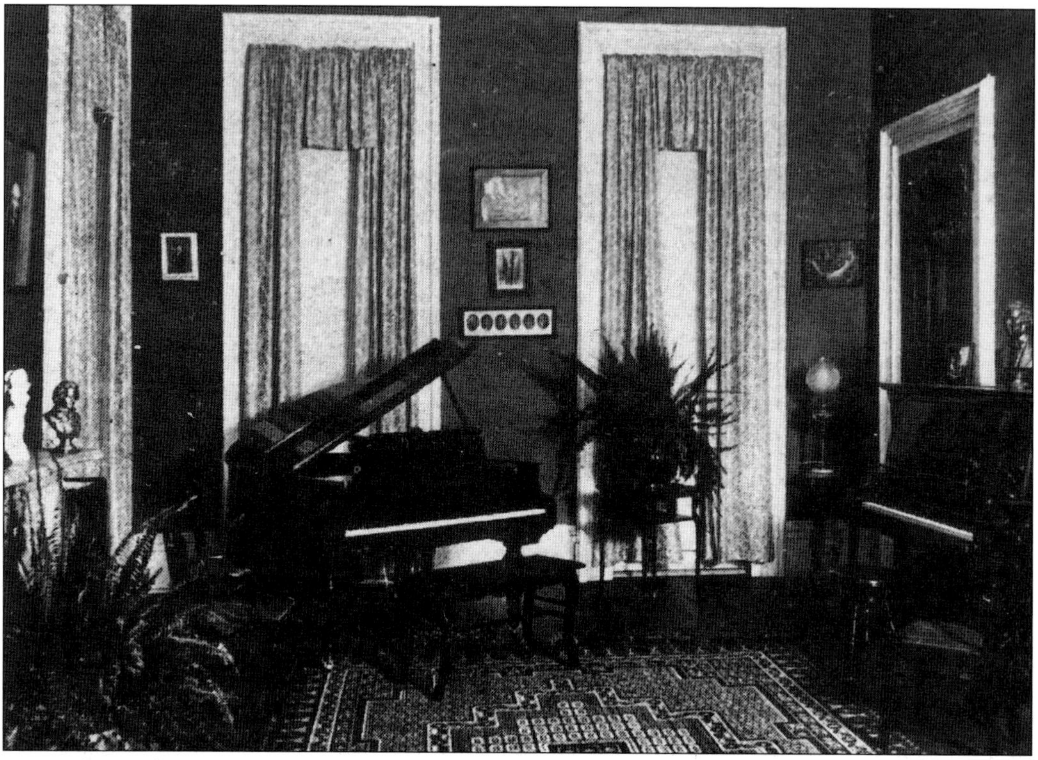

Since the study of music was stressed at Buford College, the young ladies were encouraged to practice in their leisure time. The studio contained an upright piano as well as a baby grand. The white woodwork and Oriental-style rug were *de rigueur* in the decade before World War I. As seen in the photograph below, the library walls were lined with Globe-Werneke bookcases, and Colonial Revival chairs surrounded the center library table.

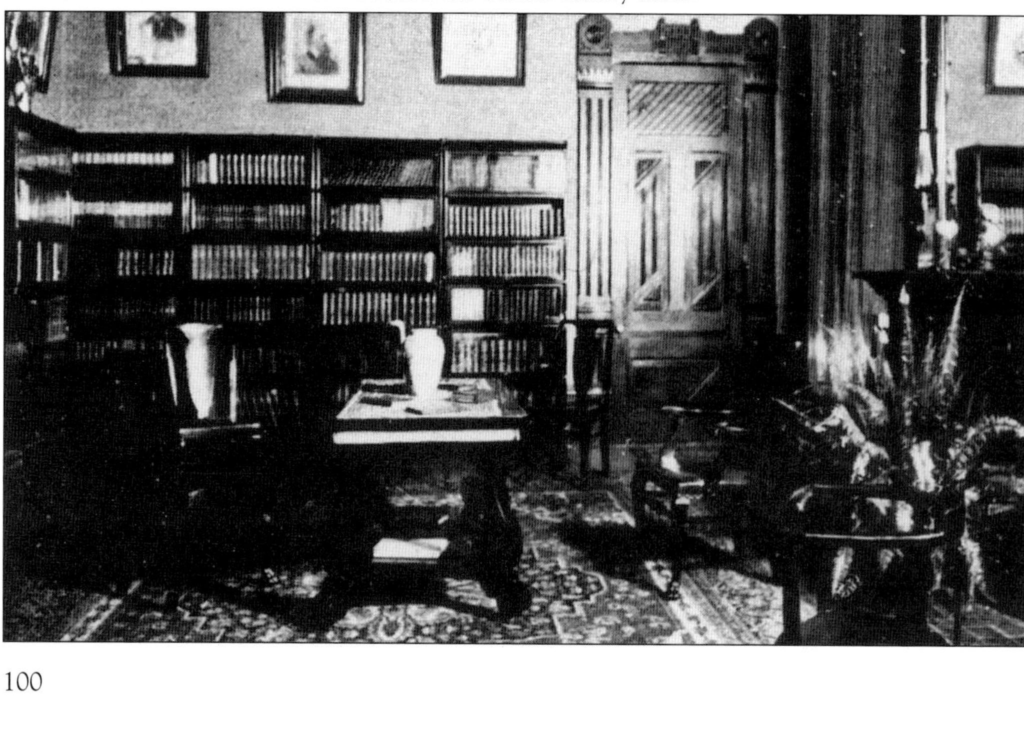

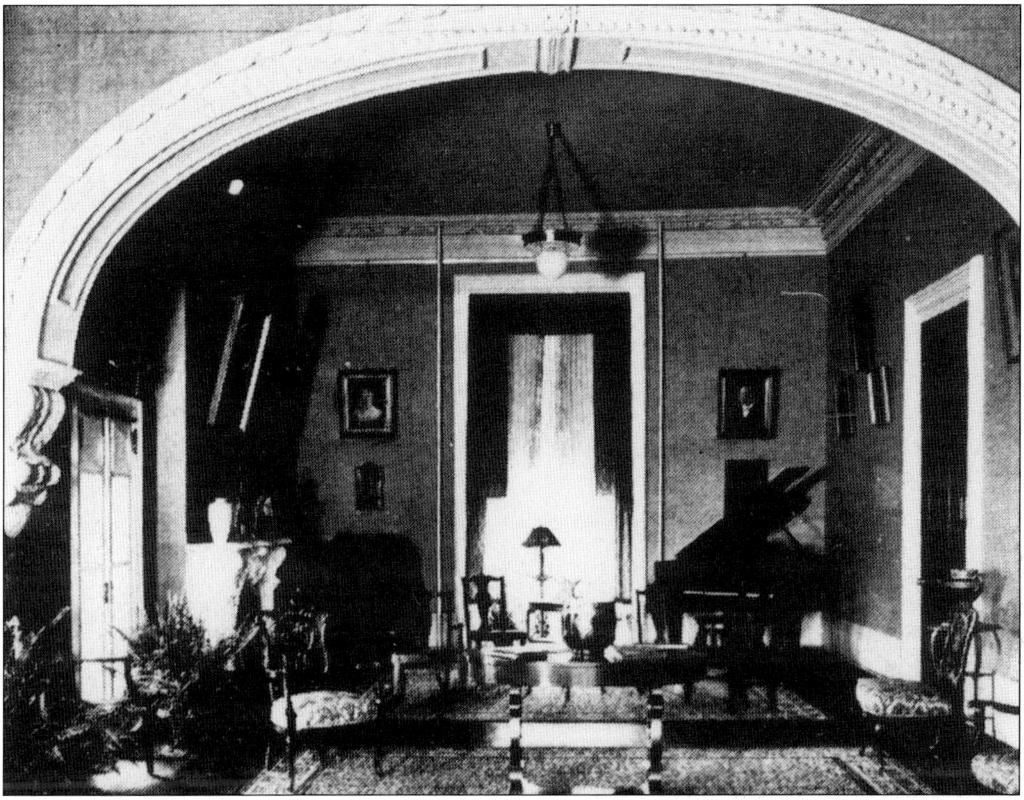

Like many girls' schools in this era, Buford College was located in the former home of a wealthy family. The fine millwork shown here attests to the quality of the house. The downstairs rooms were used by the young ladies to entertain their family and friends while upstairs were bedrooms for boarding students.

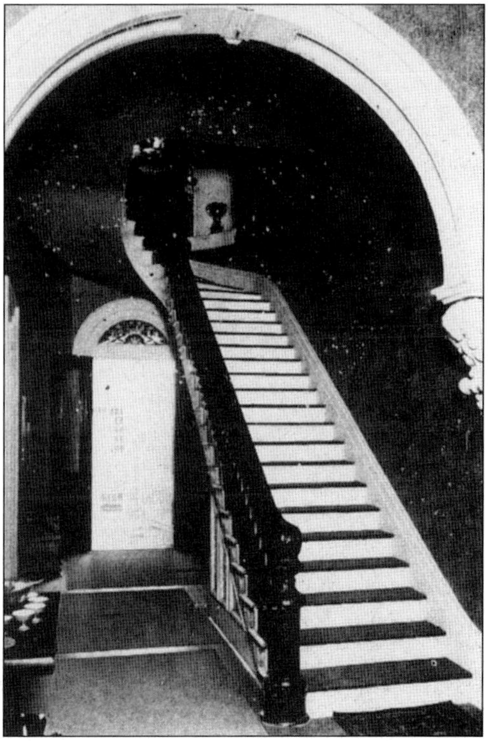

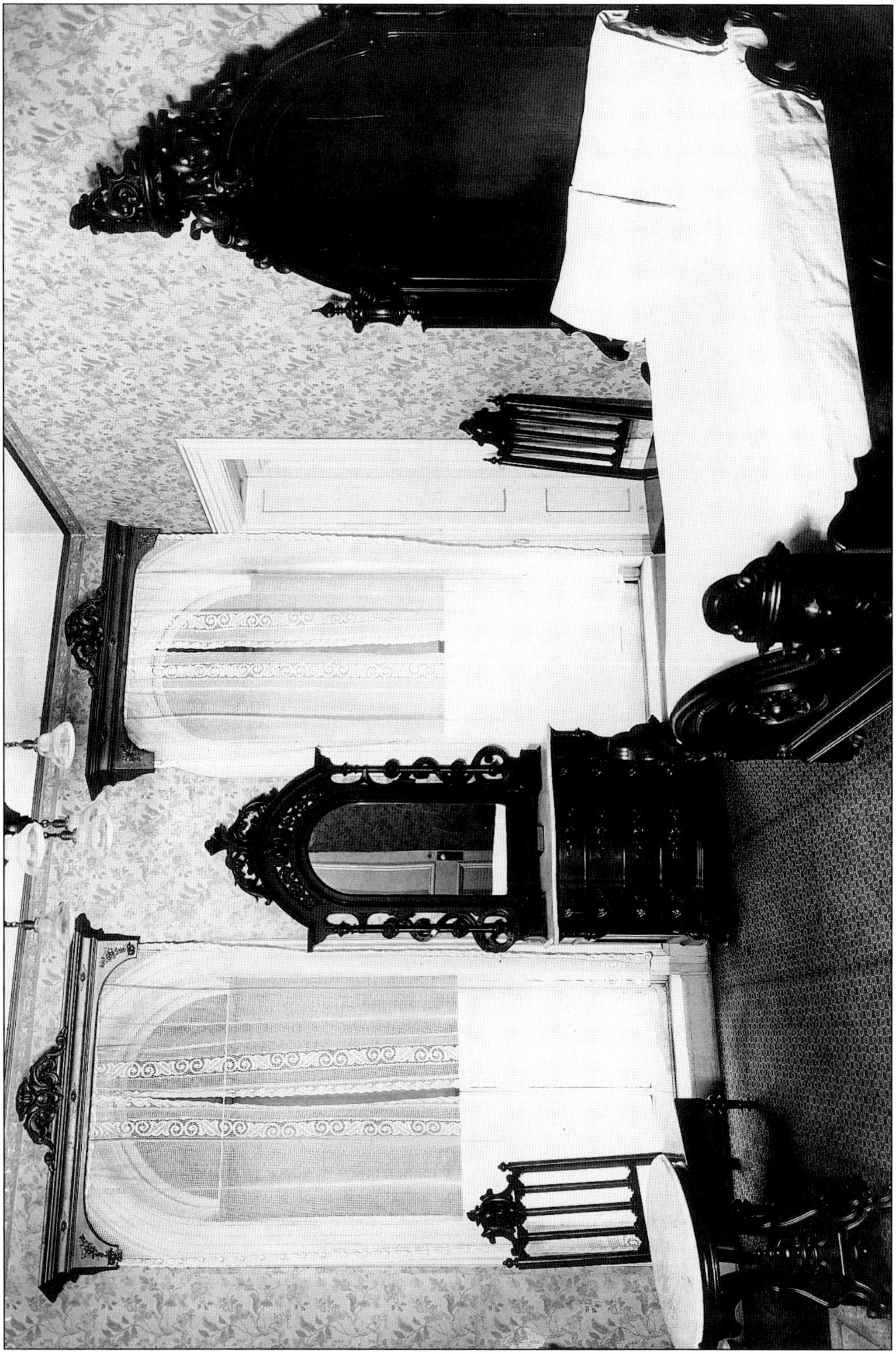

MAXWELL HOUSE HOTEL

The construction of the Maxwell House Hotel was begun by Colonel John Overton Jr. of Travellers Rest in 1859. His wife was Harriet Maxwell, and he selected her maiden name for his large luxury hotel.

Although the hotel was unfinished at the beginning of the Civil War, it was used by both the Confederate and Union troops as a barracks, a hospital, and a prison. During the war it was called the Zollicoffer Barracks in honor of Confederate General Felix K. Zollicoffer, a Congressman from Nashville who was killed in 1862.

The building was completed in 1869 and opened as a hotel. It was famous for almost a century for its fine cuisine and luxurious appointments. Adding to its fame was the popularity of Maxwell House coffee developed by Joel Cheek of Nashville, who named his blend for the well-known hotel. President Teddy Roosevelt is credited with the coffee company's advertising phrase "good to the last drop." United States presidents who stayed at the Maxwell House were Andrew Johnson, Rutherford B. Hayes, Grover Cleveland, William McKinley, and Theodore Roosevelt.

The guest room at the Maxwell House, shown on the opposite page, was known as the Bridal Suite. It was furnished with an ensemble representing the popular Renaissance Revival style. The bed, with its high, heavily carved headboard, is similar to the bed in the Lincoln Room at the White House.

The Maxwell House burned in 1961. The site is now occupied by Suntrust Bank.

Photographed: Exterior, *c.* 1863; interior, *c.* 1915
From the collection of William Fisher, Tennessee State Library & Archives

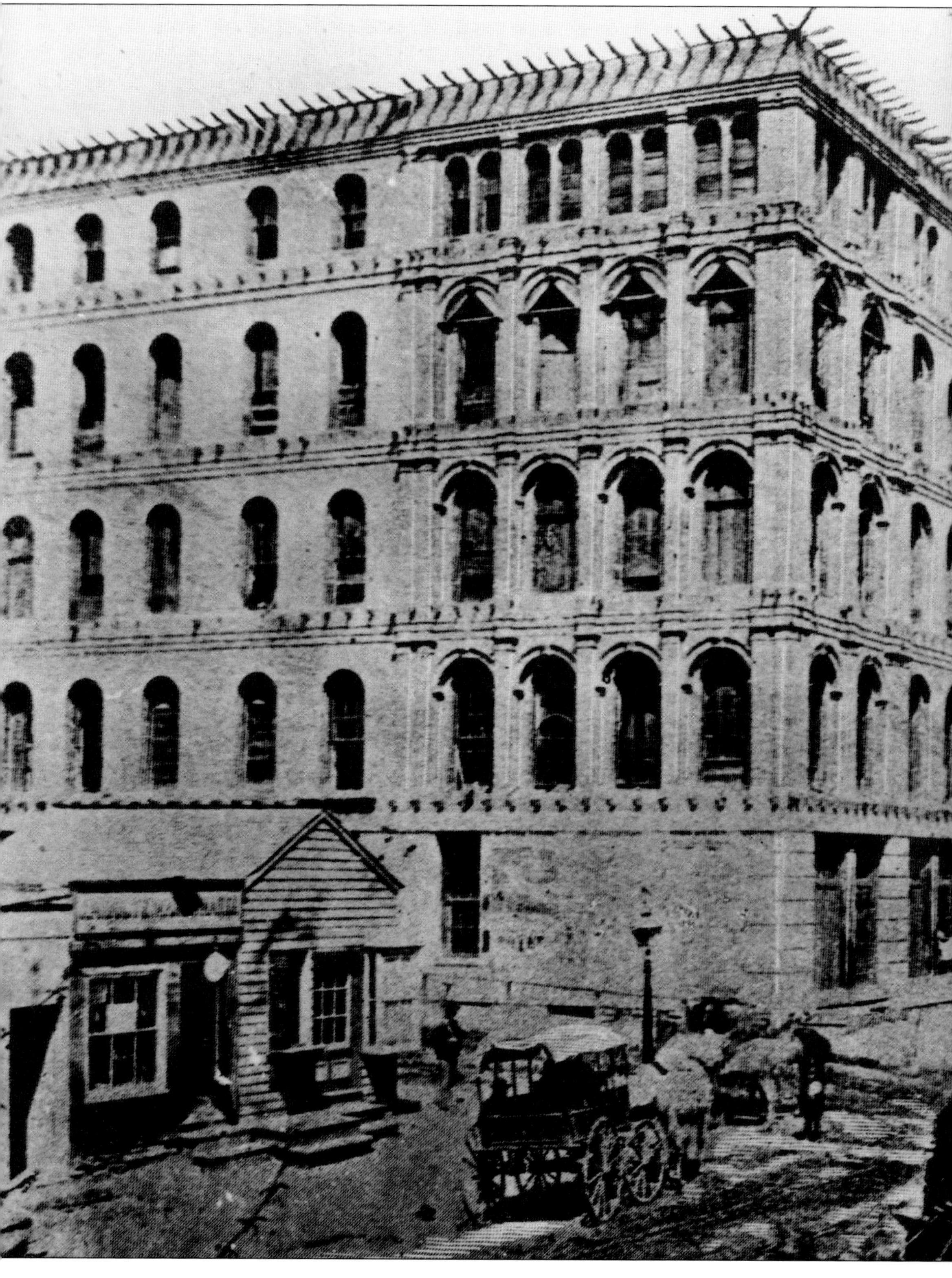

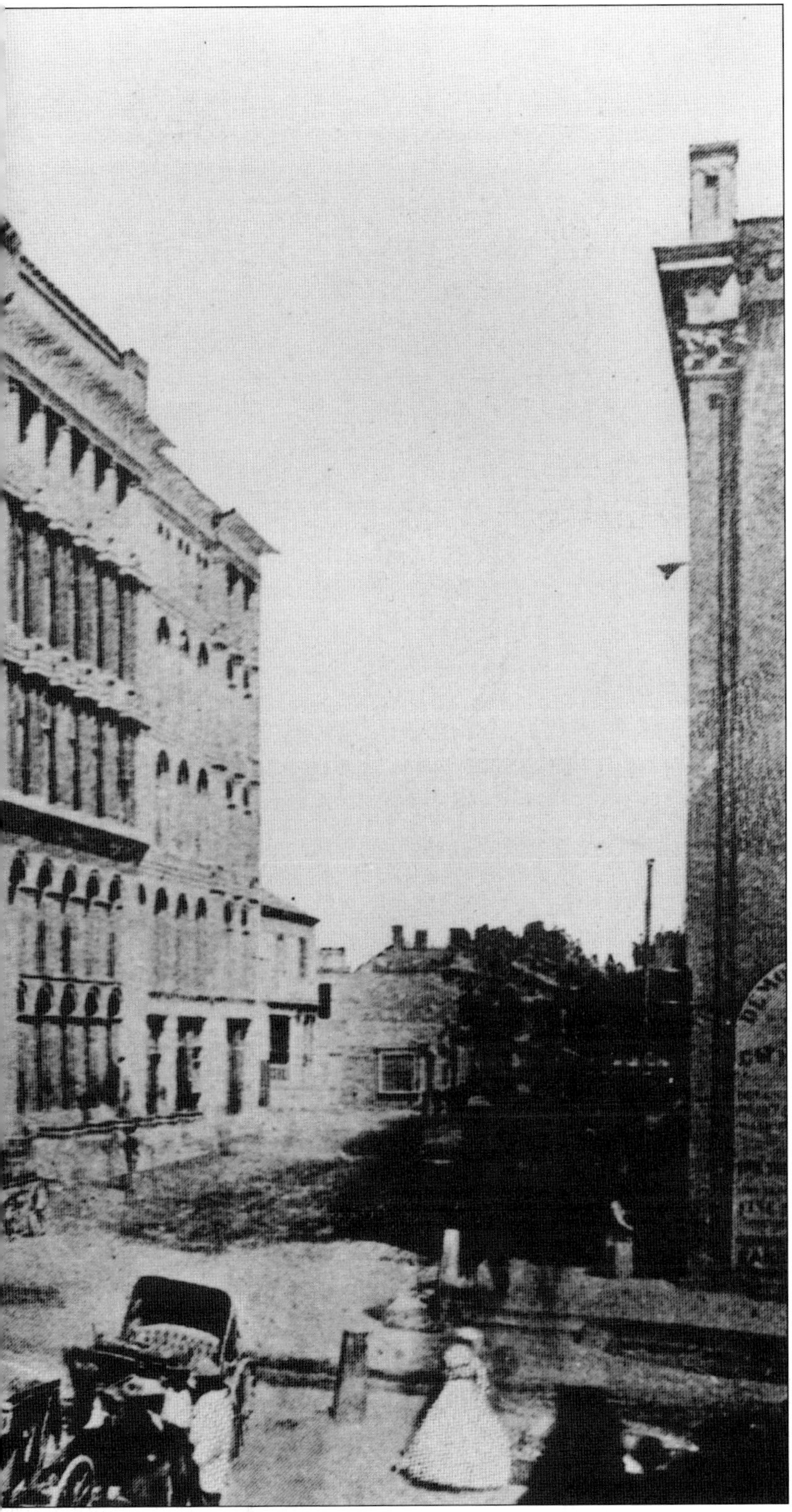

This Civil War photograph of the Maxwell House Hotel at Church and Cherry Streets identified the building as the Zollicoffer barracks. The building on the far right was occupied by Demoville and Company, the city drugstore. The small-frame building on the left occupied the present site of the Life and Casualty Tower. No telephone and electricity poles or lines had yet appeared to pollute the view.

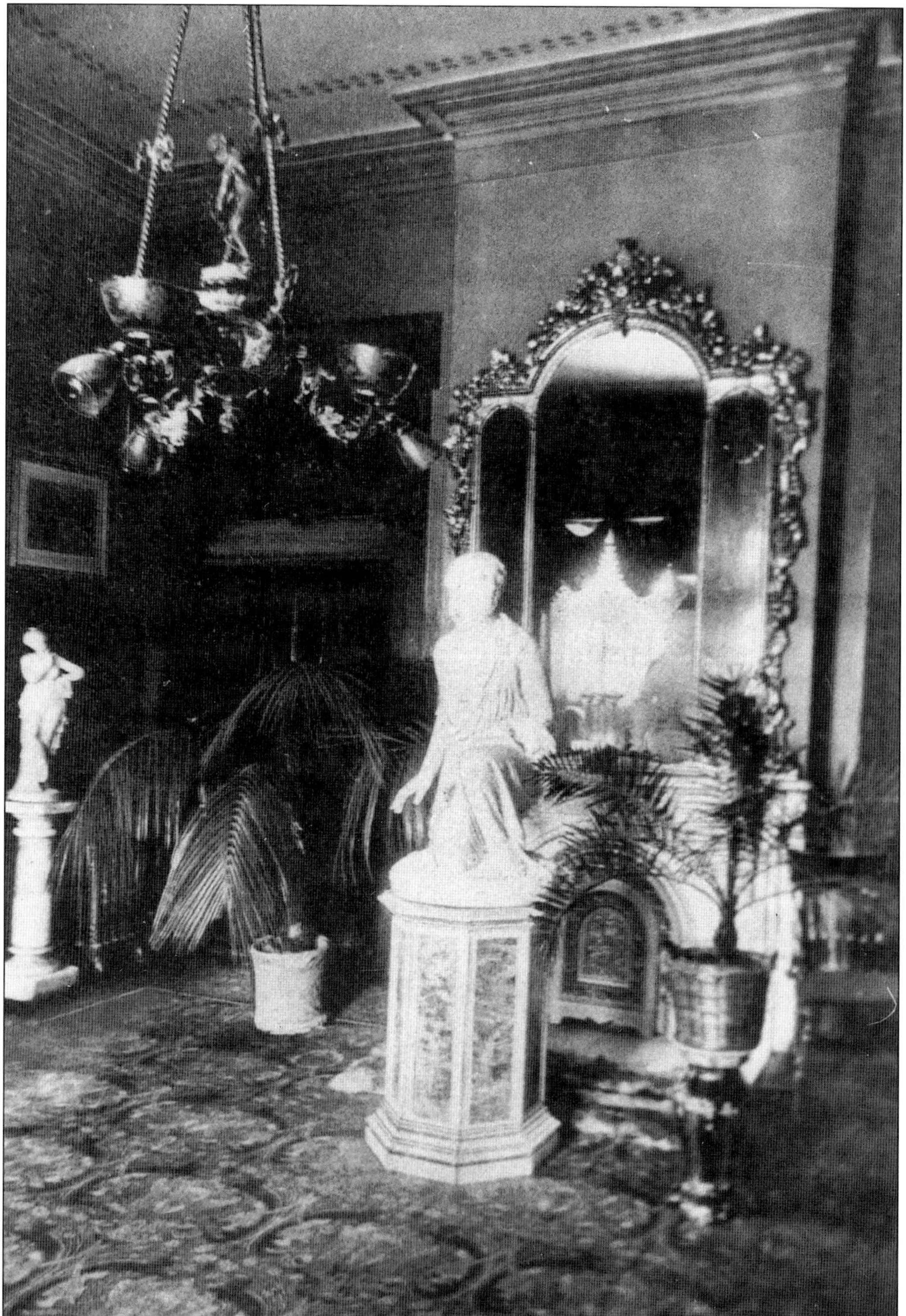

Belmont College for Young Women
Ward-Belmont School

In January of 1887, Adelicia Acklen sold Belmont to Lewis T. Baxter. She died suddenly the following May in New York City while shopping for furnishings for her new home in Washington, D.C. Baxter, who never lived in the mansion, sold it in 1889 to Ida Hood and Susan L. Heron. In September of 1890, Miss Hood and Miss Heron admitted the first students to the school they established as Belmont College for Young Women.

The second floor and part of the first floor were partitioned into small dormitory rooms. The basement was used for the dining hall and classrooms. Ultimately, three large additions were attached to the mansion: one on each side for classrooms and dormitory rooms and a columned auditorium addition on the north side facing Nashville.

In 1913, Belmont College for Young Women merged with Ward's Seminary, and the name was changed to Ward-Belmont School. This school closed in 1951. The Tennessee Baptist Convention then acquired the property and established Belmont College, a co-educational, four-year college. In recent years, the name of the school was changed to Belmont University.

In 1971, Belmont Mansion was placed on the National Register of Historic Places. The following year Historic Belmont Association, later known as Belmont Mansion Association, was formed. The aim of this organization is to restore and furnish Belmont Mansion as the home of Adelicia and Joseph Acklen. While much has been done, the restoration is still in progress. Belmont is open daily for tours and is also used for special events. The photographs shown in this section cover the early period of school occupation, from the 1890s until 1920.

Although this hallway photograph (on opposite page) was made some 40 years after the C.C. Giers's photograph shown in Chapter One, the central statue, mantel mirror, and gasolier are the same. In this photography, the woodwork is now dark, and the wallpaper has disappeared. The Art Nouveau–patterned rug is a fashionable addition. On the left, behind the smaller statue, a radiator may be seen. Belmont had an early central heating system, perhaps dating from the Acklen's era.

Photographed: between 1890 and 1920
From the collection of the Belmont Mansion Association

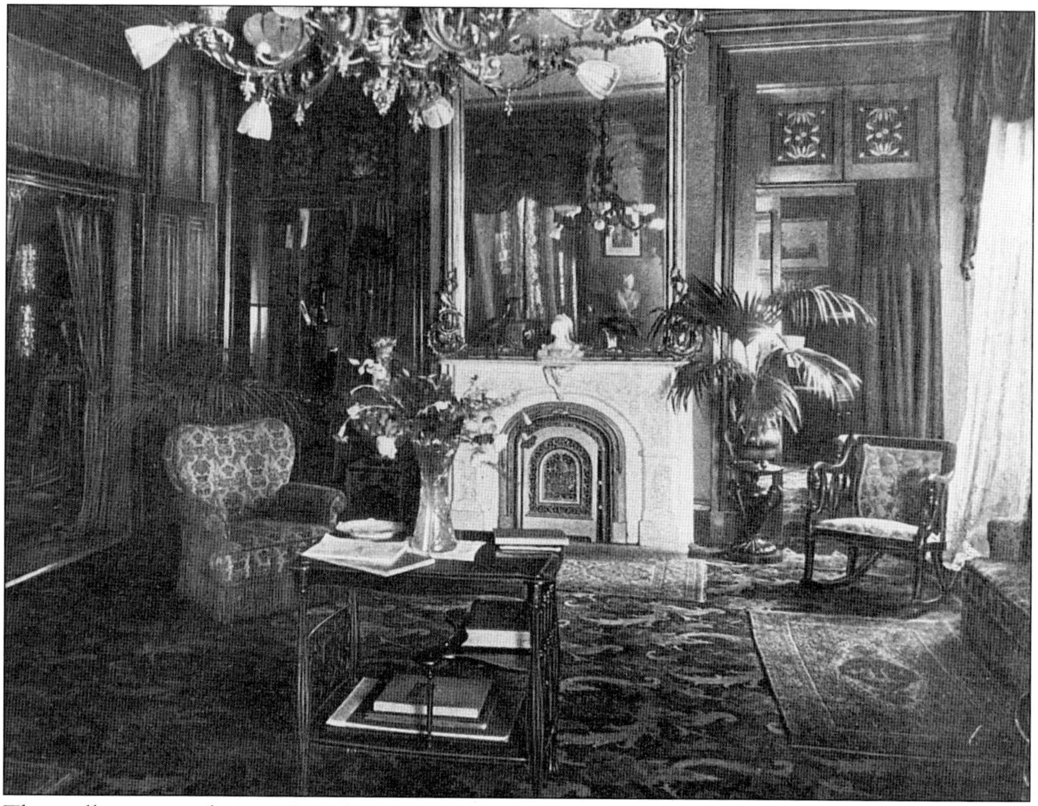

The well-appointed central parlor attests to the success of the school. While lace curtains and a swag adorn the window, heavy portières cover the door openings. The fringed and overstuffed parlor set, as well as the rocker, were examples of the emphasis on comfort in the years immediately preceding World War I.

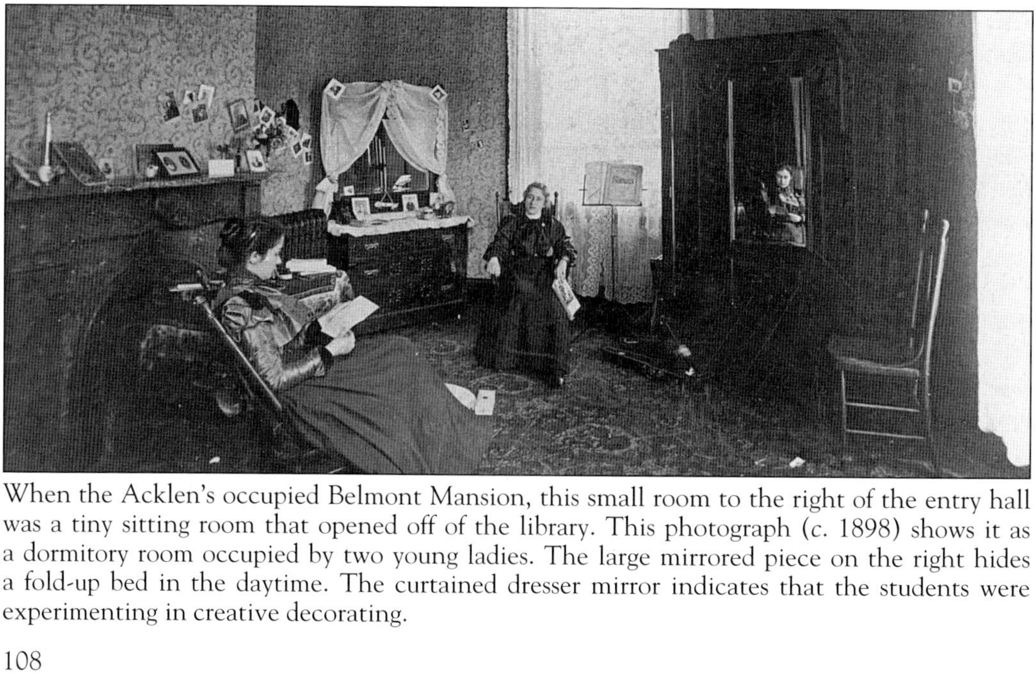

When the Acklen's occupied Belmont Mansion, this small room to the right of the entry hall was a tiny sitting room that opened off of the library. This photograph (*c.* 1898) shows it as a dormitory room occupied by two young ladies. The large mirrored piece on the right hides a fold-up bed in the daytime. The curtained dresser mirror indicates that the students were experimenting in creative decorating.

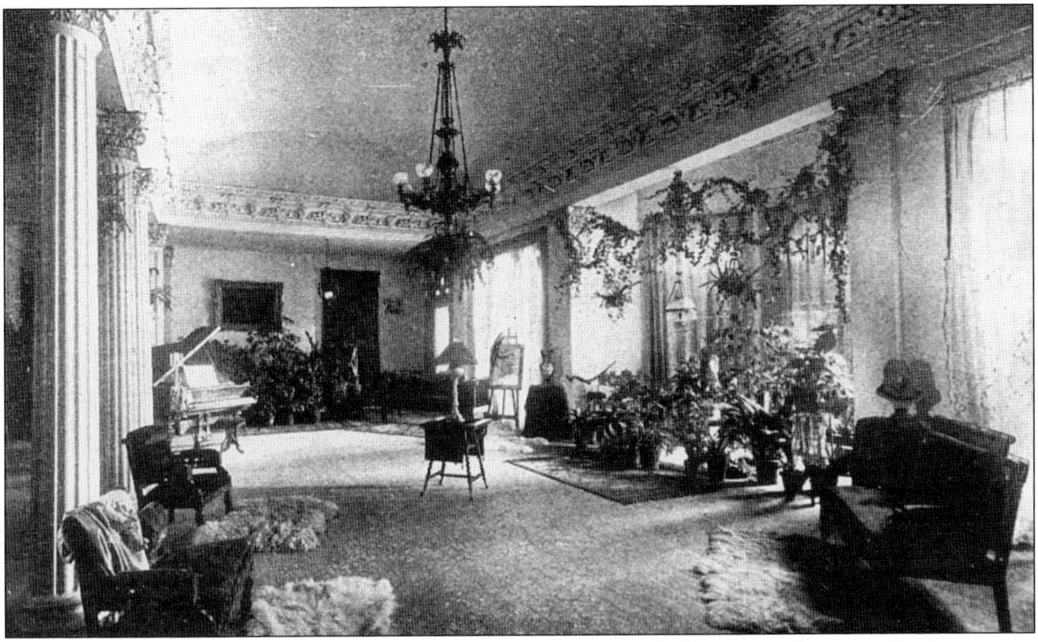

The Grand Salon at Belmont Mansion is probably one of the most photographed interiors in Nashville. In this early school photograph, the tessellated floor was bare, except for the scattered animal skin rugs. With the exception of a piano and a few seating pieces, the room is furnished mainly with plants. The radiators have not yet been installed in this room.

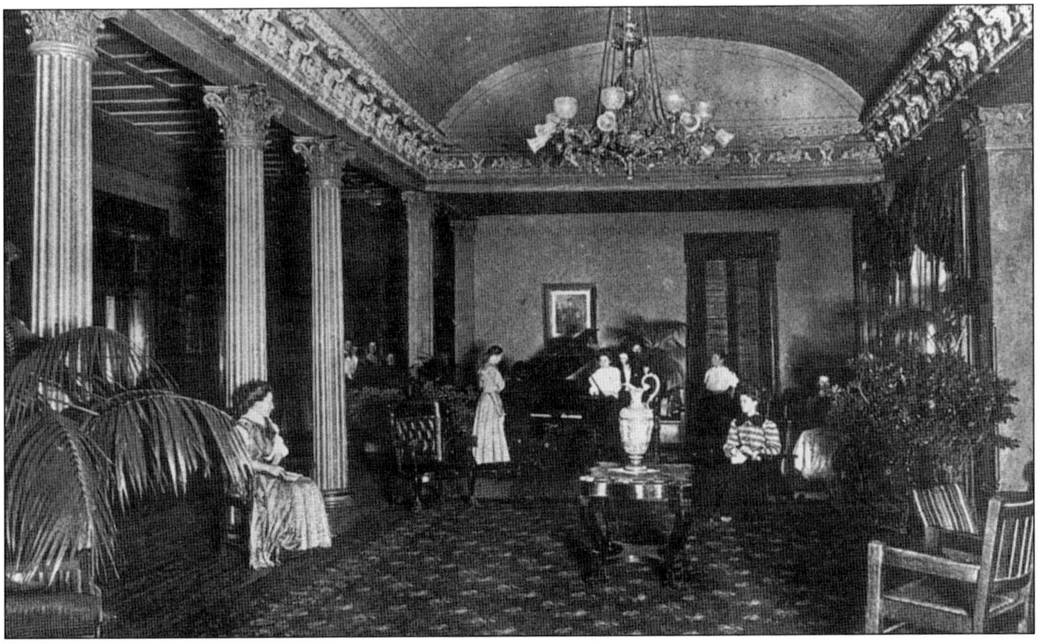

In this c. 1900 photograph of the Grand Salon, considerable upgrading has been done since the previous photograph was made. A new hardwood floor has been laid over the old floor, electric down lights have been added to the gasolier, and decorative borders have been added to the ceiling, as well as new window hangings and a large rug.

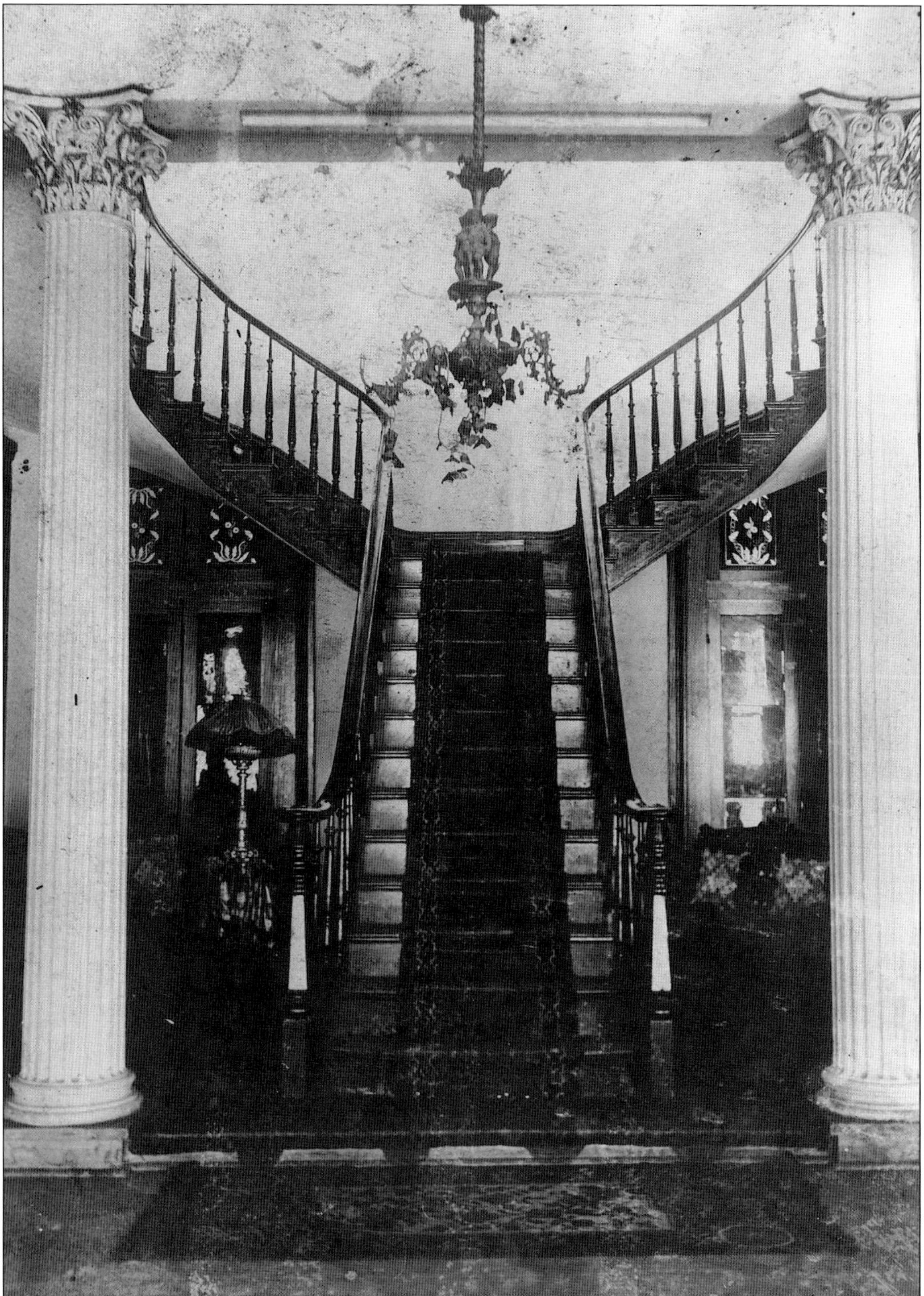

This photograph was made in 1895 by photographer Thuss. It shows the staircase that led off the Grand Salon to the dormitory rooms above.

Four

Commercial Interiors

1. Chamber of Commerce
2. L.R. Freeman's Store
3. Gier's Art Studio
4. Mitchell's Candy and Confectionaries
5. The Blouse Shop

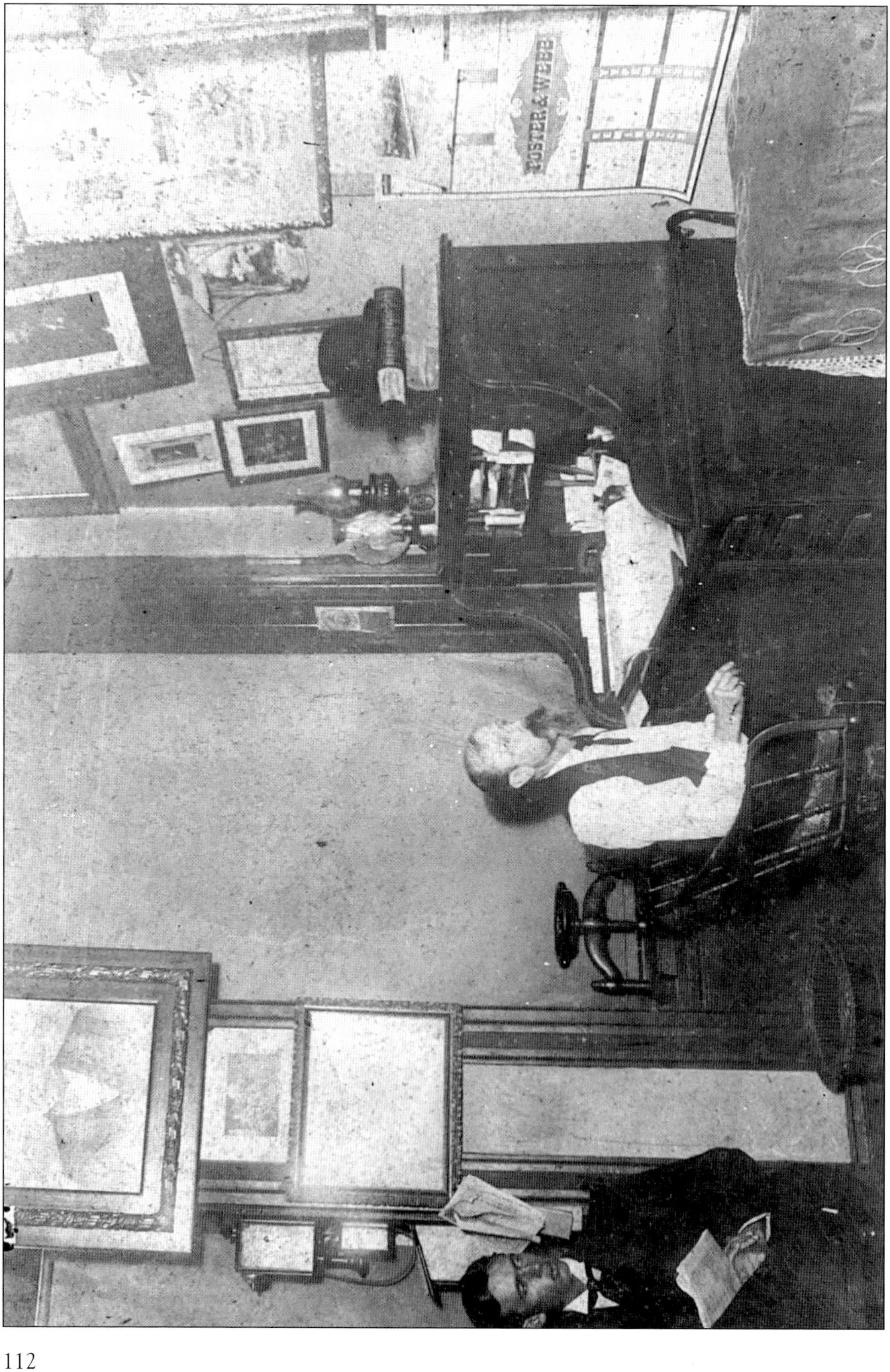
FOSTER & WEBB

Chamber of Commerce office
Baxter Court
307–311 Church Street

In May of 1894, Nashville's Board of Trade and the Commercial Club consolidated to form the Nashville Chamber of Commerce. Captain A.J. Harris was elected president. In November of that year, a mass meeting was held at the Chamber of Commerce to promote the Tennessee Centennial with Mark Cockrill presiding.

When this photograph was made in 1897, the Chamber of Commerce was located in Baxter Court at 307-311 Church Street. Although the men are unidentified, the office furnishings are typical of this period. The wire wastebasket and the spittoon were standard office fixtures. Hanging on a nail beside the wall telephone was the tiny Nashville telephone directory. Electricity had been available in Nashville since 1882, and electric ceiling fixtures undoubtedly furnished general lighting for this room. Atop the roll-top desk, however, were two oil-burning lamps to aid the bespectacled clerk in recording ledger entries.

Baxter Court was designed by Nashville architect Hugh Cathcart Thompson in 1887. Thompson also designed the Ryman Auditorium.

In 1890, Jere Baxter advertised rental space here, as well as a cafe and dining room with an Italian orchestra playing on special occasions. Baxter, a lawyer, businessman, and politician, is best remembered for his development of the Tennessee Central Railroad, first organized in 1893 to break the power of the L & N Railroad and its subsidiary, the N.C. & St.L Railroad. After his death in 1904, his statue was placed in the triangle of the intersection of Broad Street and West End Avenue. The statue now stands on Gallatin Road in front of Jere Baxter School.

The Chamber of Commerce has occupied numerous downtown locations since its formation. Between World War I and World War II, it occupied the old Vanderbilt Law and Dental School Building on the west side of Fourth Avenue North, between Deadrick and Union. The building was then known as the Chamber of Commerce Building. It was demolished in 1970.

Photographed: October 22, 1897
From the collection of Tennessee State Library & Archives
Architect: Hugh C. Thompson

L.R. Freeman's Store
423 Union Street

Lewis Ross Freeman "had a fashionable shop in the city at 423 Union Street where he sold such items as window shades and looking glasses." Shown on page 114 is the shop as photographed by Otto Giers.

It is probable that many of the items, especially the wallpaper, shown in other photographs in this volume were purchased from Mr. Freeman. He advertised himself as "the wallpaper pioneer." In the rear of the shop under the skylight is a curved sign designating the window shade department. In the foreground is the omnipresent spittoon.

Mr. Freeman and his family lived in Edgefield at 939 Russell Street. The family attended the Cumberland Presbyterian Church. One of the Freeman granddaughters, Frances Barthell Hall, reminisced that Granny Freeman always sat on the front row at church. She also sewed for the needy and entertained visiting missionaries.

The Freeman's daughter had married Nashville attorney E.E. Barthell. The Barthells lived at 934 Russell Street. After Mr. Freeman died, his wife moved across the street to live with her daughter's family.

Mrs. Freeman grew up near the Hermitage and had seen Andrew Jackson once at a barbecue. She liked to tell that she had seen every president since Jackson except for Lincoln and Harrison and that she had seen them all in Nashville. When a president came to town, there would be a parade on Union Street. Mr. Freeman would remove the large mirrors from his store window so that Mrs. Freeman and her guests could have a good view of the president.

The Freeman store at 923 Union Street later became the office of Nashville architect James Yeaman. It is now the Old Heidelberg Restaurant.

Photographer: Otto Giers
Photographed: c. 1900
From the collection of Tennessee State Library & Archives

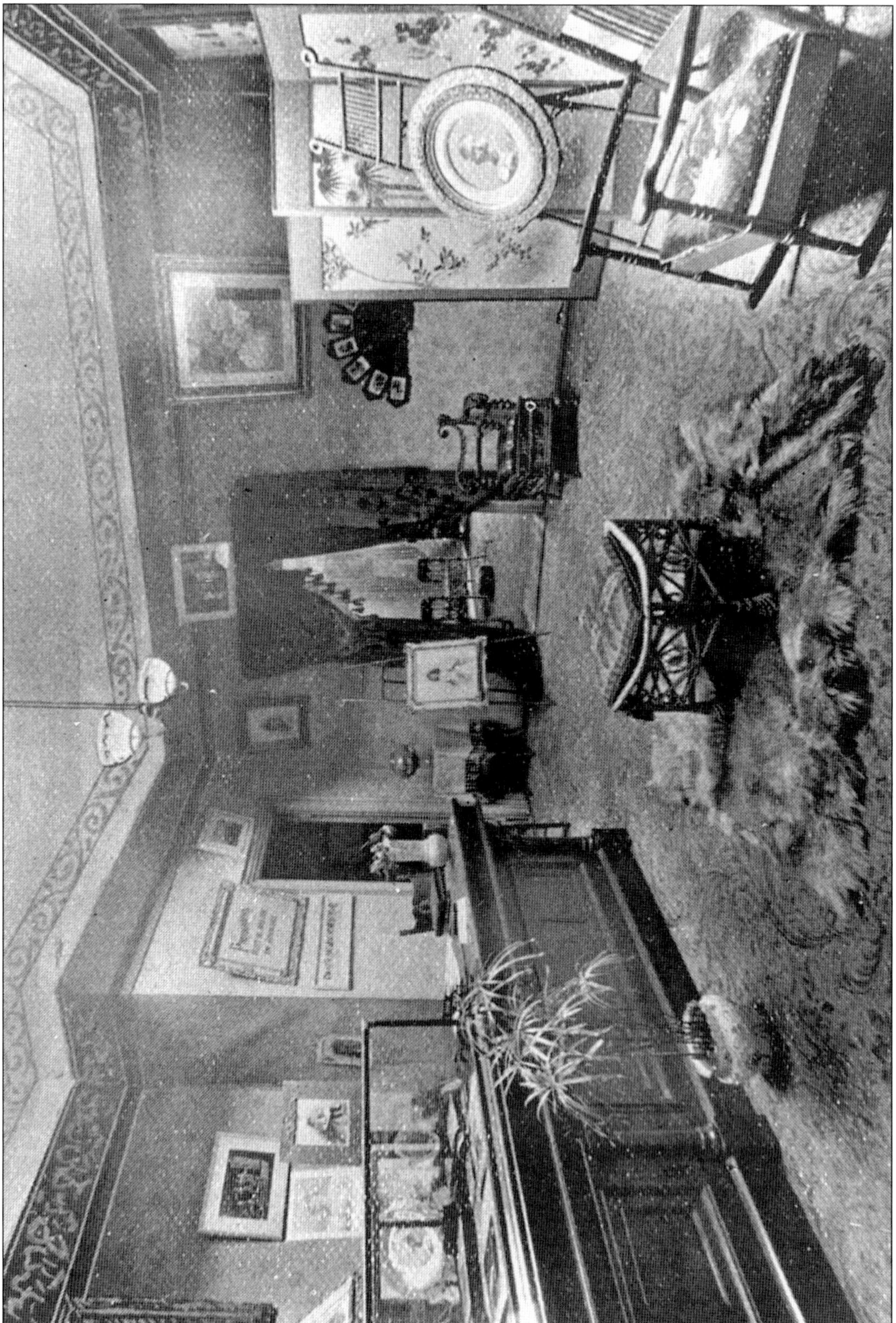

Giers Art Studio

Both C.C. Giers and his son, Otto Giers, were prominent photographers in Nashville during the last half of the nineteenth century. C.C. Giers first conducted a daguerreotype business on the Public Square. When photographs succeeded daguerreotypes, he moved his shop to Union Street. C.C. died in 1877. His son, Otto, came into the business on Union Street before moving to 415 Church Street between Cherry (Fourth Avenue) and Summer (Fifth Avenue) in the 1890s.

Although this photograph could be the Giers' Union Street address, it is more likely to be the Church Street location. Elaborately framed portraits for easel or wall display were on view in the Giers Art Studio. A large fan with photographs on each spoke was shown as an example of how portraits could be artistically hung. The wicker stool on the fur rug and the Oriental screen were in high fashion at the turn of the century.

Other photographs in this book attributed to the Giers are those of Belmont Mansion, The Hermitage, and L.R. Freeman's store. Nashvillians are indeed indebted to these two photographers for the visual record they left of the late nineteenth and early twentieth century.

Photographer: Otto Giers
Photographed: *c.* 1900
From the collection of Tennessee State Library & Archives

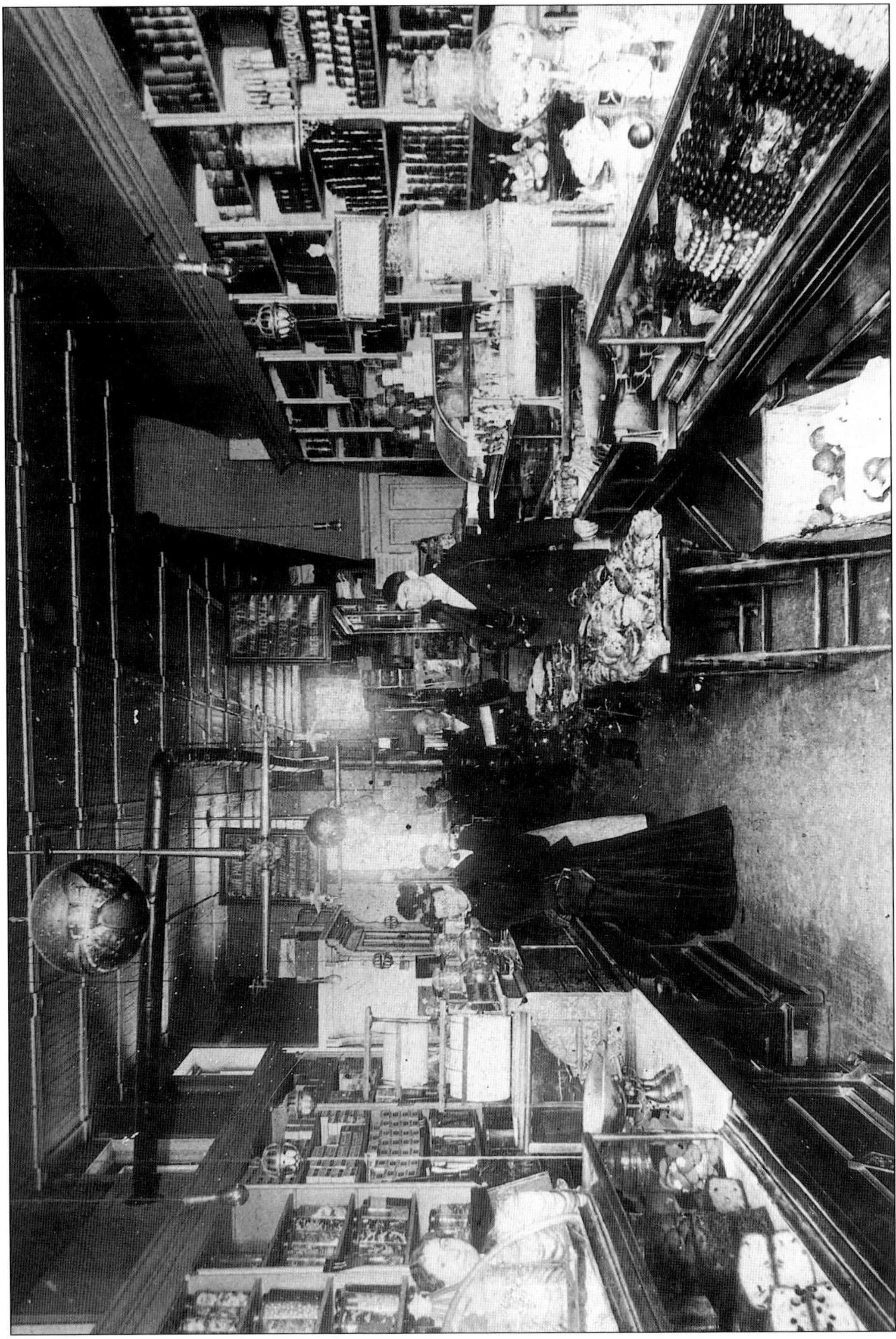

Mitchell's Candy and Confectionaries
323 Union Street

Mitchell's Candy Shop, at the corner of Union Street and Printer's Alley, was a Nashville treasure for over 100 years. The building, designed by Nashville architect James Yeaman, still stands today. In this turn-of-the-century photograph, we have a rare view of the family and their wares.

The center of the room is lighted with a plain gas fixture and reflecting globes. On either side, over the counters, were suspended bare bulb electric fixtures. The gentleman in the rear fits a contemporary description of Charles Mitchell Sr.—"a nice looking little man with gray hair and a gray mustache." The gentleman in the foreground is probably Charles Mitchell Jr., a well-known Nashvillian until his death in 1952.

Charles Mitchell Sr. inherited the family business from his wife's mother and father, Mr. and Mrs. Grieg. The family lived upstairs over the store, where the four Mitchell children were born. In his recollections, Charles Mitchell Jr. (1873–1952) says that his Grandmother Grieg lived with his family until she died. In the back of the store, she had a room with a fireplace and rocking chairs where she entertained special customers. Other contemporary accounts report on the hospitality of the proprietors. The name of the store was not changed to Mitchell's until after Mrs. Grieg died.

About 1879, when Charles Mitchell Jr. was six years old, the family moved to 314 High Street (Sixth Avenue North) near the site of the present Tennessee Performing Arts Center. Charles Mitchell Jr. would be happy indeed that great performances now take place near his old home. In his reflections, he stated that the love of his life had always been the theatre.

In addition to their residence in Nashville, the Mitchells also had a house in Beersheba Springs, Tennessee. It was next door to the R.W. Turner family home. Both Beersheba houses are occupied and well kept today.

Photographed: *c.* 1900
From the collection of Tennessee State Library & Archives
Architect: James Yeaman

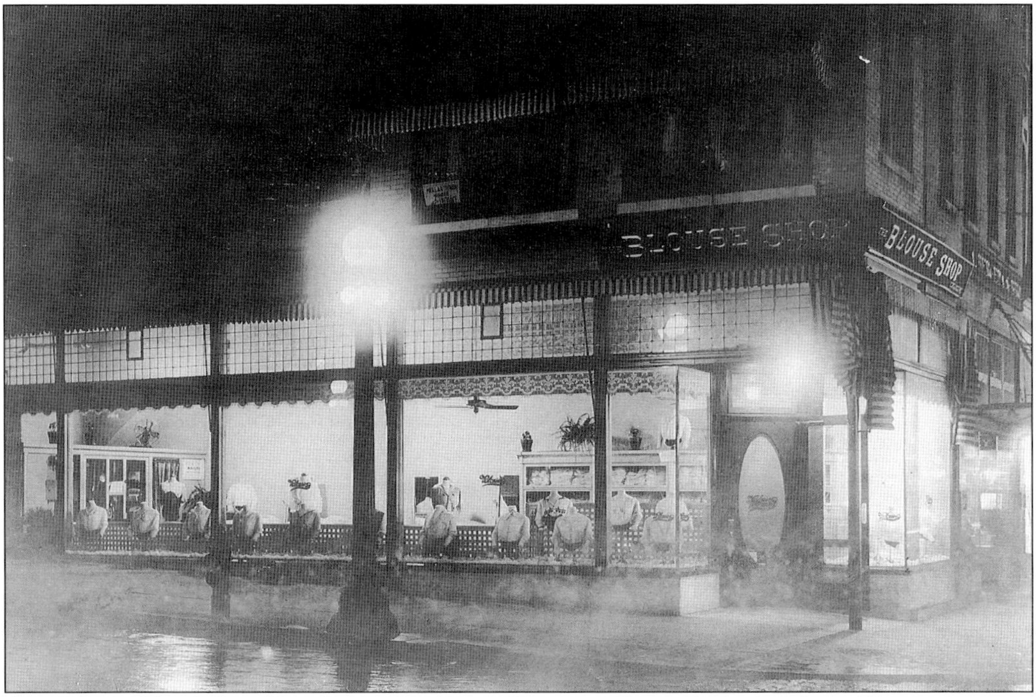
BLOUSE SHOP
BLOUSE SHOP

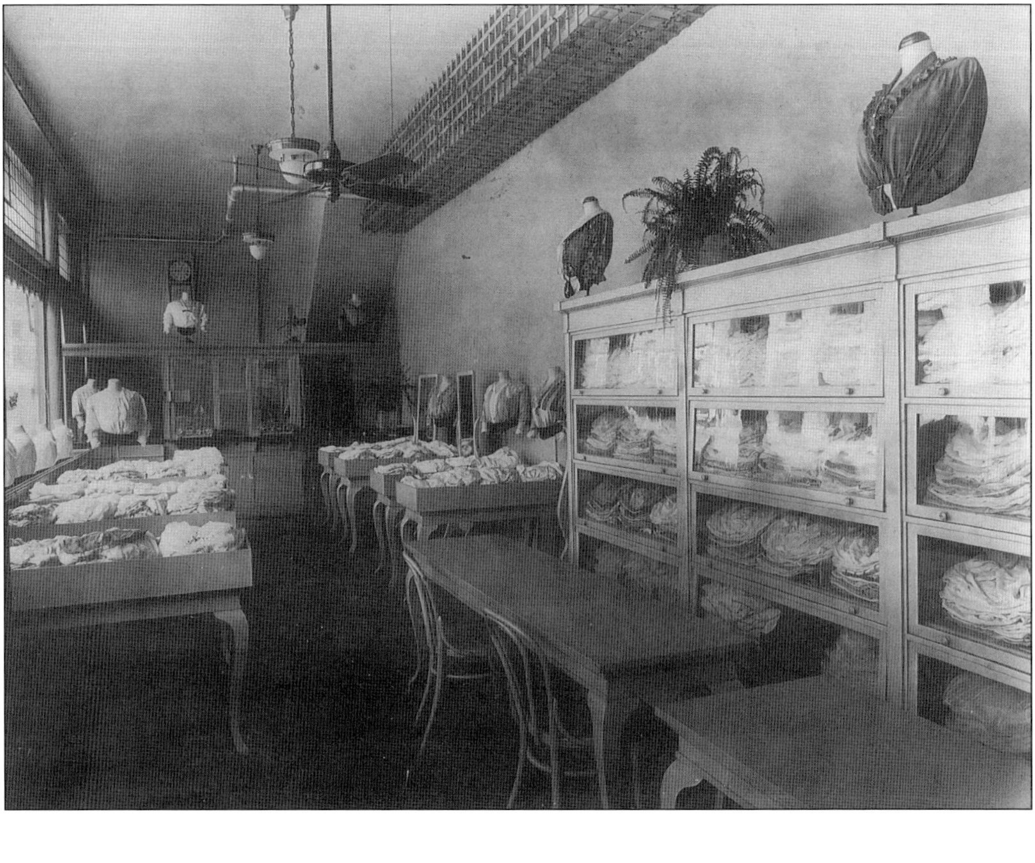

The Blouse Shop
Church Street at Capitol Boulevard

From 1916 to 1920, The Blouse Shop occupied the northeast corner of Church Street and Capitol Boulevard. The manager of this establishment was Grace White Trammell, who, in 1925, founded Grace's, the premier ladies' ready-to-wear shop in Nashville since its opening day.

A native of Seneca, Kansas, Miss Grace spent her early life in Enid, Oklahoma. Before coming to Nashville, she had worked for Frost Brothers Department Store in San Antonio, Texas. In Nashville, she was the manager of The Blouse Shop and the lingerie buyer for Rich-Schwartz & Joseph before she and her husband, George Marshall Trammell, opened Grace's on Sixth Avenue. Both Mr. and Mrs. Trammell died in the 1940s. The high standards of Grace's, however, have been maintained by their children and grandchildren.

The style and panache of The Blouse Shop manager, Miss Grace, is evident in the light and airy decor seen here. The square pattern of the upper window glass has been repeated in the square lattice work covering utility pipes and was later used as the show window background.

The walls and furniture are all painted in a light tint: probably the fashionable "Colonial buff" to blend with the cabriole legs of the display tables. Globe-Werneke bookcases have been used for blouse storage. Electric fans were a welcome addition in this space with stationary windows.

Another famous occupant of this building at Church Street and Capitol Boulevard was the painter Gilbert Gaul.

Photographer: Wiles
Photographed: c. 1916
From the collection of Polly Trammell Murphy, Historic Nashville

Index

Sources

Baxter, Nathaniel Jr. Residence

1. Cornwell, Ilene. *Biographical Directory of Tennessee General Assembly, Vol. 3.* Nashville: Tennessee Historical Commission, 1988: 38.
2. Hembree, Paul P. *The Role and History of the Nashville Electric Service.* Nashville, 1973.
3. Myers, Denys Peter. *Gas Lighting in America: A Guide to Historic Preservation.* Washington: U.S. Department of the Interior, 1978: 181–207.

Belle Meade Plantation

1. Myers, Denys Peter. *Gas Lighting in America: A Guide to Historic Preservation.* Washington: U.S. Department of the Interior, 1978: 39.
2. Wills, Ridley II. *The History of Belle Meade Mansion, Plantation and Stud.* Nashville: Vanderbilt University Press, 1991.

Belmont Mansion

1. Brown, Mark, Director, Belmont Mansion. Interview with author. Nashville.
2. *Daily American*, 30 May 1888 and 31 May 1888.
3. Patrick, James. "The Architecture of Adolphus Heiman 1854–1862." *Tennessee Historical Quarterly* 38 (1979).
4. Wardin, Albert W. Jr. *Belmont Mansion: Home of Joseph and Adelicia Acklen.* Nashville: Belmont Mansion Association, 1981: 16–24.

Belmont College for Young Women / Ward-Belmont

1. Brown, Mark, Director, Belmont Mansion. Interview with author. Nashville.

Benson, William and Mary G. Residence

1. Benson, John T. Jr. *Bensons—Early Settlers from North Carolina to Middle Tennessee 1796–1820.* Nashville, 1974.

Blouse Shop

1. "Miss Grace Given Award," *Nashville Tennessean.* 14 June 1986.

Buford College

1. Crabb, Alfred L. *Personality of a City.* New York: Bobbs-Merrill Co., 1960: 203.
2. Waller, William. *Nashville in the 1890s.* Nashville: Vanderbilt University Press, 1972: 85–186.

Burlington
1. Caldwell, Mrs. Jas. E. *Historical and Beautiful Country Homes near Nashville, Tennessee*. Nashville, 1911.
2. Farrell, Josephine E. and Mallie W. Farrell. *Burlington: A Memory*. Unpublished manuscript.
3. Hoobler, James. "T.M. Schleier, Photographer," *Tennessee Historical Quarterly* Vol. 1,005 (Fall 1986): 238.
4. Lynn, Catherine. *Wallpaper in America*. New York: W.W. Norton & Company, 1980: 191.
5. Patrick, James. "The Architecture of Adolphus Heiman 1854–1862." *Tennessee Historical Quarterly* 38 (1979): 281.

Cantrell, Dempsy Weaver and Nora Johnson Cantrell Residence
1. Aiken, Leona T. *Donelson, Tennessee: Its History and Landmarks*. Nashville, 1968.
2. Mr. and Mrs. DeWitt Ezell Sr. Interview with author. Nashville, May 1999.

Carter-Savage Residence
1. Lynn, Catherine. *Wallpaper in America*. New York: W.W. Norton & Company, 1980: 396.
2. Tennessee Historical Society. *Art Work in Nashville 1894–1901*. Nashville: Tennessee Historical Society, reprint.

Chamber of Commerce
1. Adams, G.R. and R.J. Christian. *Nashville: A Pictorial History*. Virginia Beach, VA: Donning Company Publishers, 1980: 86.
2. Edgerton, John. *Nashville: The Faces of Two Centuries*. Nashville: Plus Media Inc., 1979: 170.
3. Hembree, Paul P. *The Role and History of the Nashville Electric Service*. Nashville, 1973.
4. McGaw, Robert A. *The Vanderbilt Campus: A Pictorial History*. Nashville: Vanderbilt University Press, 1978: 68.
5. Patrick, James. *Architecture in Tennessee 1768–1897*. Knoxville: University of Tennessee Press, 1981: 210.

Cloverbottom
1. Brandau, Roberta S. *History of Homes and Gardens of Tennessee*. Nashville: Parthenon Press, 1936: 197.
2. McClellan, Nancy. *Historic Wallpapers*. Philadelphia and London: J.B. Lippincott, 1924: 167, 199, 443.

Elliott, Elizabeth P. Residence
1. Elliott. Papers. 1816–1932. Tennessee State Library and Archives, Nashville.

Fall, J. Horton Residence
1. Waller, William. *Nashville in the 1890s*. Nashville: Vanderbilt University Press, 1970: 204.
2. Zibart, Carl F. *Yesterday's Nashville*. Miami, FL: E.A. Seeman Publishing, 1976: 59.

L.R. Freeman's Store
1. Waller, William. *Nashville 1900 to 1910*. Nashville: Vanderbilt University Press, 1972: 218.

Giers Art Studio
1. Price, Dave. "Thuss, Koellein & Giers." *Nashville Historical Newsletter #13*.
2. Waller, William. *Nashville in the 1890s*. Nashville: Vanderbilt University Press, 1970: 52.

The Hermitage
1. Dorris, Mary C. *Preservation of the Hermitage 1889–1915*. Nashville, 1915.

2. Horn, Stanley F. *The Hermitage: Home of Old Hickory*. Nashville: Ladies Hermitage Association, 1950: 63.
3. Mullin, Marsha, Curator, The Hermitage. Interview with the author. Nashville, 1999.
4. "Rokeby." The *Nashville Tennessean* Magazine. 22 June 1947.

McGavock-Lindsley Residence
1. National Society of Colonial Dames in America. *Portraits in Tennessee Painted Before 1866*. 1964.
2. Warden, Margaret L. *Nashville: A Family Town*. Nashville, 1978: 81.
3. Windrow, J.E. *Nashville:A Family Town*. Nashville, 1978: 111.

Maxwell House Hotel
1. Adams, G.R., and R.J. Christian. *Nashville: A Pictorial History*. Virginia Beach, VA: Donning Company Publishers, 1980.
2. Hoobler, James A. *Cities Under the Gun*. Nashville: Rutledge Hill Press, 1986.

Mitchell's Candy and Confectionaries
1. Waller, William. *Nashville in the 1890s*. Nashville: Vanderbilt University Press, 1970: 164–262.

Overton Hall-Crieve Hall
1. The *Nashville Tennessean*. Undated newspaper article in the collection of Travellers Rest Historic House Museum, Nashville.

Renraw
1. Frazer, Percy Warner. Interview with the author. Nashville.
2. Killebrew, J.B. *Life and Character of J.C. Warner: Ironmaster of the South*. Nashville, 1897.
3. Tidwell, Oscar Cromwell Jr. *Belle Meade Park*. Nashville, 1983: 75.

Royal Oaks
1. Greenlee, Margaret W. Interview with the author. Nashville, 1975.
2. Tidwell, Oscar Cromwell Jr. *Belle Meade Park*. Nashville, 1983: 75.
3. Warden, Margaret L. Interview with the author. Nashville, 1999.

Turner Residence I: West End Avenue
1. Coppinger, Margaret Brown. *Beersheba Springs: A History*. Beersheba Springs Historical Society, 1983.

Turner Residence II: Kensington Place
1. Lynn, Catherine. *Wallpaper in America*. New York: W.W. Norton & Company, 1980.
2. McGaw, Robert A. *The Vanderbilt Campus*. Nashville: The Vanderbilt Press, 1978: 100.
3. Waller, William. *Nashville in the 1890s*. Nashville: Vanderbilt University Press, 1970: 208.
4. Wells, Judi. "C.K. Colley and James Yeaman: 1982–1983." Nashville Room Paragraph Lecture Series.

Williams / Gray / Governor's Mansion
1. Herndon, Joseph L. "Architects in Tennessee until 1930." Masters Thesis, Columbia University, 1975.
2. Waller, William. *Nashville in the 1890s*. Nashville: Vanderbilt University Press, 1970: 203.
3. White, Robert H. "The Governor's Mansions of Tennessee." *Tennessee Historical Quarterly* Vol. 25 (1966).